Incompatibilism's Allure

Incompatibilism's Allure

PRINCIPAL ARGUMENTS FOR INCOMPATIBILISM

Ishtiyaque Haji

CRITICAL ISSUES
IN PHILOSOPHY

broadview press

LIBRARY AND ARCHIVES CANADA CATALOGUING IN PUBLICATION

Haji, Ishtiyaque
Incompatibilism's allure : principal arguments for incompatibilism / Ishtiyaque Haji.

Includes bibliographical references and index.
ISBN 978-1-55111-919-9

1. Free will and determinism. 2. Responsibility. I. Title.

BJ1451.H33 2008 123'.5 C2008-906134-9

BROADVIEW PRESS is an independent, international publishing house, incorporated in 1985. Broadview believes in shared ownership, both with its employees and with the general public; since the year 2000 Broadview shares have traded publicly on the Toronto Venture Exchange under the symbol BDP.

We welcome comments and suggestions regarding any aspect of our publications—please feel free to contact us at the addresses below or at broadview@broadview press.com/www.broadviewpress.com.

NORTH AMERICA
Post Office Box 1243,
Peterborough, Ontario,
Canada K9J 7H5

2215 Kenmore Ave.,
Buffalo, New York, USA 14207
TEL: (705) 743-8990
FAX: (705) 743-8353

customerservice@broadviewpress.com

UK, IRELAND, & CONTINENTAL EUROPE
NBN International, Estover Road,
Plymouth, UK PL6 7PY
TEL: 44 (0) 1752 202300
FAX: 44 (0) 1752 202330
enquiries@nbninternational.com

AUSTRALIA & NEW ZEALAND
UNIREPS University of New South Wales
Sydney, NSW Australia 2052
TEL: 61 2 96640999
FAX: 61 2 96645420
infopress@unsw.edu.au

Broadview Press acknowledges the financial support of the Government of Canada through the Book Publishing Industry Development Program (BPIDP) for our publishing activities.

Cover design and interior by Em Dash Design

This book is printed on paper containing 100% post-consumer fibre.

Printed in Canada

Table of Contents

Acknowledgments

It is my happy duty to acknowledge the help that I have received from others in the writing of this book.

I thank the students in my course on incompatibilism given at the University of Calgary in the fall of 2007. Special thanks to Tyler McGraw and Kathleen Ganley for their comments and suggestions on an early draft of the manuscript.

A number of anonymous referees, both for Broadview Press and for certain journals, provided highly instructive criticism and helpful advice regarding sections of the manuscript. I am very thankful for this help. Parts of this book are based on previously published works of mine. They are listed in the References as: Haji (1998); (2000a); (2000b); (2000c); (2002); (2003); (2004); (2005); and (2006).

Many thanks to Robert Martin for proofreading the manuscript and his helpful recommendations; to Alex Sager, Philosophy Editor at Broadview for his diligent work; to Ryan Chynces, former Philosophy Editor at Broadview who initiated this project; and to Tara Lowes, Production Editor at Broadview; their valuable contributions are very much appreciated.

For comments on various, chapters, sections, or topics, I am deeply indebted to Joe Campbell, Randy Clarke, John Fischer, Leonard Kahn, Bob Kane, Michael McKenna, Derk Pereboom, and Michael J. Zimmerman.

I owe a special debt to Alfred Mele. Al provided helpful written comments on a late draft of the entire manuscript. In addition, I have had many, many extremely fruitful conversations with Al on almost every topic in the book. His penetrating insights on free will, agency, and the philosophy of action have been invaluable to me. Anyone acquainted with his work will immediately see how much I have lifted from it. It is to Al that I dedicate this book with great pleasure, gratitude, and respect.

1 Introduction

1.1 THE ROBERT HARRIS CASE

Robert Alton Harris' heartrending story is the sort of tragic drama that impels many of us to think deeply about free action, responsibility, and moral luck. The kind of impact, pertinent to our concerns, which Harris' case may well have on our moral thinking can be highlighted perspicuously by following Gary Watson's presentation of its details (Watson 1993). The picture of Harris that emerges from the *Los Angeles Times* article, "Icy Killer's Life Steeped in Violence," is one of a ruthless, brutal murderer (Corwin 1982).[1] This is a portrayal which, at least initially and customarily, foments attitudes of anger and resentment toward Harris. But as the history of the young man's life on Death Row unravels—as we learn, Watson explains, about how Harris came to be the mean and perverse youth that he was—typically, our negative attitudes are held in check. Some of the details of the case should bear this out.

On July 5, 1978, Robert, 25, and his brother, Daniel, 18, were trying to hotwire a car that they intended to use in a bank robbery. Unable to start the car, Harris decided to take another car in which two youths, John Mayeski and Michael Baker, on their way to a nearby lake for a day of fishing, were eating lunch. Approaching the car and pointing a Luger at Mayeski's head, Harris crawled into the back seat and ordered the 16-year-olds to drive east. Daniel followed in the Harrises' car. On reaching a secluded canyon area, Harris informed the boys about the planned robbery, and assured them that they would not be hurt. He even offered to leave some of the stolen money in their car to pay for its use. It was agreed

1 Copyright, 1982, *Los Angeles Times*.

that the Harris brothers would leave to rob the bank and that Mayeski and Baker would walk back into town and report the car stolen. As the two boys started to walk away, Harris slowly raised the Luger and shot Mayeski in the back. Harris then chased Baker down a hill and shot him four times. Mayeski was still alive when Harris made his way back. Harris walked over to the boy, put the Luger to his head and fired. Recalling the aftermath of the shooting, Daniel remarked, "[Robert] was swinging the rifle and pistol in the air and laughing. God, that laugh made blood and bone freeze in me" (Watson 1993, p. 132).

After the shooting, the Harris brothers drove to a friend's house. Harris began to feast on what was left of the slain youths' lunch. He offered his brother an apple turnover; Daniel became nauseated and ran into the bathroom. "Harris was in an almost lighthearted mood. He smiled and told Daniel that it would be amusing if the two of them were to pose as police officers and inform the parents that their sons were killed" (Watson 1993, p. 132). Thinking that somebody might have heard the shots and that the police could be searching for the bodies, Harris told Daniel that they should scout the street near the bodies and perhaps kill some police in the area. Later, as they prepared to rob the bank, "Harris pulled out the Luger, noticed blood stains and remnants of flesh on the barrel as a result of the point-blank shot, and said, "I really blew that guy's brains out." And then, again, he started laughing" (Watson 1993, p. 132).

Does it matter to our first reaction—that Harris is an archetypal candidate for blame—how he came to be so? The article is sensitive to this issue as well. During an interview with one of Robert's sisters, Barbara, Barbara "put her palms over her eyes and said softly, 'I saw every grain of sweetness, pity and goodness in him destroyed.... It was a long and ugly journey before he reached that point'" (Watson 1993, p. 134).

Harris, was born on January 15, 1953, several hours after his mother, six and one-half months pregnant, was kicked in the stomach by her insanely jealous husband who claimed that the child was not his. Because of the premature birth, Robert was a tiny baby; he was kept alive in an incubator and spent months at the hospital. All of the children had horrendous childhoods, but Robert fell victim to abuse that was unusually brutal even in the Harris family. The pain and permanent injury Robert's mother suffered because of the birth, and the constant abuse to which her husband subjected her, turned her against her son. She began to blame all of her problems on Robert and grew to hate the child. Harris suffered from a learning disability and a speech problem. There was no money, though, for therapy. Barbara reported that when he was at school Harris felt stupid and his classmates teased him, and when he was at home he was abused.

> "He wanted love so bad he would beg for any kind of physical contact.... He'd come up to my mother and just try to rub his little hands on her leg or her arm. He just never got touched

> at all. She'd just push him away or kick him".... All nine children are psychologically crippled ... [Barbara continued], but most have been able to lead useful lives. But Robert was too young, and the abuse lasted too long ... for him ever to have had a chance to recover.... [At age 14] Harris was sentenced to a federal youth detention center [for car theft]. He was one of the youngest inmates there, Barbara Harris said, and he grew up "hard and fast.".... Harris was raped several times ... and he slashed his wrists twice in suicide attempts. He spent more than four years behind bars as a result of an escape, an attempted escape and a parole violation.... The centers were "gladiator schools," Barbara Harris said, and Harris learned to fight and to be mean. By the time he was released from federal prison at 19, all his problems were accentuated.... "The only way he could vent his feelings was to break or kill something," Barbara Harris said. "He took out all the frustrations of his life on animals. He had no feeling for life, no sense of remorse. He reached the point where there wasn't that much left of him." (Watson 1993, pp. 135–36)

Reflecting on this section of the *Times*' report, it is natural to wonder to what extent Harris was responsible for becoming the sort of person that he was. Was the pathway of his life fully set in stone by parental and societal neglect, social or genetic conditioning, sheer bad luck, and the like, or did he have any hand in molding it? If the former, and this inclines us to mitigate or remove blame, then we may be well on the way toward *incompatibilism*, loosely, the view that blameworthiness—or, more generally, moral responsibility—is incompatible with being "determined" in certain ways. We might see Harris's actions as "determined" in the sense that their sources—the desires, beliefs, values, and so forth—the springs of action that collectively made up his psychological life—were "foreign" or "alien" to him; "foreign" in a robust sense in which, for example, we are comfortable in proclaiming that the desires that a child acquires as a result of *indoctrination* rather than as an outcome of *education* are not "really" the child's own. Is this ever the case? Real-life cases are engagingly (and sometimes, for purposes of analysis, distressingly) messy. For this reason, to unearth different routes to incompatibilism, which is a prime objective of this book, it may be more helpful to turn to thought experiments in which various parameters can be controlled.

1.2 THE ANN/BETH CASES

Ponder, then, a more clinical imaginary case that Alfred Mele advances. The case resembles Harris' in one vital respect: the central figure's springs of action do not seem to be "truly the agent's own" in that she did not have a hand in their acquisition. Ann and Beth are both philosophy professors but Ann is far more dedicated to the discipline. Wanting more production out of Beth and not scrupulous about how he gets it, the dean of the University enlists the help of new-wave neurologists who "implant" Ann's hierarchy of values into easy-going Beth. Understand 'values' in this way: "*S* at least *thinly values X* at a time if and only if at that time *S* both has a positive motivational attitude toward *X* [for instance, *S* is favorably inclined toward *X* or *S* wants *X*] and believes *X* to be good" (Mele 1995, p. 116). The pro-attitudes "implanted" in Beth are *practically unsheddable*. A pro-attitude is practically unsheddable for a person at a time if, given her psychological constitution at that time, ridding herself of that attitude is not a "psychologically genuine option" under any but extraordinary circumstances (Mele 1995, p. 172; 2006, pp. 164–65). It is important to keep in mind that if, for example, a desire is unsheddable for a person at a time, that desire need not be irresistible at that time. A parent's desire to care for her child may be unsheddable at some time but it need not then be irresistible. This "induction" of values into Beth results in her becoming the psychological twin of Ann in some respects. But the induction leaves unscathed values, beliefs, desires, and so forth which pre-manipulated Beth possessed and which can co-exist more or less harmoniously with the newly engineered-in pro-attitudes. Such psychological tempering is, thus, consistent with failing to undermine personal identity: pre-manipulated Beth is identical to her post-manipulated later self.[2]

An agent's action expresses a belief, or it expresses a pro-attitude such as a desire, or, more generally, it expresses an actional spring, only if that actional spring plays a (nondeviant) causal role in the production of that action.[3] Again, an actional spring just is a causal antecedent of an action such as a desire, belief, or value. Regarding the first few actions of Beth which express engineered-in actional springs, we would want to say that these implanted elements are not "truly Beth's own." Owing to their not being Beth's own, a number of us would be inclined to agree that these

2 Walter Glannon (1998, esp. sec IV) has argued that our practices of holding people morally and criminally responsible require only a low threshold of psychological connectedness and bodily continuity. Mele (1995, p. 175, n. 22) suggests that in such transformation cases, the pre- and post-surgery agents may be strongly psychologically connected, in Parfit's sense (Parfit 1984, p. 206)). They may be such that the number of direct psychological connections between them "is *at least half* the number that hold, over every day, in the lives of nearly every actual person." In addition, Mele argues that the pre-surgery agent (*t*-Beth) just before her transformation is much more similar, on the whole, to the post-surgery agent (*t**-Beth) than she is to neonate Beth or toddler Beth. Still, *t*-Beth is the same person as the neonate and toddler Beths, in a familiar "personal identity" sense of "same person." So what is to prevent her from being the same person, in the same sense, as *t**-Beth? On the supposition of personal identity, see also, Haji 2000a.

3 The concept of nondeviance is explained in the next chapter (in section 2.4.1.1).

actions of Beth are not free and that Beth is not morally responsible for them. We may refer to this case as "**Ann/Beth-1**."

"**Ann/Beth-2**" is just like **Ann/Beth-1** save that in **Ann/Beth-2** the implanted desires are both unsheddable for Beth *and* irresistible. Again, many of us would be drawn to the view that victimized Beth's actions that express these desires (and other implanted antecedents of action) in this second variation of the case are not ones for which she is responsible. And at least some of us would want to add that Beth is not responsible for these actions because, among other things, they are the inevitable causal upshots of antecedents, such as irresistible engineered-in desires, with respect to the acquisition of which she had no control. But then it is a short step from this sort of reasoning to the much more troubling conclusion that all our actions are already determined—"in the cards" so to speak, because they are the *inevitable* causal consequences, not of manipulators, but of facts in the far distant past and the laws of nature. And if this is so, then none of us is responsible for any of our actions. As some theorists steeped in the free will literature will put it, it appears that causal determinism is incompatible with free action and moral responsibility, or more simply, it appears that incompatibilism may well be true.

1.3 RESPONSIBILITY, CAUSAL DETERMINISM, AND FREE ACTION

Before dwelling further on the different trajectories to incompatibilism that these cases suggest, we should say something more about responsibility, causal determinism (henceforth, I use the label "determinism" as shorthand for "causal determinism"), and free action. The readers of this book should have an adequate pre-theoretical grasp of the concepts of *being morally praiseworthy*, *being morally blameworthy*, and *being morally responsible*. Giving an analysis of these concepts, though, is something else altogether.

1.3.1 Two Views About the Concept of Responsibility

Regarding the notion of *being responsible*, for our purposes it should suffice to note the following. First, judgments of moral responsibility—judgments concerning moral praiseworthiness and blameworthiness—should be distinguished from morally deontic judgments which have to do with moral right, wrong, and obligation. The judgments that it is morally obligatory for Ish to make this book accessible to its readers, or that it is morally wrong for some not so savvy but powerful political leader to wage war on Iraq are instances of morally deontic judgments. We may appreciate that these two sorts of judgement concern different types of moral appraisal by noting that the judgement can "diverge" in the following way:

you may, for example, do moral wrong but not be blameworthy for the wrongdoing. In such cases, you have an excuse. Imagine, for instance, that you have been assured, on excellent authority, that the rifle is not loaded and that its trigger may be pulled with no untoward consequences. Aiming at a highly valuable vase, you squeeze the trigger. To everyone's shock, the rifle fires and the bullet shatters the beautiful piece. Presumably, you have done moral wrong—you have destroyed an heirloom. But you are not blameworthy for the destruction. (I think it is also possible that you may do no wrong but still be blameworthy for what you do.) Similarly, you may do something that is morally obligatory but not be morally praiseworthy for doing this thing. (I believe, too, that you can do something that is wrong but still be praiseworthy for what you do.) An important contrast between responsibility judgments and morally deontic judgments lies in a difference in the objects of their appraisals. Responsibility judgments are "agent-focused" in that, first and foremost, they concern an appraisal of the *agent*, and only derivatively, if at all, an appraisal of what the agent does (or fails to do). When we hold an agent blameworthy, we are primarily faulting the agent and not what she does. In contrast, morally deontic judgments are "act-focused" insofar as, fundamentally, they concern an assessment of an *action* (or intentional *omission*) and only secondarily, if at all, an appraisal of the agent.

Judgments of responsibility should also not be conflated with axiological judgments that concern good and evil, such as the judgments that it is intrinsically good that Ryan takes pleasure in the fact that a cold beer is going down his hatch, or that it may be intrinsically bad that someone takes displeasure in something, or that some possible world is intrinsically better than another. Nor should responsibility judgments be confused with aretaic judgments that have to do with virtue or vice and the evaluation of character. Examples of such judgments include the judgment that Jack acted from virtue in forgiving Jill, and the judgment that it is unquestionable that Michael is generous and honest.

Second, I mention two prominent views about what judgments of moral responsibility are judgments of—these are two views concerning the concept of *being morally responsible*. The first is that to be morally responsible just is to be the appropriate object of what Peter Strawson has called the "reactive attitudes"—evaluative reactions to people's behavior—such as, gratitude, resentment, indignation, and the like. Strawson explains that it matters to us whether the actions of other people "reflect attitudes towards us of good will, affection, or esteem on the one hand or contempt, indifference, or malevolence on the other" (P. Strawson 1962, p. 63) The reactive attitudes are "natural human reactions to the good or ill will or indifference of others towards us as displayed in *their* attitudes and actions" (P. Strawson 1962, p. 67); and they express "the demand for the manifestation of a reasonable degree of good will or regard, on the part of others, not simply towards oneself, but towards all those on whose behalf moral indignation may be felt" (P. Strawson 1962, p. 71). According to Strawson, to be responsible is to be part of a moral community in which people can appropriately adopt the reactive attitudes toward one another, thereby holding each other responsible. On this view, for instance, an individual such as Data of *Star Trek* fame, who, let us suppose, cannot feel any emotion or have any moral sentiments, is not a morally responsible agent; he is not so because an inability to feel or experience the moral sentiments, such as indignation or resentment, is itself an exempting condition of responsibility.

On the second view of what judgments of responsibility are about—the "ledger view"—to be morally responsible is to be such that one's moral standing or record as a person is affected by some episode in, or aspect of, one's life. On this second view, when a person is praiseworthy, her moral standing has been enhanced in virtue of some episode in her life; when blameworthy, her moral standing has been diminished. Metaphorically speaking, when blameworthy, a negative mark has been entered into her appropriate moral ledger. The ledger view has it that it is because one's moral standing has been diminished that one is a suitable candidate for things such as resentment and indignation. So this second view denies that one's being susceptible to the reactive attitudes is *constitutive* of responsibility. As Michael Zimmerman explains, the first and the second views are allied. The difference between the two is that "whereas the former identifies responsibility with susceptibility to certain reactive attitudes, the latter identifies responsibility with that in virtue of which one is susceptible to such attitudes" (M. Zimmerman 2002, p. 555; see, also, M. Zimmerman 1988, pp. 38–39). We need not settle which of these competing analyses has the upper hand.

1.3.2 Free Action

It is standardly acknowledged that responsibility has a metaphysical component having to do with freedom or control, and an epistemic component having to do with knowledge or belief of various factors pertaining to whatever it is for which one is responsible: an intentional action, a choice or decision, an intentional omission, or a consequence of an action or omission. In an imaginary case I shall call "**Sweet Deception**," you invite your friend over for some coffee. Unbeknownst to you, someone has replaced the lumps of sugar in the bowl with a deadly look-alike. "One lump or two?" you ask your friend. She says "three please." To your horror, after the first sip, your friend drops dead. Though you presumably have "freedom-level" control in placing the cubes in the coffee, you are not to blame for this action. You had a legitimate excuse: you acted in relevant nonculpable ignorance (ignorance for which you were not blameworthy). In addition to the freedom and epistemic components, I believe that responsibility also has an authenticity or autonomy component, as the

Ann/Beth cases strongly suggest. This component has to do with whether the springs of one's actions are "truly one's own," or "authentic," or ones with respect to which one is autonomous.[4] In what follows, when I speak of "free action" the freedom at issue is the freedom that moral responsibility requires. More precisely, add to a set of necessary and otherwise sufficient conditions for responsibility—perhaps the set consisting of the epistemic and authenticity conditions—the requisite freedom or control condition, and this set of conditions suffices for moral responsibility. I take free will simply to be the power or ability to act freely. If we understand what free action is—if, for instance, we can defend an account of free action—then we will thereby understand what free will is (Clarke 2003a, p. 4, n. 2; Mele 2006, p. 17).

1.3.3 Causal Determinism

As for the concept of causal determinism, we start with a distinction. A *temporally relational fact* is, roughly, a fact that includes a reference to various times and whose truth-value depends on what happens (or fails to happen) at times other than some of the times to which this fact makes reference. For example, that *Scott awakens at 8:00 a.m., three hours before the alarm rings*, is a temporally relational fact. A "genuine fact" (alternatively, a "temporally non-relational fact") is not a temporally relational fact. For example, that *Tim falls asleep at 10 p.m.* is a genuine fact. We might better grasp the distinction between these two sorts of fact by dwelling on the difference between genuine facts (or "hard facts") about the past and temporally relational facts (or "soft facts" about the past). Intuitively, hard facts about the past are facts that are wholly about the past; they are "settled" or "over and done with." In contrast, soft facts about the past are facts that are not wholly about the past—they have a "future-infected component." For example, relative to 2 p.m., the fact that *Michael begins to eat noodles at 1 p.m.* is a hard (temporally non-relational) fact about the past, whereas, the fact that *Michael eats noodles for three hours after having started to eat them at 1 p.m.* is a soft (temporally relational) fact.

Now we can understand (causal) determinism to be the thesis that a complete statement of the non-relational or genuine facts of the world at a time, together with a complete statement of all the laws of nature, entails all truths. Roughly, on this view if all the facts of the world at a time were "plugged into" the laws of nature—whatever these laws turn out to be—the result would be propositions expressing truths about the world, including truths involving human choices and actions. Take "deterministic universe" to mean "universe of which determinism is true." Then we can streamline the notion of determinism in this way: If the universe is deter-

4 For a defense of the view that authenticity of our springs of action is a condition of responsibility, see Haji 1998; and Haji and Cuypers 2008.

ministic, then at any instant, the state of the universe at that instant and the laws of nature entail that, at that instant, there is exactly one physically possible future (van Inwagen 1983, p. 3). On this picture there are no alternative pathways for any of us into the future; rather, the future is like a forkless trunk line that is an extension of the past.

1.3.4 Some Definitions: Incompatibilism, Compatibilism, and Libertarianism

With these brief explanations of the notions of *free action*, *moral responsibility*, and *determinism*, the essential idea of incompatibilism should be pretty evident. *Incompatibilism* is the thesis that free action and moral responsibility are incompatible with determinism. *Compatibilism* is the denial of incompatibilism in both domains: it is the thesis that determinism and moral responsibility, and determinism and free action, can co-exist. *Libertarianism* is the conjunction of incompatibilism and the thesis that at least some of us, at times, perform free actions for which we are morally responsible. If libertarianism is true, then determinism is, of course, false.

1.4 DIFFERENT PATHWAYS TO INCOMPATIBILISM

Reverting to the cases that we have introduced, it is not so difficult to see why one might think that determinism rules out free action and, thus, moral responsibility on the credible assumption that if a person is morally responsible for an action, then that action is free. In the second version of the **Ann/Beth** case—**Ann/Beth-2**—Beth's first post-transformation action, *A*, causally issues from an irresistible desire. (Assume that *A* consists in Beth's expending considerable time on refereeing a paper.) Some may find it tempting to argue in this way:

THE LACK OF FREEDOM ARGUMENT

(1) The causal antecedents of Beth's *A*-ing (her pertinent desires, for example) are irresistible.
(2) If the causal antecedents of Beth's *A*-ing are irresistible, then Beth cannot but do *A*.
(3) If Beth cannot but do *A*, then Beth does not do *A* freely.
(4) If Beth does not do *A* freely, then Beth is not morally responsible for *A*-ing.
(5) Therefore, Beth is not morally responsible for *A*-ing.

What underlies this argument is the intuitive and highly attractive picture that *free* agents have more than one path or option genuinely open to them on various occasions in their lives. On this picture, the paths into the future branch out from the present—"the future is a garden of forking paths," as

John Martin Fischer following Borges says—and it is "up to us" on which pathway we tread; it is "up to us" how we choose and act (Fischer 2007, p. 46). So although we may have chosen and acted in one way, we could, given the same past and the laws, have chosen and acted in another way. If determinism is true, though, then at every instant, the future is a branchless extension of the past. So if determinism is true, no one is free to choose among alternative pathways into the future.

It is worth probing deeper into how, precisely, **Ann/Beth-2** motivates *incompatibilism*—it's worth examining how exactly this case helps to energize the view that determinism is incompatible with free action and responsibility. Among others, Peter van Inwagen has argued that if determinism is true, then none of our actions is "up to us"; they are not up to us in the sense that *we could not have done otherwise*. He summarizes his intriguing **Consequence Argument** in this way:

> If determinism is true, then our acts are the consequences of the laws of nature and events in the remote past. But it is not up to us what went on before we were born, and neither is it up to us what the laws of nature are. Therefore, the consequences of these things (including our present acts) are not up to us. (1983, p. 16)

Conjoined with the premise that if our acts are not up to us—if we lack the freedom to do otherwise—we do not perform them freely and are not morally responsible for them, the **Consequence Argument** yields incompatibilism as its conclusion. In **Ann/Beth-2**, Beth's first post-transformation act, *A*, is inevitable because this action is performed, in part, on the basis of a desire that is irresistible. Suppose we accept van Inwagen's conclusion that if determinism is true, then we never have the freedom to do other than what we in fact do; all our actions are inevitable insofar as they are the causal upshots of the distant past and the laws. We can then avail ourselves of this sort of argument:

THE PROTO-CONSEQUENCE ARGUMENT

(1A) If determinism is true, then Beth cannot but do *A*.

(2A) If Beth cannot but do *A*, then Beth does not do *A* freely.

(3A) If Beth does not do *A* freely, then Beth is not morally responsible for *A*-ing.

(4A) Therefore, if determinism is true, then Beth is not morally responsible for *A*-ing.

The second version of the **Ann/Beth** case suggests another route to incompatibilism. One might reason that manipulated Beth is not responsible for acquiring the engineered-in springs of action, including the irresistible desire, on the basis of which she exerts considerable efforts in refereeing a paper. Nor is she responsible for the fact that if she acquires these springs, then she referees the paper. But then it seems to follow that she is not responsible for refereeing the paper either. In short, this line of reasoning relies on a principle of this sort: if you are not responsible for one thing, and you are not responsible for this thing's leading to a second—that is, you are not responsible for the "conditional fact" that if the first occurs or obtains, so does the second—you are not responsible for the second thing. Exploiting this principle, it may be proposed that, pretty clearly, no one is even partly morally responsible for the state of the universe at a distant time in the past—a time at which there were no human beings, for instance—and no one is even partly morally responsible for the laws being what they are. Assuming that determinism is true, no one is even partly morally responsible for the fact that the combination of the distant past (the complete state of the universe at a time in the past) and the laws entail all events, including our actions. These two claims appear to sanction the result that no one is even partly responsible for one's actions. Unlike the **Proto-Consequence Argument**, in working toward incompatibilism this **Direct Argument** does not invoke the **Principle of Alternative Possibilities**—that persons are morally responsible for what they have done only if they could have done otherwise. It appears to sidestep this principle altogether. In brief, compare this direct argument for Beth's not being responsible—*direct* because it works around the **Principle of Alternative Possibilities** altogether—with the prior argument for the same conclusion:

THE DIRECT ARGUMENT

(1B) No one is even partly responsible for what the state of the universe at a time close to the Big Bang was and for the laws being what they are.

(2B) Assuming determinism, no one is even partly responsible for the fact that the combination of the distant past (the complete state of the universe at a time close to the Big Bang) and the laws entails that Beth performs *A* (at the time when she does perform *A*).

(3B) If (1B) and (2B), then Beth is not morally responsible for performing *A*.

(4B) Therefore, Beth is not morally responsible for performing *A*.

Inspection reveals that there is no premise in the **Direct Argument** that neatly corresponds to premise (2A) of the **Proto-Consequence Argument**. So, it seems, there is no premise in the **Direct Argument** that appeals to the **Principle of Alternative Possibilities**.

Reflecting on Harris' case, we might be tempted by the view that it is obvious that Harris did moral wrong in killing the youths; he ought not to have killed them. If we think of the morally deontic notions of right, wrong, and obligation, it would not be unusual to be drawn to the principle that "ought" implies "can": if you morally ought to do something, then you can do it. If it is true, for example, that you cannot open the safe and defuse the bomb therein because you don't know the combination, then you can't have a moral *obligation* to open the safe. The moral "ought" expresses a kind of necessity or requirement. Morality cannot *require* you to do what you *cannot* do. But if "ought" implies "can," then surely "ought not" implies "can refrain from"; if you ought not to do something—if it is wrong for you to do it—then you can refrain from doing it. So it seems that there is a requirement of alternative possibilities for wrongness: you can't do wrong unless you could have refrained from doing what you do. Suppose, though, that determinism *does* undermine alternative possibilities; suppose, that is, that if determinism is true, then you cannot refrain from doing what you do. We now have another pathway that the **Deontic Argument** exposes to incompatibilism:

THE DEONTIC ARGUMENT

(1C) If determinism is true, then you can't refrain from doing what you do.

(2C) If you can't refrain from doing what you do, then whatever you do is not wrong (because you can't do wrong unless you could have avoided doing what you did).

(3C) If whatever you do is not wrong, then you can't be morally blameworthy for anything that you do.

(4C) Therefore, if determinism is true, you can't be morally blameworthy for anything that you do.

Harris' case and both **Ann/Beth** cases invite yet another argument for incompatibilism. Various varieties of manipulation, or social conditioning, or indoctrination undermine moral responsibility. Arguably, the kind of treatment to which Harris was subject during his early childhood is responsibility-subverting. The manipulation in the **Ann/Beth** cases also seems to be manipulation of a responsibility-subverting sort. Focusing on the **Ann/Beth** cases, one might plausibly propose that the type of manipulation involved in these cases undercuts responsibility because its victim (Beth), as a result of being manipulated, is not the "ultimate originator" of her engineered-in springs of action; so she is not the ultimate source of the actions that causally derive from these springs. To be responsible, though, for our choices, actions, and so forth, these things must originate "in us." It is a condition of responsibility that we be the ultimate originators or sources of our intentional behavior. As Beth fails to satisfy this condition, Beth is not morally responsible for them. *She* is not the ultimate source of her actions that express her implanted desires, beliefs, etc.; maybe the *manipulator* carries the burden of responsibility. But now assume, again, that determinism is true. Then there is a sense in which all our actions, including all our decisions, originate in the distant past and the laws of nature, sources over which we have no control. Given the thought that if we are not the ultimate sources of our actions we are not responsible for them, it follows that if determinism is true, we are not responsible for any of our actions. So we have this sort of argument for incompatibilism:

THE MANIPULATION ARGUMENT

(1D) Actions that result from manipulation of the sort displayed in the **Ann/Beth** cases are actions for which an agent is not morally responsible. (Or, as we may say, actions that derive from a causal history involving *menacing manipulation*—manipulation that undermines responsibility—aren't ones for which an agent is responsible.)

(2D) Actions that result from a deterministic causal history are relevantly similar to those that derive from a causal history involving menacing manipulation (in either case, the agent is not the ultimate source of her actions).

(3D) If (1D) and (2D), then determinism undermines moral responsibility.

(4D) Therefore, determinism undermines moral responsibility.

This version of the **Manipulation Argument** attempts to convince us that cases of responsibility-undercutting manipulation are relevantly similar to actions that are causally determined: just as, in virtue of being manipulated in the manner in which she is, Beth is not the ultimate originator of her actions, and, thus, is not morally responsible for them, so in virtue of her actions being causally determined, Beth is not their ultimate originator and, hence, bears no responsibility for them.

Finally, all the cases with which we commenced might spur an argument—the **Impossibility Argument**—for the stronger conclusion that we are not responsible for any of our actions *regardless* of the truth of determinism. This conclusion is, of course, consistent with the incompatibilist's claim that determinism rules out moral responsibility. In roughly hewn strokes, the line of reasoning for this forceful conclusion unfolds in this way: If Beth is not responsible for the way she is at a particular time—if she is not, for example, responsible for having the desires, values, or beliefs with which she finds herself at a particular time—then she is not responsible for actions that express these causal antecedents. But if she is to be responsible for these causal antecedents—if she is to be responsible for these desires, for instance—she must be responsible for earlier actions or behavior as a result of which she acquired these desires. To be responsible, though, for these earlier actions, she would have had to have been responsible for the springs of these earlier actions. But to have been responsible for these earlier springs, she would have had to have been responsible for still earlier actions that led to the acquisition of these earlier springs, and so forth. Thus, responsibility for an action requires what is impossible: it requires having made an *infinite* number of choices. In premise and conclusion form, the **Impossibility Argument** can be restated in this way:

THE IMPOSSIBILITY ARGUMENT

(1E) The actions we perform depend on certain facts about what we are like in relevant mental respects, or *how we are*.

(2E) If (1E), then if we are responsible for any of our acts, then we are responsible for being in the relevant ways how we are.

(3E) If we are responsible for being in the relevant ways how we are, then we can or could be responsible for an *infinite* series of "character-forming" actions.

(4E) It is not the case that we can or could be responsible for an *infinite* series of "character-forming" actions.

(5E) Therefore, it is false that we are responsible for any of our acts.

The **Impossibility Argument** and the **Manipulation Argument** share a common kernel: both place a great deal of stock in the idea that if we are to be responsible for our actions, these actions must originate "in us"; we must be their "final source." The **Manipulation Argument** seeks to convince us that, just as in cases involving manipulation that is responsibility-undermining, we are not responsible for our actions because our actions ultimately originate in sources external to us (they originate in the manipulator), so with causally determined actions, we are not responsible for them because they have their ultimate sources in the distant past and the laws. The **Impossibility Argument**, in slight contrast, seeks to persuade us that responsibility does require that we be the ultimate originators of our actions, but that it is impossible for us to be such originators. If this skeptical argument is sound, then it indirectly supports incompatibilism in this way: if we are not responsible for our actions regardless of whether determinism is true, then we are not responsible for our actions even if determinism is true.

Some theorists may be drawn to incompatibilism via yet another route. These theorists may first affirm that we *are* morally responsible for at least some of our behavior. This leaves open two possibilities:

(1) the incompatibilist account is true, so this moral responsibility is consistent only with a libertarian account of action.

(2) The *compatibilist account of free action and responsibility* is true: this attempts to show that free action and responsibility are compatible with determinism.

Then they might reason that, among the leading competing compatibilist and libertarian accounts of free action and responsibility, the best account is a libertarian one. They may, for example, call upon the **Manipulation Argument** to cast doubt on compatibilist rivals. Or, for instance, they might reason that ultimate origination is a requirement of free action and responsibility but no compatibilist competitor is up to the task of providing a suitably rich account of such origination. Their overall strategy would be to examine critically both compatibilist and libertarian contenders and then see which wins the day. In the view of these theorists it is a form of libertarianism that prevails. But if some version of libertarianism is true, then incompatibilism is victorious.

On one libertarian snapshot of free action, if you perform an action at a certain time, that action is free only if, given *exactly* the same past and the laws up until the time (or just prior to the time) at which you perform the action, you could then have performed some alternative instead. If determinism is true, this is impossible; you do not have such "genuine alternatives." For, assuming determinism, if you perform an action at a certain time, the past and the laws entail that you perform that action at that time. So if the past and the laws are "held fixed" right up to or just prior to the time at which you perform an action, it appears that it is not possible that, at that time, you perform some alternative instead. What may underlie this libertarian vision of free action? Either the garden-of-forking-paths picture of free action—the thought that free action and responsibility require that you have genuine alternatives so that it is "up to you" on which pathway into the future you tread; or the idea that responsibility requires that you be an ultimate originator of your choices or actions, something that is not possible if determinism is true; or, perhaps, both of these things.

I can now summarize the key aims of this book. I pay close attention to the case for incompatibilism by enlisting a two-fold strategy. First, I lay out more carefully the arguments for incompatibilism that I have previously sketched. I offer relatively little that is innovative on the **Consequence Argument** and the **Impossibility Argument** because there is already a wealth of literature on them. I say more that might be of interest on the **Deontic Argument**, offer something that is novel on the **Direct Argument**, and devote a fair bit of attention to the **Manipulation Argument**. Second, as I explained, I suspect that many theorists may be drawn to incompatibilism because they believe both that some libertarian account of free action and moral responsibility is true or overall superior to its best compatibilist rival, and that the existence of moral responsibility is a reality. In assessing the case for incompatibilism, I thus examine an objection, the **Luck Objection**, to prominent versions of libertarianism. At the core of this objection is the thought that, given any of the libertarian views at issue, an action deemed free in light of the view under evaluation, cannot in fact be free because its performance by its agent or its occurrence is merely a matter of freedom- and responsibility-subversive luck. The sort of luck at issue is incompatible with free action and moral responsibility.

1.5 PROSPECTUS

The book has the following structure. Chapter 2 begins with an outline of the **Consequence Argument**. In its standard formulation, the **Consequence**

Argument's association with control is not transparent. To expose clearly this association, I reformulate the **Consequence Argument**. I propose that if we disambiguate 'control,' then this reworked argument is not as forceful as one might have initially taken it to be. Also discussed in this chapter is a relatively recent, powerful successor of the **Consequence Argument**, the **Basic Version**. We said that the **Consequence Argument** works its way to the conclusion that determinism and moral responsibility are incompatible by courting the **Principle of Alternative Possibilities**—persons are morally responsible for what they have done only if they could have done otherwise. Chapter 3 scrutinizes this principle. Chapter 4 examines the **Direct Argument**. I defend the view that a crucial inference rule to which this argument appeals is susceptible to counterexample. Chapter 5 is devoted to the **Deontic Argument**. I propose that two principles on which it essentially relies, the principles that one is blameworthy for an action only if it is wrong for one to perform that action, and that one is praiseworthy for an action only if it is obligatory for one to perform that action, are suspect. Chapter 6 addresses the **Manipulation Argument**. Derk Pereboom has done as much as anyone else to advance the prospects for a potent version of this argument (1995; 2000; 2001; 2002; 2005; 2007). He reasons that, with respect to moral responsibility, there is no germane difference between a case of clandestine manipulation (such as **Ann/Beth-1** or **Ann/Beth-2**) in which the pertinent agent is not morally responsible for her apt actions, and mundane cases in which an agent performs similar actions in deterministic worlds. Regarding the former cases, I agree with Pereboom that the victimized agent, such as Beth, is not morally responsible for her actions that express engineered-in springs of action because these springs are not "truly her own" or not "authentic." After detailing an instructive objection to the verdict that manipulated Beth in either of the **Ann/Beth** cases is not responsible for her pertinent actions, Chapter 7 first gives an outline of authentic springs. Then this objection is rebutted. Finally, armed with compatibilist conditions on authenticity, a response is advanced to Pereboom's challenge to the compatibilist to produce reasons to believe that while an agent, such as Beth, is not responsible for the actions that she is manipulated into performing, ordinary cases involving garden-variety deterministic causation can be cases in which the relevant agent may be responsible. Chapter 8 contains a discussion of the **Impossibility Argument**. Chapter 9 is concerned with establishing that, with respect to leading versions of libertarianism, the **Luck Objection** does indeed have bite.

Anticipating some of the overall conclusions of the book, when it comes to establishing the incompatibility of determinism and freedom to do otherwise, I believe that the Basic Version of the Consequence Argument is plausible. This argument gives us powerful reason to think that determinism rules out our having genuine alternatives. To get to the further conclusion that determinism undermines moral responsibility, the Basic Version, just like van Inwagen's original version, invokes the Principle of

Alternative Possibilities—persons are morally responsible for having done something only if they could have done otherwise. I have strong doubts about this principle. I believe that various considerations (such as so-called "Frankfurt-type examples") tell against this principle. Further, I am not convinced that the other arguments that I discuss in this work for the incompatibility of determinism and moral responsibility escape serious difficulties. So I tend to agree with Fischer's "semicompatibilism" position (see, for example, Fischer and Ravizza 1998; Fischer 2007) that whereas determinism undermines freedom to do otherwise, it does not undermine moral responsibility. I said previously that a number of thoughtful people might be drawn to libertarianism. The libertarian affirms that determinism is incompatible with moral responsibility and free action but at least some of us, at times, perform free actions for which we are morally responsible. These people might reason that it seems much more plausible that we are, at least on occasion, morally responsible for what we do than that we are not responsible for any of our behavior. They may go on to argue that in the battle among competitors for the true account of free action and responsibility, a libertarian view takes the prize. I aim to argue, though, that some of our leading libertarian accounts of free action have significant shortcomings. So if we are drawn to the view that overall, it seems more credible that we are morally responsible than that we are not, and we are convinced, perhaps by the Basic Version of the Consequence Argument that determinism is incompatible with freedom to do otherwise, then we should be receptive to semicompatibilism.

2 The Consequence Argument

2.1 THE CONSEQUENCE ARGUMENT

This chapter is devoted to the **Consequence Argument.**[1] As we noted, the **Consequence Argument** attempts to show that determinism and moral responsibility are not friendly partners indirectly by establishing the incompatibility of determinism with *something else*—the freedom to do otherwise—that is allegedly required for free action and moral responsibility. 'The agent could not have done otherwise' means that the agent is not able, at a time, to render false a true proposition regarding what she does at that time. So, for instance, if for some reason, I cannot now render it false that I now stop writing, then I cannot now do other than write. On one of its constructions the principal burden of the **Consequence Argument** is to establish that it is indeed the case that, if determinism is true, no agent is ever able to render false any true proposition concerning what she does at any time.

2.1.1 The Logical Modalities

To formulate and understand the **Consequence Argument**, a slight digression on the *logical modalities* such as *necessity*, *contingency*, *impossibility*, and *possibility* will be valuable. Of special concern to us is that these modalities can be predicated on the truth-values of propositions.

1 Carl Ginet introduced the **Consequence Argument** in his 1966. He refines this argument in 1990 and 2003. Wiggens advances a version of the **Consequence Argument** as well in his 1973.

Every proposition has a truth-value.[2] According to classical logic, there are just two truth-values: truth and falsehood. So, assuming classical logic, each proposition is either true or false.

A true contingent proposition can instead be false (and a false one can instead be true). Necessarily true propositions cannot be false (and a false one cannot be true). The concepts of a proposition's *being contingent*, a proposition's *being necessarily true*, and a proposition's *being necessarily false* can be understood in terms of the notion of a *possible world*. I assume that a possible world is an abstract entity—a conjunction of propositions which is maximal or suitably complete, and which does not imply a contradiction. (A proposition, *p*, is maximal or suitably complete if and only if, for any proposition, *q*, either *p* entails *q*, or *p* entails the negation of *q*, but not both.) Assume, in addition, that a possible world is itself a proposition.[3] We may, very roughly, explicate the notion of a possible world in this way: Start with the history of the real (actual) world. True propositions expressing all the facts of the world, past, present, and future, comprise its history. Now imagine some change in this history. Imagine, next, all the other changes that would be required in order to accommodate this initial change into an internally coherent story. The result is the history or description (expressed by a large conjunction of propositions) of some other possible world. So long as such a history is internally consistent and complete, it may be taken to be the history of a possible world.

Redefining the notion of a contingent proposition, a proposition is contingent if and only if it is true in at least one possible world and it is false in at least one possible world. *That Stefaan is a cheery person* and *that Calgary is in Alberta* are contingent propositions; these propositions are both possibly true and possibly false. A proposition is necessarily true if and only if it is true in all possible worlds; it is not false in any world. The proposition that *if something is red, then it is colored* and the proposition

---

2 Some people have denied that every proposition has a truth-value. So, for instance, Aristotle (1966, ch. 9) argues that some propositions, so-called "future contingent" propositions, are neither true nor false. For example, the proposition that *Al will fight a sea battle tomorrow* (a proposition that is contingent and future relative to now), or that the *stars will shine tomorrow* are examples of such propositions. Standard logic implies that either it is true that Al will fight a sea battle tomorrow or it is false that Al will fight a sea battle tomorrow.

3 There are different positions on the ontological status of possible worlds. According to the conceptualist position, possible worlds are mental constructions, for example complexes of concepts (see, for instance, Rescher 1975). On the combinatorial position, the actual world is the set or collection of everything there is, and other possible worlds consist of all of the possible combinations of the basic entities that exist in the actual world (see, for example, Cresswell 1972). According to the abstract worlds position (which I favor), a possible world is an abstract entity, a very large conjunction of propositions, a conjunction that is maximal or suitably complete, and which does not imply a contradiction. (This view is associated with Plantinga 1974.) On the concrete worlds position, a possible world is a concrete entity, for example, a causally isolated collection of concrete things (see, for instance, Lewis 1968).

that *if some person is a bachelor, then that person is male* are necessarily true. A proposition is necessarily false (or impossible) if and only if it is false in all possible worlds; there are no worlds in which it is true. The proposition that *some square has five sides* and the proposition that $2 + 2 = 5$ are necessarily false. Contingent and necessarily true propositions are possible (or possibly true): there is at least one possible world in which they are true. Contingent and necessarily false propositions are possibly false: there is at least one world in which they are false. Each necessarily true proposition and each necessarily false proposition is a non-contingent proposition.

2.1.2 Peter van Inwagen's Version of the Consequence Argument

To secure the conclusion that no agent is able to render false any true proposition concerning what she does at any time, van Inwagen introduces two rules of inference. Let '$\Box$' represent logical necessity (truth in all possible worlds), '$\vdash$' stand for 'therefore,' '$p \supset q$' symbolize 'if p then q' (the material conditional), and 'Np_{at}' abbreviate 'proposition p is true, and person a at time t is powerless to render p false.' (For simplicity, in future occurrences of this operator, the indexing to persons and times will be assumed but suppressed.) The rules can be expressed in this way:

> **Rule α**: $\Box p \vdash Np$ (van Inwagen 1983, p. 94).

In other words, we may infer from a proposition's being necessarily true that each person is powerless to render it false. For example, no person can render false the proposition that *all men are mortal* (1983, p. 93). Similarly, no person can render false the proposition that $2+2 = 4$.

> **Rule β**: $N(p \supset q), Np \vdash Nq$ (1983, p. 94).

This rule says, roughly, that if p and one is powerless to render p false, and if $p \supset q$ and one is powerless to render this conditional—*if p, then q*—false, then one is powerless to render q false. Or, more intuitively, if one is powerless over one thing, and one is powerless over this thing's leading to a second, then one is powerless over the second. Powerlessness "transfers" through logical implication. For example, if you are powerless over your being six feet tall, and you are powerless over its being the case that if you are six feet tall, then you are at least five feet tall, then you are powerless over your being at least five feet tall.

In addition to relying on **Rule α** and **Rule β**, the **Consequence Argument** also appeals to two premises. The first, the principle of the fixity of the past, says that the past is "fixed"; one is powerless to render false any truth about the past. The second, the principle of the fixity of the laws, says that no one can so act as to violate a law of nature; one is powerless to render false any true proposition that expresses a law of nature.

Assuming the truth of determinism, the **Consequence Argument** proceeds to show that no person can do otherwise—no person can render false a true proposition concerning what she does at any time. Recall, if determinism is true, then at any instant, the complete state of the universe at that instant and the laws of nature entail that, at that instant, there is exactly one physically possible future. Let '**Past**' stand for a proposition expressing the complete state of the universe at a time when no human being existed, '**Laws**' stand for a proposition expressing the laws of nature, and '**Action-Now**' stand for any true proposition about the state of the world now. Then from the assumption that determinism is true, it follows that:

$\Box$ (Past and Laws $\supset$ Action-Now).

To elaborate, suppose **Action-Now** is identical to the true proposition that *Ish writes on April 3, 2007*. Assuming determinism, we may infer:

(P) Necessarily, if the past and laws are what they are, then Ish writes on April 3, 2007.

Since a necessary truth obtains independently of what anybody does or fails to do, an application of **Rule α** to **(P)** yields **N(P)**, that is, it yields:

(1) If the past and the laws are what they are, then Ish writes on April 3, 2007, and Ish is powerless to render false this "conditional fact."

The fixity of the past implies that Ish cannot now render false any true proposition about the past, and the fixity of the laws implies that Ish cannot now render false any true proposition that states a law of nature. We may put the point in this way:

(2) *The past and the laws are what they are*, and Ish is powerless to render false this "conjunctive fact."

An application of **Rule β** to (1) and (2) yields the conclusion:

(3) *Ish writes on April 3, 2007*, and Ish is powerless to render this false.

In other words, if determinism is true, then we may conclude from (1), (2), and **Rule β** that Ish cannot do other than write on April 3, 2007.

Somewhat more rigorously, what we may dub the **Original Consequence Argument** may be formulated as follows.

THE ORIGINAL CONSEQUENCE ARGUMENT

1. The thesis of determinism is true.	[Assumption]
2. $\Box$ (**Past** and **Laws** $\supset$ **Action-Now**)	[from 1]
3. $\Box$ (**Past** $\supset$ (**Laws** $\supset$ **Action-Now**))	[from 2, by logic]
4. N (**Past** $\supset$ (**Laws** $\supset$ **Action-Now**))	[from 3, **Rule α**]
5. N **Past**	[Assumption, the past is "fixed"]
6. N (**Laws** $\supset$ **Action-Now**)	[4, 5, **Rule β**]
7. N **Laws**	[Assumption, the laws are "fixed"]
8. N **Action-Now**	[5, 6, **Rule β**]

In van Inwagen's words, this "deduction shows that if determinism is true, then no one ever has any choice about anything" (1983, p. 95).

The argument may be simplified in this way. Suppose determinism is true. Then the complex proposition (call it "**PL**") which is the conjunction of proposition **Past** (a complex proposition expressing facts about the distant past) and proposition **Laws** (a complex proposition expressing the laws of nature) entail all true propositions about the future, including propositions about my choices and actions. The proposition, *if* **PL** *is true, then I will choose to do what I in fact choose to do* (proposition **C**), is a necessary truth. Since I lack causal power over the past and the laws, I can't render **PL** false. Since nobody can see to it that a necessary truth is false, I can't render **C** false. Hence, applying **Rule β** to **PL** and **C**, we may conclude that I can neither choose nor do anything other than what I in fact choose and do.

Again, as we have noted, if the conclusion that "no one ever has any choice about anything" is conjoined with the **Principle of Alternative Possibilities**—persons are morally responsible for having done something only if they could have done otherwise—we derive the incompatibilist's thesis that determinism and moral responsibility are incompatible.

There has been copious discussion of this absorbing argument. Some people have tried to unseat the argument at premise 5; they have proposed that one *is* able to act in such a way that, if one were to so act, some fact about the past would not be a fact about the past (Saunders 1968). Others have argued that premise 7 is false; they have claimed that, given a certain understanding of the laws of nature, one is able to act in such a way that, if one were to so act, the laws of nature that do obtain at a world would not in fact obtain (Beebee and Mele 2002, Lewis 1981). Yet others have questioned the validity of **Rule β** (Huemer 2000; McKay and Johnson 1996; Slote 1982).[4] Still others have proposed that the conclusion of the **Original Consequence Argument** is false because if we understand the 'can'

4 A number of people who have argued that **Rule β** is invalid (given van Inwagen's definition of 'N*p*,') have identified an alternative definition of 'N*p*' that would both serve van Inwagen's purposes, and that, they claim, is valid on this alternative definition (see, for example, Clarke 2003b; Huemer 2000; McKay and Johnson 1996).

that is relevant to moral responsibility as an ability of a certain sort, then one can choose to do otherwise than one did even if determinism is true (Vihvelin 2000, 2004). This would be an ability analogous to the ability that I have to read a book or to refrain from reading a book, an ability or power that determinism does not threaten.

Since I have little to add to these searching assessments, I prefer to proceed in this fashion. I first summarize one criticism of the **Original Consequence Argument** that introduces material that will be handy for what is to come in later chapters. (For those who are interested, a second criticism, the local miracle compatibilist's reply, is relegated to *Appendix* below.) I then pay close attention to an underlying theme of this argument—the theme that determinism robs us of the control that responsibility requires. Among other things, focusing on this theme of control facilitates appreciating that the **Original Consequence Argument**—or at least a near cousin of it, the **Reformulated Consequence Argument**—and the **Manipulation Argument** (which will be discussed in Chapter 6) may be more closely related than one might have thought.

2.2 A PROBLEM CONCERNING THE INTERPRETATION OF 'CAN'

At various places, the **Original Consequence Argument** invokes claims about what is or what is not in one's power to do, or, what amounts to the same thing, what one can or cannot do. Its conclusion, for instance, says that *if determinism is true, then no one can do otherwise*. Care should be taken in interpreting this conclusion and the premises of the argument in which 'can' occurs because there are different senses of 'can.' We distinguish two of these senses.

2.2.1 The Hypothetical Sense of 'Can'

First, there is the hypothetical (or weak, or compatibilist) sense of 'can.' It is to be analyzed in this way:

> **Can-Hypothetical:** *S* can, at time *t*, do *A* at time t^* (*t* may be identical to or later than t^*) =df. *S* would, at *t*, do *A* at t^* if *S* were, at *t*, to choose, or want, or try to do *A*, at t^*.

The basic idea underlying this sense of 'can' is that when you say that you can do something, you are saying that there are no constraints or impediments that prevent you from doing what you want, or try, or choose to do. If you can do something, it is true that you would have done it had you wanted, or tried, or chosen to do it. Hence, to say that *S* can do other than *A* is to say that if *S* were to choose, or want, or try to do other than *A*, *S* would do other than *A*. And to say that *S* cannot do *A* is to say that even if *S* were to want, or try, or choose to do *A*, *S* would not do *A* (see, for instance, Ayer 1954; Hume 1748/1978, Section VIII, Part 1, p. 73; Moore 1911, ch. 6).

It is vitally important to appreciate that, given this hypothetical sense of 'can,' it *is* in our power (sometimes) to do other than what we in fact do even if determinism is true. Here's an illustrative example. Suppose Claudette, in a deterministic world, is pondering whether to buy a Coke or a Pepsi. She buys a Pepsi. Could she have bought a Coke instead? According to **Can-Hypothetical**, when we ask this question, we are asking: "Had Claudette wanted, or tried, or chosen to buy a Coke, would she have done so?" Surely, the answer to this question may be "yes" even if determinism is true. We can expect an affirmative answer provided that there were no constraints or impediments that would have prevented Claudette from buying the Coke had she wanted, or tried, or chosen to buy the Coke. Alternatively, on the **Can-Hypothetical** analysis, when we ask, "could Claudette have bought a Coke instead even if it is causally determined that she buy a Pepsi?", we're asking, roughly: "If conditions in the past had been different—if, for example, contrary to fact Claudette had wanted a Coke—and there were no impediments that prevented her from buying a Coke, would she have bought a Coke?" And the answer to this question is a resounding "yes."

In contrast, in the hypothetical sense of 'can,' Claudette *can't* run faster than the speed of light, or *can't* see to it that a fact about the past is not a fact about the past, or can't get hold of her keys (as naughty Ralph threw them into the well). Even if Claudette had wanted, or tried, or chosen to, Claudette wouldn't have been able to run faster than the speed of light, or wouldn't have been able to so act that a fact about the past is not a fact about the past, or wouldn't have been able to find the keys. There are constraints that prevent Claudette from doing any of this.

Notice that if 'can,' in all its appearances in the **Consequence Argument**, refers to the weak, hypothetical sense of 'can,' then the premises that *you can't alter the past* and that *you can't alter the laws are true*: even if you had wanted, or tried, or chosen to alter these things, you would have failed. But the conclusion of the argument—*if determinism is true, you can't do otherwise*—would be false: on the hypothetical analysis of 'can,' as we have just explained, you *can* do other than what you in fact do even if determinism is true (for instance, Claudette could have done other than buy a Pepsi). It stands to reason, then, that it could not be *this* weak, hypothetical concept of *can* that is operative in van Inwagen's **Consequence Argument**. If it were, the argument would not be valid. So let's introduce a second stronger, categorical, or incompatibilist sense of 'can.'

2.2.2 The Categorical Sense of 'Can'

It will be easier to understand this alternative by asking what, on this alternative, it would mean to say that you can do other than something, *A*, that you do. The basic idea is that you can do other than, say, *A*, at *t* just in case, given exactly the same past up to, or just prior to *t*, you do something else instead. We may state the analysis in this way. Suppose, *S*, at *t*, does *A* in the actual world, *w*.

> **Can-Categorical:** In world, *w*, *S*, at time *t*, can, at *t*, do other than *A* at time *t** (again, *t** may be identical to or later than *t*) =df. There is a possible world with (i) exactly the same laws as *w* until *t*, and (ii) exactly the same past right up to, or just prior to *t*, as *w*, in which *S*, at *t*, does something other than *A* at *t**.

Compare **Can-Categorical** with **Can-Hypothetical:**

> **Can-Hypothetical:** *S*, at *t*, can, at *t*, do other than *A* at time *t** =df. *S* would, at *t*, do other than *A* at *t** if, at *t*, *S* wanted, or tried, or chose to do something other than *A* at *t**.

'**Can-Categorical**' is a strong sense of 'can' because it implies (unlike the weak, hypothetical sense) that if you perform some action at a time—you buy a Coke, say, at *t*—you cannot do other than buy a Coke at *t*, *given* exactly the same past and the laws right up to or just prior to *t*. Clearly, it is in this strong sense of 'can' that van Inwagen intended that we interpret 'can' in all its occurrences in the **Consequence Argument**. Given this interpretation of 'can,' the argument is valid.

But we now run smack against a problem: one might well wonder why one should interpret 'can,' whenever it occurs in the **Consequence Argument**, in the sense that van Inwagen prefers rather than in some alternative sense such as the sense that **Can-Hypothetical** captures. It is, after all, not obvious that if responsibility requires freedom to do otherwise, it must be the case that we can do otherwise in some weak sense of 'can do otherwise' or in the strong sense that incompatibilists, in general, favor. At this stage, one might try to advance the debate by careful scrutiny of each competing analysis of 'can.' So, for instance, some have argued that **Can-Hypothetical** has serious deficiencies (for elaboration, see sections A.1 in the Appendix at the end of this chapter and 4.4.2.). But **Can-Hypothetical** may well be replaced by other (relatively weak) "compatibilist" analyses of 'can' that are not obviously flawed (see, for example, Smith 2003 and Vihvelin 2004). Compatibilists who endorse this alternative (compatibilist) analysis and incompatibilists who favor the stronger analysis would once again find themselves at an impasse over the relevant interpretation of 'can.'

Concerns regarding the germane sense of 'can' are important in the context of discussing responsibility for, among other reasons, the intuitive association of what we *can do* (in the apt sense of 'can') and what it is *in our control* to do (in the pertinent sense of 'control'). This association is brought to light in the next section.

2.3 THE REFORMULATED CONSEQUENCE ARGUMENT

One might parse **Rule β** in this way: if one cannot prevent one thing, and one cannot prevent this thing's leading to a second, then one cannot prevent the second. Reformulated in this fashion, the link between what we can do and what it is in our control to do is not difficult to discern. **Rule β** can just as easily be reconceptualized as a principle regarding control. Understood in this way, its general thrust is that if one has no control over one thing, and one has no control over this thing's leading to a second, then one has no control over the second. This version of **Rule β** can be stated more carefully in the following way:

> **Rule β (Control)**: From, (C1), one lacks control over its being the case that P, and, (C2), one lacks control over its being the case that if P, then Q, infer, (C3), one lacks control over its being the case that Q.

If we ignore nuances regarding the concept of control, then the following line of reasoning for incompatibilism that the **Original Consequence Argument** suggests is seductive: "No one has any control over the complete state of the universe in the far distant past. In addition, no one has any control over the laws. No one, for instance, can now do anything, the doing of which would bring it about that some fact of the past is not a fact of the past or that some law of nature is not a law of nature. But if determinism is true, the past plus the laws 'lead to'—that is, the relevant propositions (**Past** and **Laws**) entail—all truths, and, needless to say, no one has any control over *this* conditional fact. So, it follows that no one has any control over what one in fact does; what one does is not 'up to one.' If none of one's actions, though, is 'up to one,' then none of one's actions is free. Hence, no one is morally responsible for any of one's actions." We may recast this line of reasoning so that its premises and the rationales for these premises are perspicuous.

Let '*S*' range over any person and '*A*' range over any action. (Construe 'action' broadly to include intentional omissions as well as mental actions such as decisions.) Assume that determinism is true. The **Reformulated Consequence Argument** unfolds in this way:

THE REFORMULATED CONSEQUENCE ARGUMENT

(1) *S* has no control over the past and the laws being as they are. [Assumption, the past and the laws are fixed]

(2) *S* has no control over its being the case that the past and the laws being as they are entail that *S* does *A*. [From determinism and the fact that no one has control over a necessary truth. Remember, assuming determinism and that it is true that *S* does *A*, necessarily, the conjunction of the past and the laws entails that *S* does *A*.]

(3) If (1) and (2), then *S* has no control over *A*. [(1), (2), **Rule β (Control)**]
(4) Therefore, *S* has no control over *A*.
(5) If *S* has no control over *A*, then *S* has no control in *A*-ing.[5] [Assumption]
(6) Therefore, *S* has no control in *A*-ing.
(7) If *S* is morally responsible for *A*-ing, then *S* has control in *A*-ing. [Assumption, responsibility requires control]
(8) Therefore, it's false that *S* is morally responsible for *A*-ing.

2.4 CONTROL

Suppose, however, that we *are* sensitive to niceties about control. Then the **Reformulated Consequence Argument** is suspect. In particular, it is doubtful whether **Rule β (Control)** can sustain incompatibilism. To appreciate this, distinguish, first, between *active control* and *ultimate control.*

2.4.1 Active Control

Active control concerns the direct causal production of agent-involving events, such as the agent's having certain values, desires, and beliefs, his making a certain evaluative judgment, his forming a certain intention or arriving at a certain decision, his executing an intention, and his performing a nonmental action. Suppose, on the basis of prior deliberation, you form the judgment that it is best for you to remain home and complete your paper that is due tomorrow, rather than going to the theatre. Your reasons cause your best judgment. If there is nothing untoward in the causal sequence that involves your deliberation and that culminates in your forming the best judgment, then you exert active control in forming the judgment. Members of this causal sequence may include the coming to mind of pertinent beliefs, your weighing of reasons for and against remaining home and spending time on the paper, and so forth. There is no reason to deny that we can exert this sort of control even in a deterministic world.

Another way to appreciate what active control amounts to is to reflect on the outlines of a popular theory of the nature of actions, the *event causal theory of action*.

2.4.1.1 The Event Causal Theory of Action and Deviance

Every action is an event. According to the event causal theory of action, an event is an action in virtue of being appropriately caused by mental events

5 Sometimes the phrase '*S* has control *over A*' has the connotation of *S*'s having alternatives. As I use this phrase or close variants of it in this argument, it should *not* be taken to have any such connotation. When I use this phrase (or close variants) in the premises, I do so simply because it is stylistically preferable, in the premise, to the alternative '*S* has control in *A*-ing.'

of certain sorts. Each action, for instance, is caused by the acquisition or possession of an intention. On the view that I find most plausible, intentions are not reducible to mental states such as (the having of) beliefs and desires. Among an action's mental causes are motivational elements, such as desires, and cognitive elements, such as beliefs. On the causal theory, typically, each agent's action is caused by the agent's having a certain desire and the agent's having a certain belief.

The causal theory enjoys various advantages. For example, when a person acts freely, the person usually, or perhaps always, acts for a reason. Causal theorists can readily explain what it is to act for a reason. Suppose Kate wanted to cheer up Dave, and she believed that she could do so by (freely) sharing a joke with Dave. Suppose that the having of this desire and belief causes Kate freely to tell the joke. Then we can rationally explain why Kate told the joke by citing her reasons—the having of her relevant desire and belief (a complex event), or, the having of her pertinent reason (again, an event), caused her to tell the joke. Moreover, we can say that Kate acted on her relevant reason, because *this* reason—roughly, this desire—caused her to tell the joke. It could be that the actual reason Kate told the joke was a different desire that could also be satisfied by that same action, say a desire to stop Dave from falling asleep. Causal theorists can explain the difference between the reason for which one acted and a reason that one merely had. They can say that only one was causally efficacious.

Sometimes, it appears, an action may arise from a causal chain that is *deviant* or wayward. In one of Donald Davidson's examples (1980, p. 79), a climber wants or intends to rid himself of the weight and danger of holding another man on a rope. He might believe that by loosening his hold on the rope, he could satisfy this want. This belief and want (or intention) might so unnerve him as to cause him to loosen his hold unintentionally. Here, the relevant alleged action—the climber's loosening his hold—arises from a deviant causal chain. This action is caused by the pertinent want and belief but not in the "normal" way. This example is an example of *primary deviance*. It raises a concern about causal connections between mental elements (or their physical realizers) and ensuing bodily movements. Cases of *secondary deviance* center more on the association between intentional actions and their consequences. For example, in another of Davidson's illustrations, a man attempts to kill someone by shooting at him. The killer misses his victim by a mile, but the shot stampedes a herd of wild pigs that trample the intended victim to death (1980, p. 78).

Some have taken this problem of deviance to be a decisive counterexample against causal theories of action. The objectors claim that causal theorists of action are committed to the view that the climber, in Davidson's case of primary deviance, performs *an action* of loosening his grip on the rope (because the climber's behavior issues from a germane want and belief). They insist, though, that this view is false; further, they insist that causal theorists cannot identify something of a causal nature in virtue of which it is false that the climber performed the action. Others, though, are more optimistic; a number of causal theorists have argued that this problem of nonwayward causation can be surmounted (see, for e.g., Audi 1997; Brand 1984, ch.1, Harman 1997; Mele 2000; Mele 2003, ch. 2; Mele and Moser 1997; Thalberg 1984). So, for instance, one might propose that the climber's "loosening his hold" is more faithfully described as the rope's slipping from his fingers, something that is not an action; hence, the climber's example cannot falsify a claim of the form "an event is an intentional *action* only if it is caused by relevant beliefs and desires." Others have theorized that intention has a continuous guiding function in the development of intentional action. Possibly, because the climber's loosening his hold is not guided by a pertinent intention, it is not an intentional action (Mele 2003; Mele and Moser 1997). Or maybe the climber's loosening his hold is not an intentional action because it does not have an immediate or proximate cause of the right sort.

As Randolph Clarke (2000, pp. 26–27) and Mele (1995, p. 225) explicate, active control is a constituent of different types of *direct actional control*. On the causal theory of action, any action is an exercise of some sort of direct control by the agent. An action's proximal causation consists in its being nondeviantly caused by appropriate desires, beliefs, intentions, and the like. When an agent exercises direct actional control in performing an action, this action's proximal causation is partly what constitutes the agent's having direct actional control in that instance. An agent would exert this sort of control, for example, in (nondeviantly and properly) forming an intention, something that qualifies as a mental action. Determinism, of course, does not preclude our forming intentions.[6] So, again, determinism does not bar us from exercising active control in performing mental actions. At bottom, active control is a species of causal control.

---

6 Active control can also be a constituent of indirect actional control as when an agent exercises such indirect control over the occurrence of an event that is not an action, this control deriving from the agent's direct actional control over earlier actions (Clarke 2000, p. 26). Active control may also have a nonactional form. For example, an event that would be the making of an evaluative judgment by some agent would not be an action. An agent's control over such an event, the occurrence of which is not itself the result of having performed earlier actions over which the agent had direct actional control, would be a function of the way in which the agent's deliberative causal process produced that event. This sort of event would be under its agent's active control to the extent that the (nondeviant) causal processes that produced it were free of certain sorts of influences. These would be influences that either would, as Mele proposes (1995, p. 225), undermine the freedom of the subsequent action the event produced, such as compulsion, manipulation, and insanity, or, as Clarke suggests (2000, pp. 26–27), involve certain sorts of inefficiency and irrationality that may not be so severe as to undermine the freedom of the agent's subsequent action, such as the coming to mind, while deliberating, of irrelevant considerations or akratic influences.

2.4.2 Ultimate Control

Ultimate control is concerned with forging an intimate link between an agent's putatively free action and the agent herself so that it is, minimally, plausible to maintain that the agent is the "final" or "ultimate" source of her action; her action originates "*in her*." We suppose that if an agent is the ultimate originator of her action, then she has ultimate control in performing that action. We may distinguish between three different conceptions of ultimate origination, and so three different conceptions of ultimate control. We start with a trio of conditions that all three conceptions of ultimate origination share. Assume that any free action is caused.[7] (On the causal theory of action, this would have to be true because this theory implies that an event is an action only if that event is appropriately caused.) (i) The cause, or at least a causal antecedent, of the free action must be a component of the type of cause that plays a salient role in the production of *action* or *free action* (such as the having of a suitable belief or desire). The cause could not be something like the beating of an agent's heart. (ii) This cause (or part of it) must, in some obvious sense, be internal to its agent. (iii) The cause must be at least partly constitutive of the agent in a way in which, in virtue of being so constitutive, it would be correct to say that the action (or the free action) "truly" issues *from the agent*, or is the "*agent's own*," or is one over which *the agent has control*. It is something like (iii) that conceptions of ultimate origination seek to capture. To differentiate the three conceptions of ultimate origination, we need to say something about what it is for one event to cause deterministically another event, and what it is for an event to cause indeterministically another.

One event deterministically causes another if and only if in each possible world with the same laws of nature as the actual world in which the first event occurs, and that has the same past up until the time that this event occurs, this first event causes the second; there is no chance that the second will not be caused by the first, given the occurrence of the first. *An event indeterministically causes another* if and only if it is consistent with the laws of nature that the former event occurs and not have caused the latter; there is a chance that the latter not be caused by the former even if the former occurs. Suppose, for example, that if a certain microphysical particle is fired at another such particle at a certain velocity, there is a chance (or probability) that the particle that is fired at, when hit by the first, will emit another particle, and there is chance (or probability) that the fired-at particle, when hit, will not emit this other particle. If fired at and it does emit another particle, we may have an instance in which the first triggering particle indeterministically causes the second particle to emit yet another particle. Even if the first is fired at the second and the first hits the

7 Non-causalists, such as Ginet (1990) and Goetz (1998) will not accept this assumption.

second, there is a chance that the second will not emit another particle on being hit by the first.

Let's sketch an example involving the indeterministic causation of an action by prior reasons. Imagine that on some occasion, there is a nonzero probability that is less than one that a prior event, *R1*, consisting in an agent's having (or acquiring) certain beliefs and desires will cause event *A1*, a certain mental action performed by the agent. So, for instance, we can assume that there is an 80% chance that some of Claude's relevant desires and beliefs will cause Claude to decide to buy a Coke. Suppose, in addition, that there is, as well, a nonzero probability that is less than one that a prior event *R2* consisting in the agent's having (or acquiring) certain other beliefs and desires will cause event *A2*, a certain alternative mental action, instead. We may assume that there is a 20% chance that other pertinent desires and beliefs will cause Claude to decide to buy a Pepsi. Then, given all prior conditions, it is genuinely open to the agent to perform action *A1* and genuinely open to him to perform the alternative action *A2*. Claude can either decide to buy the Coke or he can decide to buy the Pepsi. Now suppose that, in the circumstances, whichever of the available mental actions the agent performs, that action will be performed, and it will be caused by the reasons (pairs of suitable desires and beliefs) that favor it. The causation by the prior reasons of the action will be indeterministic. If Claude decides to buy the Coke, this decision of his will be indeterministically caused by prior reasons of his; even given *these* reasons, he could have decided to buy the Pepsi instead. Had he decided to buy the Pepsi, this alternative decision of his would have been indeterministically caused by the reasons that favor his buying the Pepsi.

We may now differentiate among three different conceptions of ultimate origination.

2.4.2.1 The Negative Conception of Ultimate Origination

To introduce the first conception, Robert Kane (2000, p. 66) proposes that "ultimate responsibility" for an action requires either that the action not be deterministically caused (even by its immediate causal antecedents, such as the having of desires or beliefs) or, if the action is deterministically caused, any determining cause of it either be or result (at least in part) from an action by that agent that was not deterministically caused (and for which the agent was "ultimately responsible").[8] These remarks on ultimate responsibility suggest a view of ultimate origination that is negative; the view is negative because it is characterized in terms of the absence of deterministic causation. We may take someone who endorses

---

8 "What the condition [of ultimate responsibility] requires is that there not be any sufficient ground or reason (condition, cause, motive) of our actions for which we are not ourselves to some degree responsible. Or, putting it positively, we must be responsible to some degree by virtue of our own voluntary actions for anything that is a *sufficient ground (arche)* or *reason* (condition, cause, or motive) for our acting as we do" (Kane 2000, p. 66).

this *negative conception* of ultimate origination to be committed to the following. Assuming, again, that any free action is caused, add to the trio of conditions:

> (i) The cause, or at least a causal antecedent, of the free action must be a component of the type of cause that plays a salient role in the production of *action* or *free action*. (ii) This cause must, in some obvious sense, be internal to its agent. (iii) The cause must be at least partly constitutive of the agent in a way in which, in virtue of being so constitutive, it would be correct to say that the action (or the free action) "truly" issues *from the agent*, or is the "*agent's own*," or is one over which *the agent* has control,

the fourth condition that the cause in (i), (ii), and (iii), *not* itself be deterministically caused if this cause deterministically gives rise to the action or free action, or this cause indeterministically produces the action or free action. Claude's decision to buy the coke is indeterministically caused by prior reasons of his. So in relation to this decision, Claude meets the requirements of the negative conception for being the ultimate originator of this decision; he has ultimate control in making it. With this sort of control with respect to his decision, his decision to buy the Coke was not already "written in his book of life" long before he was born. He enjoys a species of freedom from control by the past.

2.4.2.2 The Positive Conception of Ultimate Origination

Regarding the second conception, one promising construal of what we may refer to as the *positive conception* of ultimate origination (and so ultimate control) is explicated in terms of agent-causal activity. So let's first say something about *agent-causal accounts of free action*. The agent causalist affirms that *directly* free actions are *agent-caused*. To understand this view, we need to understand the distinction between actions that are directly free and those that are indirectly free, and we need to appreciate the difference between agent-causation and ordinary "event-event" causation.

Starting with the former distinction, an action is *indirectly free* if it is free and it derives its freedom from the freedom of other actions to which it is suitably related. Suppose that, if you take a magical pill, you cannot but cheat on the exam. Assume that you are free to decide to take the pill and that you are free to decide to refrain. Suppose you freely decide to take the pill, you take it on the basis of this decision, and you end up cheating. Your cheating is indirectly free insofar as its freedom traces to the freedom of your prior decision to take the pill. An action is *directly free* if it is free but not indirectly so. It has frequently been thought that decisions are prime candidates of actions that, if free, are directly free.

AGENT-CAUSAL ACCOUNTS OF FREE ACTION

Traditional agent-causal accounts of free action, like compatibilist ones, require for free agency that the agent possesses an effective capacity for conscious, reflective practical reasoning. In addition traditional agent-causal *libertarian* accounts require that a (directly) free decision or action not be deterministically caused by any events. Traditional agent-causal theories, further, introduce specifically *agent-causal requirements* on free action:

> (1) A (directly) free decision (or overt action) is caused by *the agent*. (2) Neither the decision (or action) nor the event that is the *agent's causing the decision* (or action) be deterministically caused by other *events*. (3) The causation by the agent of the decision (or action) not consist in causation by events.

To elaborate, according to agent-causal accounts, the freedom that moral responsibility requires is accounted for by the existence of agents who possess a special causal power, the power of agent- or substance-causation to make choices or perform actions, without being deterministically caused to make these choices or actions. The kind of causation involved in an agent's making a free choice is not reducible to causation among states of the agent or events (such as the having of desires or beliefs) involving the agent. Rather, the kind of causation is irreducibly an instance of *a substance* causing a choice (but, again, not by way of any states or events). The agent has the causal power to make choices without being deterministically caused to do so.

It's important to get clear on the sort of causation at issue with agent-causal theories. As Timothy O'Connor explains (2002, p. 200), we often talk loosely of inanimate objects as causing certain things to happen. We say things like "Ish's car knocked down the fence." But it would be wrong to interpret this event—the event of Ish's car knocking down the fence—as Ish's car (a substance) literally causing the fence to be knocked down. Rather, we interpret the claim as shorthand for the assertion that the movement of Ish's car, an event, caused the fence to fall down, another event. Here, we have an instance of ordinary event-event causation. The *event* involving Ish's car, and not the car, brought about the effect that is another event involving another physical object, the fence. After all, no such effects emanate from Ish's car when it is parked in Ish's garage.

With agent-causation, though, the causation at issue is not ordinary event-event causation. When the agent causalist asserts that Ish agent-caused his free decision, the claim is not to be interpreted as the claim that an event involving Ish, such as Ish's thinking about certain reasons, caused another event, Ish's making a certain decision. Rather, the claim is to be taken as asserting that Ish, a substance, himself caused an event—Ish's making some decision.

The agent causalist maintains that an agent is a substance and, hence, is not the kind of thing that can itself be an effect (though events in its life can be effects of it). On these agent-causal accounts, then, an agent is in a strict and literal sense an originator or ultimate source of her free actions; she is an uncaused cause of that behavior whose causing of that behavior is not deterministic.

Traditional agent-causal theories seem, then, to be able to accommodate the following libertarian desiderata. (1) They secure the availability of genuine alternatives. The free actions that are agent-caused have no deterministic event-causes. So, for example, if we suppose that Claude agent-caused his decision to buy the Coke, given exactly the same past right up to (or just prior to) the time at which he made this decision, and the same laws, he could instead have agent-caused the alternative decision to buy the Pepsi. (2) By agent-causing her free actions, the agent exercises active control in bringing about her free actions; after all, the agent agent-*causes* her free actions. (3) By being an uncaused agent-cause of her free actions, the agent is the ultimate originator of her actions (see, for e.g., Clarke 2003a). (4) Finally, having the power to agent-cause her actions, it appears, endows the agent-cause with a power to influence causally which open alternative—which pathway into the future—will be made actual. It is "up to" Claude to make actual either the trajectory into the future in which he decides to buy the Coke, or the trajectory in which he decides to buy the Pepsi.

To summarize some key points, all versions of traditional agent-causal views take agent-causation to be a different kind of causation from event causation. With all such versions, when an agent performs an action freely, the agent agent-causes the free action. With all such versions, the action that is agent-caused does not have any event cause. One motivation for this requirement of lack of an event cause is the thought that only with the absence of such event causation can there be two or more courses of action genuinely open to the agent. Versions of the traditional view differ with regard to what is directly caused by an agent—a bodily movement, a brain event, an intention, a decision, etc.[9]

There are some non-traditional versions of agent-causal accounts of control that attempt to combine both event causation and agent-causation in the production of free action. Clarke, for example, has defended the view that a *free* action is both indeterministically caused by apt agent-involving events, such as the agent's prior desires, intentions, and beliefs *and* co-produced by the agent's substance-causing it. He says that a "determinant" is any entity that is a cause of an event (1996, p. 28). On the traditional agent-causal view, the agent is the sole determinant of the free

9 For more on traditional agent-causal views, see, for example, Chisholm 1982; Reid 1969; Rowe 1991, and Taylor 1966; 1974.

event she directly causes. On Clarke's hybrid view, she is one determinant among others, the others being event-causes. The agent-cause co-determines the free action as does the action's event-cause. (We shall return to Clarke's view in Chapter 9.)

It is also possible that, on a different sort of hybrid view, an action of an agent's be co-caused in this way: the agent agent-causes the action and the action is also deterministically caused by prior events such as the agent's having of reasons.

We may now characterize the positive conception of ultimate origination. This conception adds to the three conditions, (i), (ii), and (iii), the additional condition that the action (or free action) be *agent-caused.*

2.4.2.3 Compatibilist Conceptions of Ultimate Origination

As for the third conception, compatibilists favor accounts of ultimate origination that are compatible with determinism. Some compatibilists may well accept conditions (i), (ii), and (iii) as sufficient for ultimate origination but may differ over what is to be true if (iii),

> (iii) The cause must be at least partly constitutive of the agent in a way in which, in virtue of being so constitutive, it would be correct to say that the action (or the free action) "truly" issues *from the agent*, or is the "*agent's own*," or is one over which *the agent* has control,

is to be satisfied.

AN HIERARCHICAL COMPATIBILIST CONCEPTION OF ULTIMATE ORIGINATION

Harry Frankfurt's early work on hierarchical motivation, for instance, suggests something along the following lines in the way of "authenticity" of desires and ultimate origination of actions (Frankfurt 1971). A higher-order desire is a desire that has some *desire* as its object; so, for example, Annie's desire that she not have a desire to be selfish is a *second-order desire*; it has, as its object, the desire not to be selfish. A first-order desire is a desire that is not a higher-order desire. Suppose that Gill both has a (first-order) desire to smoke because he has been smoking for several years, and a conflicting (first-order) desire not to smoke because he has decided to kick the habit. Assume that he also has a higher-order desire, specifically a second-order desire, that his desire not to smoke be effective; he wants it to be the case that his desire not to smoke move him all the way to action (or intentional inaction). A *second-order volition* is a second-order desire that a first-order desire be effective. Gill's second-order desire that his first-order desire not to smoke move him all the way to action is a second-order volition. Very roughly, think of second-order desires as desires that are "truly one's own." One "makes" some first-order desire that one has one's own by forming a second-order volition concerning it. As Gill has a second-order volition regarding the desire not to smoke, Gill "sides with" this first-order desire and he "distances himself" from the competing first-order desire to smoke. Determinism places no obstacles against our having second-order desires; nor does it bar us from forming second-order volitions.

On a simple hierarchical view of authenticity, a first-order desire is authentic if its agent has an unopposed second-order volition concerning this first-order desire (Frankfurt 1971). You have a second-order desire (a volition) that some first-order desire of yours be effective (in the sense that this first-order desire moves you all the way to action), and, in addition, you have no conflicting second-order volition. An agent is the ultimate originator of an action if the action causally issues from an authentic first-order desire of hers. This is one outline of an account of a compatibilist conception of ultimate origination. It is compatibilist because its requirements for ultimate origination are all consistent with determinism.

FISCHER AND RAVIZZA'S COMPATIBILIST CONCEPTION OF ULTIMATE ORIGINATION

John M. Fischer and Mark Ravizza propose an alternative compatibilist account of ultimate origination. Their overall view concerning the freedom dimension (as opposed, for example, to the epistemic dimension) of responsibility is that an agent is morally responsible for an action only if the action derives from a process (a "mechanism") for which he has taken responsibility and that is moderately responsive to reasons. This view has both a reasons-responsive component and a taking-responsibility (or ownership) component which is, in effect, Fischer and Ravizza's origination component. The central idea underlying the reasons-responsiveness component is that an agent has freedom-level control in performing an action only if that action is appropriately sensitive to reasons; the action is responsive to rational considerations. If Gill's desire to smoke were irresistible, then even if Gill had sufficient reasons not to smoke and he recognized these reasons, his pertinent conduct would not be responsive to these reasons; he would smoke despite being aware of these reasons and wanting these reasons to guide his actions. We need not dwell any further on this component of Fischer and Ravizza's view.

It is possible for an agent's actions to issue from an appropriately reasons-responsive mechanism whose primary constituents have been induced externally by clandestine manipulation, hypnosis, brainwashing, and so forth. Intuitively, in cases of this sort the agent is not morally responsible for the pertinent actions. Such cases impel Fischer and Ravizza to theorize that the way in which the agent's springs of action are acquired has a pronounced bearing on responsibility; responsibility is, consequently, an essentially "historical" phenomenon. Fischer and Ravizza's diagnosis is that in these troubling cases, the mechanism that issues in action is not the "agent's own," the agent having failed to take responsibility for it. Thus, to guard against casual springs being acquired in a manner that subverts responsibility, Fischer and Ravizza supplement the reasons-responsiveness component with an account of mechanism ownership.

Taking responsibility is part of the process by which a mechanism leading to action becomes one's own. To adumbrate this process, it will be useful to summarize central theses pertaining to taking responsibility that Fischer and Ravizza defend. As actions can have various sources (like practical reason, nonreflective habit, direct brain stimulation, etc.) they can issue from different mechanisms. When an agent takes responsibility for his actions, he is taking responsibility for actions that issue from certain sources. He doesn't take responsibility, for example, for actions that issue from actional elements that are implanted in him against his will. He takes responsibility only *for behavior which issues from certain mechanisms*. What sorts of mechanism? Well, there is first the mechanism of ordinary practical reasoning; reasoning about what one should do and how one should live (1998, p. 215). But it is also the case that many of our actions do not arise from explicit reflection or deliberation. Some are spontaneous; others might be based on imitation, and so forth. We take responsibility, too, for behavior that issues from nonreflective mechanisms (1998, p. 216). In this way the mechanisms (in their totality) become the agent's own.

Three conditions are necessary and sufficient for taking responsibility. First, the individual must view himself, when acting from various mechanisms, as a source of certain events in the world. Specifically, he must see certain events in the world as results of his deliberation, choices, or action (1998, pp. 210–11). Second, the agent must view himself as an apt target for the reactive attitudes such as indignation, resentment, gratitude, admiration, etc. (1998, p. 211) There are two versions of this condition. In the nonreflective case where there is no philosophical reflection on the relationship between determinism and the appropriateness of the reactive attitudes, the agent has to view himself as a suitable candidate for the reactive attitudes in certain circumstances, given our actual social practices. Here, the social practices are not criticized (1998, p. 211). In the reflective case where there is philosophical reflection on the relationship between determinism and the appropriateness of the reactive attitudes, the agent must at least believe that it is prima facie plausible that he is an apt candidate for the reactive attitudes and be willing to put aside any residual doubts, for practical purposes (1998, p. 227). The doubts may arise from the thought, for instance, that incompatibilism is probably true. The first two conditions involve relevant dispositional beliefs. The agent must believe, at least dispositionally, that he is a source of certain upshots in the world and that he is an appropriate candidate, under certain conditions, for the reactive attitudes. Lastly, the third condition is that the beliefs specified by the first two conditions be based, in an appropriate way, on the individual's evidence. The general import of this third condition may be summed up in the following way. The agent has certain beliefs: he is a source of certain upshots in the world, and he is a fair candidate for the reactive attitudes. The third condition requires that these beliefs must be based on the agent's evidence for them. For example, a person's view of himself as an agent needs to be based, in an appropriate way, on his experience with the effects of his choices and actions on the world. And his view of himself as an apt target for the reactive attitudes in certain circumstances needs to be based on his experiences with the social practice of things like praise and blame (1998, p. 213).

Fischer and Ravizza stress that taking responsibility is *not* an action; rather it is to have a cluster of dispositional beliefs, beliefs specified by the first two conditions of taking responsibility, in a certain way (1998, p. 217). It is important that the beliefs need not be occurrent. That is, roughly, they need not be beliefs that you currently have in mind; rather, they need simply be standing beliefs.

There is a subjective element to taking responsibility, to wit, in order for an agent to be morally responsible for his behavior that issues from certain sorts of mechanism, he must see himself as an agent who is an apt candidate for the reactive attitudes (assuming the truth of determinism). So if an agent, say an incompatibilist like Derk Pereboom, does not see himself in this way, he won't be responsible for his behavior. Fischer claims that having a certain view of ourselves, that we are indeed sources of our behavior and apt candidates for things like praise and blame is required for us to be active and in control (1998, pp. 220–23).

In summary, when an agent takes responsibility for the mechanism of an action, he makes that mechanism "his own" (Fischer and Ravizza, 1998, ch. 8). In the terminology we have introduced, when an agent takes responsibility for a type of mechanism, the mechanism is "authentic"; and the agent is the ultimate originator of an action which issues from such a mechanism provided that this action is appropriately responsive to reasons. Fischer and Ravizza argue that each of the three constituents of taking responsibility (or ultimate origination) can be satisfied by us even if our world is deterministic. Label this third conception of ultimate origination, either the Fischer and Ravizza variant or the Frankfurt variant, the *compatibilist conception.*

For what is of immediate interest to us—assessing the **Reformulated Consequence Argument**—we need not argue for the superiority of any one of these three competing conceptions. It is sufficient that we recognize that there are these competing conceptions.

2.5 ASSESSING THE REFORMULATED CONSEQUENCE ARGUMENT

We may now return to the primary component of the **Reformulated Consequence Argument** with which we are concerned, the modified version of **Rule β**. This rule says:

> **Rule β (Control)**: From, (C1), one lacks control over its being the case that P, and, (C2), one lacks control over its being the case that if P, then Q, infer, (C3), one lacks control over its being the case that Q.

Recapitulating, the proponent of the **Reformulated Consequence Argument** reasons as follows: If (C1a) one lacks control over its being true that (**Past** and **Laws**), and (C2a) one lacks control over its being true that [(if **Past** and **Laws**), then (**Action-Now**)], then (C3a) one lacks control over **Action-Now**. Alternatively, and more intuitively, if (C1b) one lacks control over the past and the laws, and (C2b) one lacks control over its being true that the conjunction of these things entails anything that one does, then (C3b) one lacks control over anything that one does. If we lack control over anything that we do, then we are not responsible for anything that we do. Therefore, we are not responsible for anything that we do.

C1, C2, and C3 are multiply ambiguous given, first, the distinction between active control and ultimate control, and, second, the different conceptions of ultimate control. So **Rule β** requires disambiguation by disambiguating 'control.' First, suppose that 'control,' in each of its occurrences in **Rule β** and in the Reformulated Argument, refers to active control. Then lines (1) (*S has no control over the past and the laws being as they are*), and (2) (*S has no control over its being the case that the past and the laws being as they are entail that S does A*) are true, but line (4) (*Therefore, S has no control over A*) is false. We cannot derive (4) from an application of **Rule β (Control)** to (1) and (2). We cannot do this for the simple reason that determinism does not prevent us from exercising active control in, for example, forming intentions. So even if we lack active control over the past and the laws being what they are (as we surely do), and we lack active control over its being the case that the past and the laws being as they are entails anything that one does (given determinism), it doesn't follow that we lack active control in, for example, making a decision. Put another way, this instance (or variation) of **Rule β (Control)** that we may dub "**Rule AC**" is invalid:

> **AC**: From, **(AC1)**, one lacks active control over the past and the laws being what they are, and, **(AC2)**, one lacks such control over its being the case that if the past and the laws are what they are, then one does whatever it is that one does (that is, one lacks active control over its being the case that the conjunction of propositions **Past** and **Laws** entails anything that one does), infer, **(AC3)**, one lacks active control over whatever it is that one does.

Second, suppose 'control,' in **Rule β** and in each of its occurrences in the argument, refers to Kane-style negative ultimate control. Then, arguably, lines (1) – (4) are all true (*assuming determinism*); arguably, we can accept the following inference rule (**Rule NUC**):

> **NUC**: From, (**NUC1**), one lacks negative ultimate control over the past and the laws being what they are, and, (**NUC2**), one lacks such control over its being the case that if the past and the laws are what they are, then one does whatever it is that one does (that is, one lacks negative ultimate control over its being the case that the conjunction of propositions **Past** and **Laws** entails anything that one does), infer, (**NUC3**), one lacks negative ultimate control over anything that one does.

But given that this type of control requires the falsity of determinism, premise (7)—the premise that *if S is morally responsible for A-ing, then S has (negative ultimate) control in A-ing*—straightforwardly begs the question against compatibilists. Compatibilists, such as Fischer and Ravizza, and Frankfurt, will (or should) argue that it is not clear why the relevant notion of ultimate control that free action or responsibility requires, if these things do indeed require such control, be one that entails that determinism is false.[10] Why can't some compatibilist notion of ultimate control be up to the task?

If determinism is not true, then **NUC3** does not, it appears, follow from **NUC1** and **NUC2**. In an indeterministic world in which some of our actions are indeterministically caused, although you cannot now do anything, the doing of which is indeterministically caused, to "alter" the past or laws, or to render false a necessary truth, what you do at a time may be indeterministically caused (recall the example of Claude's indeterministically caused decision to buy the Coke). So you may well exercise negative ultimate control in what you do at this time. Some might claim that if **Rule NUC** is not valid in a world that is not deterministic, then we should reject this rule altogether.

Third, suppose 'control,' whenever this term occurs in the **Reformulated Consequence Argument**, refers to positive "agent-causal" ultimate control. Then, again, though lines (1) and (2) are true, we cannot infer (4) from these premises and the apt **β**-like rule, **Rule AGC**, because **AGC** is invalid:

> **AGC**: From, (**AGC1**), one lacks agent-causal control over the past and the laws being what they are, and, (**AGC2**), one lacks such control over its being the case that if the past and the laws are what they are, then one does whatever it is that one does (that is, one lacks agent-causal control over its being the case that the conjunction of propositions **Past** and **Laws**

10 A highly insightful discussion of this issue can be found in Fischer 2006a.

> entails anything that one does) infer, (**AGC3**), one lacks agent-causal control over anything that one does.

AGC3 does not follow from **AGC1** and **AGC2** because it is possible that an agent's action be both deterministically or indeterministically event-caused by apt agent-involving events, such as the agent's having or recognizing of reasons, *and* agent-caused by the agent. Also, there seems to be no independent, plausible reason to deny that though we lack agent-causal control over the past and the laws being what they are, and we lack such control over these things "leading to" anything that we do, we may well exercise agent-causal control over some of the things we do (assuming, of course, that there are no other concerns with agent-causation).

Premise (7)—*if S is morally responsible for A-ing, then S has (agent-causal) control in A-ing*—will also strike many, libertarians and compatibilists, as controversial. They will claim that it is not obvious that moral responsibility requires agent-causal control.

Finally, suppose 'control' refers to "compatibilist" ultimate control. (Pick your favorite candidate of such control; it might be Fischer and Ravizza's, or the simple hierarchical view, or yet some other compatibilist variant.) The relevant **β**-like rule, this time, is **CUC**:

> **CUC**: From, (**CUC1**), one lacks compatibilist ultimate control over the past and the laws being what they are, and, (**CUC2**), one lacks such control over its being the case that if the past and the laws are what they are, then one does whatever it is that one does (that is, one lacks compatibilist ultimate control over its being the case that the conjunction of propositions **Past** and **Laws** entails anything that one does), infer, (**CUC3**), one lacks compatibilist ultimate control over anything that one does.

Premises (1) and (2) are true if 'control' denotes compatibilist ultimate control, but applying **CUC** to these premises won't yield (4); this inference rule is, again, invalid. For even if determinism is true, one can, for example, exercise Frankfurt-style hierarchical control in performing an action, or one's actions can issue from a suitably reasons-responsive mechanism for which one has taken responsibility.

I conclude that the notion of control, if there is one, which sustains the **Reformulated Consequence Argument** is elusive.

2.6 THE BASIC VERSION OF THE CONSEQUENCE ARGUMENT

Both van Inwagen's original version and the reformulated version of the **Consequence Argument** have shortcomings. One of these that they share is that **Rule β** seems to be problematic. Adversaries of either of these versions may argue that depending upon how we interpret 'can' (or 'control'), neither **Rule β** nor a version of **Rule β Control** that may legitimately be employed to argue for incompatibilism is valid. Regarding **Rule β** and the original version of the **Consequence Argument**, for instance, we are supposed to infer from the fact that there is nothing we can now do to alter the past and the laws, and the fact that there is nothing we can now do to alter its being the case that our actions are the upshots of the past and the laws (given determinism), that we cannot now do otherwise than what we actually do. On the hypothetical analysis of 'can,' while it is true that we cannot alter the past and the laws, and we cannot do anything to alter the fact that the past plus the laws entail all that we do (given determinism), it is false that we cannot now do otherwise than what we actually do. To evade this sort of problem, some theorists have developed a version of the **Consequence Argument**—what Fischer calls the "**Basic Version**"—that seemingly circumvents any appeal to a **β**-like rule. Briefly outlining this version will be instructive.

Fischer proposes that the **Basic Argument** employs the following principle (the "**Extension Principle**"): an agent can do *X* only if his doing *X* can be an extension of the actual past, holding the laws fixed (1994, p. 88). He elaborates:

> Put metaphorically, if an agent can do *X*, then one could in principle "trace a path" (along which the actual natural laws obtain) between the actual past and his doing *X*. Imagine various pathways into the future. The point is that the only such pathways that indicate what an agent has it in his power to do are the ones which are extensions of the actual past and along which the actual natural laws obtain: these are paths whose initial segments correspond to the actual world up to the relevant time of the action. (1994, p. 88)

Ted Warfield advances a similar sort of principle. He says that "I am free only to add to the past consistent with the laws of nature. Surely all of the actions open to me are actions that, if performed, would add to the past of my world" (2003, p. 627). Warfield has an interesting explication of part of what motivates this principle:

> Consider a large book containing a list of all the true statements about my world up to the present moment. Imagine further that the book is continuously being updated. As I go about my daily business, what I do is add to the list of truths about my world. My actions add to the actual past in ways consistent with the laws of nature. My actions don't 'erase' earlier truths. And none of the additions my actions make are

> additions that involve my doing things in violation of natural laws. This picture strongly suggests that my being free to do something is that my doing so be consistent with the actual past and laws. (2003, p. 628).

Given the **Extension Principle**, the **Basic Consequence Argument** may be summarized in this way: Assume that determinism is true. Suppose Finn tosses a ball at *t2*. The state of the world at an earlier time, *t1*, and the laws entail that Finn tosses the ball at *t2* (assuming determinism). Holding fixed the laws, if determinism is true, there is only one extension of the past into the future, an extension that includes Finn's tossing the ball at *t2*. The **Extension Principle** entails that an agent can do something only if his doing it could be an extension of the actual past (holding fixed the laws). Thus, holding the natural laws fixed (and assuming determinism), it is false that Finn's refraining from tossing the ball at *t2* could be an extension of the actual past. It follows that Finn cannot refrain from tossing the ball at *t2*. (See Fischer 1994, p. 88; Ginet 1990, pp. 102–06; Ginet 2003, pp. 590–92). A suitably generalized version of this argument yields the intermediate conclusion that no one can do other than what one actually does. Combining this intermediate conclusion with the **Principle of Alternative Possibilities**—one is morally responsible for having done something only if one could have done otherwise—secures the incompatibility of determinism with moral responsibility.

Some people might take issue with the **Extension Principle**. They might claim that it is not transparent that the following modification of the **Extension Principle** is defective: if an agent can do *X*, then one could in principle "trace a path" (along which the actual natural laws obtain) between what is *very close to* or *very much like* the actual past and his doing *X*. On this modification, my actions add to what is very close to the actual past in ways consistent with the laws of nature. (Of course, the proponent of the modified principle shoulders the burden of specifying, in a non-arbitrary way, what elements of the past remain fixed; this is no easy task.) Suppose, again, that Finn tosses the ball at *t2*. Could he have done something else instead at that time, holding fixed the laws (and the assumption of determinism)? If *all* elements of the past, and the natural laws, are held fixed, then the original **Extension Principle** (together with the assumption of determinism) entails that Finn could not have done other than toss the ball at *t2*. But if some elements of the past are not fixed, then given the natural laws and the modified, attenuated **Extension Principle**, we cannot rule out Finn's being able to do other than toss the ball at *t2* even if determinism is assumed. Roughly speaking, slightly different pasts and the laws may entail that Finn does different things at *t2*.

The intuitive pull of the original **Extension Principle** is undeniable. If this principle is without fault, then the **Basic Consequence Argument** may well establish that determinism is incompatible with *freedom to do otherwise*.

But as we have stressed, the argument still has a way to go to secure the further conclusion that determinism is incompatible with *moral responsibility*. We need a principle that bridges having (or not having) alternatives with responsibility or (non-responsibility). This principle is the **Principle of Alternative Possibilities** to which we turn in the next chapter.

Appendix

Local Miracle Compatibilism

Van Inwagen's version of the **Consequence Argument** (what I have dubbed the "original version") has as a premise (premise 7) that the natural laws are fixed—one cannot render false a true proposition that states a law of nature. In this appendix, I summarize the local miracle compatibilist's view that there is a sense in which we are free to break the laws.

A.1 LOCAL MIRACLE COMPATIBILISM

In the meeting which you are attending raising your hand at a certain time signifies your voting in favor of a proposal. You fail to raise your hand at that time because you're against the proposal. Could you, nevertheless, have raised your hand at that time? Intuitively, if you were not subject to coercive forces, you were not phobic, you were mentally and physically healthy, you thought well of the proposal, etc. you could have done so. However, you cannot run faster than the speed of light. To run faster than the speed at which light travels would require the occurrence of a miracle—it would require your doing something that violates or breaks a law of nature. But such miracles just don't occur—no one can violate a natural law.

Some compatibilists, appealing to the hypothetical sense of 'can,' claim that even if determinism is assumed, it is easy to see why you could have raised your hand but could not have run faster than light: had you wanted, or tried, or chosen to do so, then (provided there were no relevant impediments) you would have raised your hand. But despite your having wanted, or tried, or chosen to do so, you would not have run faster than the speed of light.

A familiar incompatibilist retort is that, given determinism, and given that you did not choose (try, want) to raise your hand, you were not able to choose to raise your hand. It's true that if you had so chosen, you would have raised your hand. But you did not (at the relevant time and in the relevant circumstances) so choose. To have so chosen would have required a miracle, but no one is able to perform miracles.

Another compatibilist reply, proposed (among others) by David Lewis (1981), is that you *were* able to raise your hand even though a miracle would have had to have occurred for you to have done so. Helen Beebee explains:

> [A]ccording to Lewis, while (1) deterministic agents are able to do things, the doing of which would *require* a miracle to happen, (2) they are not able to *perform* miracles: they are

> not able to do things, the doing of which would *be* a miracle.... [C]all this view—the conjunction of claims (1) and (2) ... 'local miracle compatibilism' (so called because the view appeals to Lewis's theory of counterfactuals, and in particular on the notion of a 'local miracle'). (2003, p. 260)

To understand Lewis's position, some preparatory work is called for. A counterfactual is a conditional proposition of the form, if *p* were the case, *q* would be the case as well. First, according to Lewis, a counterfactual is true if and only if in all those worlds (if any) that are most similar (or "closest") to the actual world and in which *p* is true, *q* is true, too. Suppose you did not raise your hand. To assess the counterfactual, *if (counter to fact) you had raised your hand, the proposal would have passed*, we need to figure out which of all the worlds in which you raise your hand are (or is) most similar to the actual world, and whether the proposition, *the proposal passes*, is true in these most similar worlds.

Second, Lewis theorizes that similarity of one world to another is a function of two factors: the extent to which the two worlds' laws are the same and the extent to which the matters of particular fact are the same. He trades off similarities (or dissimilarities) in matters of fact and laws in accordance with these principles:

> (1) It is of the first importance to avoid big, widespread, diverse violations of law.
> (2) It is of the second importance to maximize the spatio-temporal region throughout which perfect match of particular fact prevails.
> (3) It is of the third importance to avoid even small, localized, simple violations of law.
> (4) It is of little or no importance to secure approximate similarity of particular fact, even in matters that concern us greatly. (Lewis 1979, pp. 47–48)

Third, the notion of a miracle is an *inter-world notion*. To say that the closest world *w* in which some event, *e*, occurs contains a miracle is not to say that event *e* violates *w*'s laws. There is no such world; no event occurs at a world that violates the laws of that world. Rather, to say that world *w* where event *e* occurs contains a miracle is to say that this event violates the laws of nature of the *actual world* (and not of its world, *w*). If, in the closest world, you do raise your hand in the meeting, the event that is the raising of your hand in this world breaks the laws of the actual world. More generally, an event in another possible world, *w1*, is miraculous, from the perspective of *w2* if and only if the occurrence of that event is inconsistent with the laws of *w2*.

Fourth, the spatio-temporal region of perfect match of matters of particular fact between w and the actual world is to be traded off against the "size" of the miracle required to bring about e. Beebee elaborates:

> For example, suppose that in fact I remain seated at my desk for the next half hour. Which is the closest world in which I arrive at the pub in ten minutes' time (event e)? At one e-world, w_1, I remain seated at my desk for, say, 9 minutes and 59.9 seconds, so that the whole of the past up until that moment is exactly the way it is at the actual world, and then I spontaneously disappear, reappearing in the doorway of the pub a tenth of a second later. At another e-world, w_2, something happens to me after, say 5 minutes—the whole of the past up until that (earlier) time being exactly the way it is at the actual world—which induces me to walk in the usual fashion to the pub, arriving exactly 5 minutes later. Let's suppose the thing that happens to me after 5 minutes at w_2 is that I suddenly acquire a strong desire for beer.... Assuming determinism, both w_1 and w_2 contain miracles relative to the actual world. Facts about the distant past of both worlds are exactly the same as they are at the actual world, so those facts plus the *actual* laws of nature are incompatible with e's occurrence. w_1 preserves perfect match of matters of particular fact for several minutes longer than does w_2; on the other hand, the miracle that occurs at w_1 is arguably much bigger than the miracle that occurs at w_2. At w_2, all that is required by way of a miracle is that I acquire a strong desire for beer—and perhaps this can be brought about by a few extra neurons firing, say. The miracle required at w_1, however, is much bigger. Extremely large numbers of molecules need to vanish from one place and reassemble, in just the right configuration, in another. Hence (arguably), since a large miracle occurs at w_1 and only a small one occurs at w_2, w_2 is closer to the actual world—despite the slightly longer match of matters of particular fact at w_1. (Beebee 2003, p. 262)

Fifth, distinguish between weak and strong abilities.

> *Weak ability*: The ability to do some act, A, such that, were you to do A, an actual law of nature would have been violated but not by A or by any effects of A.

If, for instance, you have the ability to raise your hand at t—at the meeting, say—even though you don't actually raise your hand at t, this ability, according to Lewis, is a weak ability. The closest world where you raise your hand is a world where a tiny miracle occurs just prior to your hand-raising. This tiny miracle is a law-breaking event that is *not* an action of yours occurs. Thereafter, the course of events (including the hand-raising itself) unfolds in accordance with the actual laws of nature. So the *act* of hand-raising itself, were you to do it, would neither be, nor cause, a law-breaking event (Beebee 2003, p. 263).

> *Strong ability*: The ability to do some act, *A*, such that were you to do *A*, *A* itself would be or would cause, a law-breaking event. (Roughly, event *e* is a law-breaking event if and only if in every possible world, if *e* occurs then the proposition that is the conjunction of all the actual laws of nature is false. This amounts to more or less the following: necessarily, the occurrence of *e* violates the actual laws.)[11]

If, for example, you have the ability to run faster than the speed of light, this ability is a strong ability. Your running faster than the speed of light is something that is itself (relative to the actual world) a law-breaking event (Beebee 2003, p. 263).

According to Lewis, it is plausible to suppose that agents in a deterministic world sometimes have weak abilities but that these agents never have strong abilities.

We can now finally appreciate how all these different strands fit together to enable the local miracle compatibilist, such as Lewis, to offer a rebuttal of the **Original Consequence Argument**. We may focus only on the part of the argument (presented in simplified form) that is of interest to us: Assuming determinism,

> (1) All my actions are the upshots of propositions about the distant past and propositions that state the laws.
> (2) I can't render propositions about the past false.
> (3) I can't render propositions stating the laws of nature false.
> (4) If (1), (2), and (3), I can't render the upshots of propositions about the distant past and propositions that state the laws—propositions that express the actions that I perform—false.
> (5) Therefore, I can't render the upshots of propositions about the distant past and propositions that state the

11 Beebee (2003, pp. 266–67) indicates problems with this definition of 'law-breaking event.' As a replacement, she suggests: Event *e* is a law-breaking event at world w_a, relative to world w_b, if and only if *e*, together with the circumstances under which it occurs at w_a, is incompatible with *L*, where *L* is the conjunction of all of w_b's laws. This change is not of import in our outline of local miracle compatibilism.

laws—propositions that express the actions that I perform—false.

Having distinguished between weak and strong abilities, line (3) is ambiguous between:

(3a) I can't perform any act such that that act would be or its effects would cause a law-breaking event. In other words, I, just like anybody else, do not have strong abilities.

(3b) I can't perform any act such that were I to do that act, an actual law of nature would be false (and hence would not be a law). (3b) amounts to the claim that I have neither strong nor weak abilities.

As we have noted, according to Lewis, (3b) is false. We do have some weak abilities. So if (3b) replaces (3), the argument is valid but not sound. (3a), in contrast, is true. But replacing (3) by (3a) would render the argument invalid; (5) would not follow from premises (1) – (4). Given determinism, assume that it is true that I cannot alter the past—I cannot render false a true proposition about the past. Assume, also, that I cannot do anything the doing of which would be or would cause a law-breaking event—I cannot, for example, run faster than the speed of light. Still, it doesn't follow from these premises that I lack *weak* abilities. If determinism is true, even if I didn't raise my hand, I may well have the weak ability to raise my hand: it may well be the case that I can perform an act of hand-raising such that if I were to perform it, an actual law of nature would be violated.

One might still be puzzled about the local miracle compatibilist's claim that deterministic agents sometimes have weak abilities; they are sometimes able to do things such that, were they to do them, a law of nature would be broken (but not by the action itself). For suppose one has the following *necessitarian* picture of the laws. On this picture, the laws constrain all the events, including our actions, which occur in the actual world. According to the necessitarian, what events in the actual world transpire depends, in some robust sense, on what the laws are.[12] Suppose, then, that you are in a deterministic world and you refrain at noon from raising your hand at noon. If the laws *constrain* what happens in the actual world, and determinism is true, on this conception of the laws, it really seems that you cannot raise your hand. If the laws do constrain, how could it plausibly be the case that if you were to do something, a natural law would be violated and, thus, would not be a law in the first place? How can what we do "determine" what the laws are? Shouldn't things be the other way around?

12 For development of the necessitarian view, see Armstrong 1983, esp. chs. 6 and 11.

That is, on the necessitarian view of laws, shouldn't it be that what the laws are "determines" what it is in our power to do?

Fortunately, the local miracle compatibilist need not accept the necessitarian picture of the laws but may argue, instead, for a *Humean* picture. On this picture, the laws are simply facts about regularities (perhaps the deepest, most explanatory regularities). On the Humean view, laws place no constraints on what happens; rather, it is the regular course and succession of events that determines what the laws are.[13] If one set of regularities pans out in the actual world, then the actual world will have one set of laws; if a different set of regularities pans out, the actual world will have different laws. Given a Humean conception of the laws, the local miracle compatibilist's claim that agents are sometimes able to do some things such that, were they to do them, a law of nature would be violated (and so would not be a law) seems far more reasonable. For on the Humean view, roughly what laws a world has depends on the regularities that obtain in the world and what regularities obtain in a world depends, in part, on what agents in that world do. Different sets of regularities and so different laws obtain in possible worlds other than the actual world. So there is little reason, if any, to think that (given the Humean view of laws), the fact that raising my hand (at a non-actual world) would require violation of the actual laws undercuts my ability (at the actual world) to raise my hand.

A.2 AN OBJECTION TO LOCAL MIRACLE COMPATIBILISM

This fascinating response on the part of the local miracle compatibilist is not without its share of problems. I mention only one that Beebee develops. Beebee argues that local miracle compatibilism "embodies an inherently unstable attitude towards laws of nature, since it requires that laws have a special kind of jurisdiction over events that are acts, which they do not have over events that are not acts" (2003, p. 273). As we have summarized, Beebee explains, first, that the local miracle compatibilist's claim that deterministic agents sometimes have weak abilities looks plausible from a Humean perspective but *not* from a necessitarian perspective. (Having weak abilities, these deterministic agents are sometimes able to do things which are such that, if they were to do them, a law of nature would be broken and so would not be a law.) But she says that the opposite is true of the other half of the local miracle compatibilist creed, the denial that agents ever have strong abilities (that is, the ability to do something such that, were they to do it, a law would be broken by their acts themselves, or by some of their effects). A necessitarian, of course, would have no difficulty in agreeing with the local miracle compatibilist about this: the laws constrain what we do; so we can't ever do anything the doing of

13 See Beebee 2000 and Loewer 1996.

which itself or the effects of the doing of which would violate the laws. But Beebee adds that, from a Humean perspective, it is very hard to see what reason there could be to believe this second half of the local miracle compatibilist's claim:

> If miracles are relatively cheap when it comes to events that are *not* actions of mine, or effects of actions of mine—as they must be if we are to hold that deterministic agents have weak abilities—why should they not be equally cheap when it comes to events that *are* actions of mine? Actions are, after all, merely a species of event, and the laws of nature manifestly do not care about the distinction between events that are and are not actions. So how could the laws of nature constrain my abilities in the sense that they render me unable to violate them *by my acts*, yet not constrain my abilities in the sense that they do *not* render me unable to perform acts that *require* them to be violated?.... In short, local miracle compatibilism needs a Humean view of laws to motivate the claim that agents have weak abilities, and a necessitarian view of laws in order to motivate the claim that agents never have strong abilities. That is why I said that local miracle compatibilism embodies an unstable attitude towards laws of nature, and that, in the end, is why it fails to be a viable version of compatibilism. (2003, pp. 274–75)[14]

14 For further critical discussion of local miracle compatibilism see Fischer 1994 and Vihvelin 1991.

3 Alternative Possibilities and Moral Responsibility

3.1 THE CONSEQUENCE ARGUMENT AND FREEDOM TO DO OTHERWISE

In connection with the original and the **Basic Version** of the **Consequence Argument**, it is important, once again, to appreciate their feature of *being indirect arguments* for incompatibilism. We have seen that advocates of either of these versions proceed from the intermediate conclusion of these arguments—no one is free to do otherwise—*via* the **Principle of Alternative Possibilities** to the skeptical conclusion that no one is morally responsible for anything that one does. In this chapter, we discuss two objections against this principle, one having to do with a counterexample, and the other with considerations of luck.

3.2 FRANKFURT-TYPE EXAMPLES AND FREEDOM TO DO OTHERWISE

It is well known that famed "Frankfurt-type examples," so christened after Frankfurt's presentation of them (Frankfurt 1969), seem to cast serious doubt on the principle that persons are morally responsible for doing something only if they could have done otherwise. In a typical Frankfurt example, in Stage 1, an agent, Jones, chooses (or decides) to do something, *X*, and intentionally *X*-s. We are to assume that whether you are a libertarian or compatibilist, on your account of free action and moral responsibility, Stage 1 Jones *is* morally responsible for choosing to *X* (and for *X*-ing). In Stage 2, the scenario is developed in such a fashion that something ensures that Jones (Stage 2 Jones) chooses to *X*; this thing supposedly precludes Jones from choosing to do other than *X* *without* in any way interfering in Jones's choosing to *X*. We are meant to draw the conclusion that since Stage 1 Jones is morally responsible for choosing to *X*, and since Stage 2 Jones does not differ relevantly from Stage 1 Jones with respect to choosing to *X*, Stage 2 Jones is also morally responsible for choosing to *X* even though he could not have refrained from choosing to *X*. Individual Frankfurt-type examples may differ by way of what is offered in Stage 2 as the "ensuring mechanism." In Frankfurt's original case (1969, pp. 835–36), a "counterfactual intervener"—Black—who can manipulate Jones's mind is supposed to turn the trick. Stage 2 Jones chooses and does exactly what Black wants him to choose and do, and Black never intervenes. Had Stage 2 Jones, though, showed any involuntary sign of not choosing to *X*, Black would have intervened and forced Jones to choose to *X*.

Elaborating, suppose Jones believes that in his circumstances it is wrong for him to lie to prevent embarrassment. In spite of this, he decides to lie and lies anyway. As he has no excuse or justification for lying, it seems that he is deserving of blame for deciding to lie. Unbeknownst to Jones, though, he could not have refrained from deciding to lie due to the presence of Black who has the power to read and control Jones's mind. Black wields this power partly in virtue of possessing the following knowledge. Had Jones been about to refrain from deciding to lie, he would have displayed some involuntary sign—a neurological pattern, N^*, in his brain—whereas if he had been about to decide to lie, he would have displayed a different neurological pattern, *N*. Had Black detected N^*, she would have interceded in Jones's deliberations via direct stimulation of Jones's brain and would, in this way, have caused Jones to decide to lie. But Black detects *N*, the reliable sign for Black that she need not show her hand at all. As Jones decides to lie on his own, in the absence of Black's intervention, it seems highly reasonable that Jones decides freely and is morally blameworthy for deciding to lie despite not having alternative possibilities with regard to his germane decision (and subsequent action). It has, thus, been thought that Frankfurt cases provide strong prima facie reason to believe that alternative possibilities are *not* required for blameworthiness or responsibility in general.[1]

3.3 THE DILEMMA OBJECTION

Not surprisingly, Frankfurt examples have not gone unchallenged. Perhaps the most potent objection against such examples—the "**Dilemma Objection**"—was initially suggested by Kane (1985, p. 51; 1996, pp. 142–44, 191–92) and then developed independently by Carl Ginet (1996)

1 The literature on Frankfurt-type examples is voluminous. An excellent collection of papers on Frankfurt examples is to be found in Widerker and McKenna 2003.

and David Widerker (1995, 247–61). The objection is in the form of a dilemma. If, on the one hand, sign *N* is reliable, in the sense of being infallible, it can only be so because states of the agent (Jones) prior to the occurrence of the supposedly free choice (or action) are causally sufficient for this choice, and the sign indicates this. But if that is the case, then a *deterministic* relation obtains between the prior sign and Jones's subsequent choice, and this begs the question against incompatibilists who believe that determinism is incompatible with freedom or responsibility. On this first horn of the dilemma, the incompatibilist will insist that Jones is not responsible for his choice, for his choice was deterministically caused. If, on the other hand, sign *N* is not infallible and is only reliable in some weaker sense, then an agent (such as Jones) who acts freely in a Frankfurt example retains the ability to do otherwise when he acts on his own. On this second horn, the connection between the prior sign and subsequent choice is not deterministic. The presence (or absence) of the prior sign is, thus, consistent with the agent choosing or acting in a manner other than the manner in which he does. So on this second horn, Jones could well be responsible for his choice; but as he could have chosen otherwise, the incompatibilist will claim that the **Principle of Alternative Possibilities** remains unscathed.

In reply to the **Dilemma Objection**, Frankfurt defenders have responded in many different ways (see, for example, Fischer 1999; 2006b; Hunt 2005; McKenna 2003; Mele and Robb, 1998; 2003; Pereboom 2000; 2001; 2003; Widerker 2006).

3.4 MELE AND ROBB'S REPLY TO THE DILEMMA OBJECTION

A number of theorists have addressed the second horn by attempting to construct Frankfurt examples in which the relevant decision of the agent, such as Jones's decision to lie, is indeterministically caused, consistent with its being true that Jones could not have refrained from making the decision that he did. In an intriguing example that Mele and David Robb develop, for instance, Bob is not determined to make his allegedly free decision to steal Ann's car at any moment prior to the precise moment, *t*, at which he indeterministically makes this decision. But the example also features a mechanism, totally independent of Bob's own indeterministic reasoning, that will deterministically cause Bob to arrive at the very decision that he does (to steal Ann's car) at the precise time *t* in every condition save one: the condition in which Bob himself indeterministically decides, at *t*, to steal Ann's car. Under just this condition, the mechanism's causal powers will be rendered inert, and it will be Bob himself and not the mechanism that indeterministically brings about the relevant decision. Here is Mele's summary of the case:

> Black initiates a certain internally deterministic Process *P* in Bob's brain at *t1* with the intention of thereby causing Bob to decide at *t2* (an hour later, say) to steal Ann's car. The process, which is screened off from Bob's consciousness, will culminate in Bob's deciding at *t2* to steal Ann's car unless he decides on his own at *t2* to steal it or is incapable at *t2* of making a decision (because, for example, he is dead by *t2*). The process is in no way sensitive to any "sign" of what Bob will decide. As it happens, at *t2* Bob decides on his own to steal the car, on the basis of his own indeterministic deliberation about whether to steal it, and his decision is not deterministically caused. But if he had not just then decided on his own to steal it, *P* would have issued, at *t2*, in his deciding to steal it. Rest assured that *P* in no way influences the indeterministic decision-making process that actually issues in Bob's decision.... Two further points about Bob's story ... merit emphasis. First, *P*, the internally deterministic process in Bob's brain, makes it impossible for Bob to avoid deciding at *t2* to steal Ann's car, given that he is capable of making a decision then. *P*'s internal operations are deterministic, and unless *P* is preempted by some event or process external to it, it will cause Bob to decide at *t2* to steal Ann's car. Given that Bob is capable of making a decision at the time, the only thing that can preempt *P* is Bob's deciding on his own at *t2* to steal Ann's car. Thus, all worlds with the same laws of nature as *W* and the same past up to *t2* are worlds in which Bob decides at *t2* to steal Ann's car. *P* makes it inevitable that Bob will decide at *t2* to steal the car, if he is capable of making a decision at *t2*, but because *P* does not actually cause Bob's deciding to do that, it does not deterministically cause it. (2006, pp. 88–89, note omitted)[2]

Adding some details, Mele and Robb suppose that there are "decision nodes" in Bob's brain:

> The "lighting up" of node *N1* represents his [Bob's] deciding to steal the car, and the "lighting up" of node *N2* represents his deciding *not* to steal the car. Under normal circumstances and in the absence of preemption, a process's "hitting" a decision node in Bob "lights up" that node. If it were to be the case both that *P* hits *N1* at *t2* and that *x* does not hit *N1* at *t2*, then *P* would light up *N1*. If both processes were to hit *N1* at *t2*, Bob's indeterministic deliberative process, *x*,

2 See, also, Mele and Robb 1998 and 2003.

would light up *N1* and *P* would not. (Mele and Robb 1998, p. 104)

Many would agree that in virtue of Bob's indeterministically deciding on his own at *t1* to steal Ann's car at *t2*, this decision of Bob is free and he is morally responsible for it. They would insist that Bob would be responsible despite lacking alternatives. Others, though, might worry about how, precisely, it can be that only one of the causal pathways to Bob's decision is causally efficacious. How can it be that the deterministic pathway "fizzles out" and, thus, its causal constituents do not also co-cause Bob's decision at the very time when Bob indeterministically causes the decision?[3]

3.5 ANOTHER REPLY TO THE DILEMMA OBJECTION

Reflection on Mele's example suggests a line of resistance to the *first* horn. Consider an amended version of a Frankfurt-type scenario that I have advanced (Haji 2000c). Pemba decides on his own to squeeze the trigger at *t1*, and he does squeeze the trigger at *t1*, thereby bringing it about that Rubens is killed by *t2*. Assume that his decision to squeeze the trigger, just like Bob's decision to steal Ann's car, is not causally determined: there is a possible world that is exactly like the actual world in every detail up (or just prior) to the moment at which Pemba decides to squeeze the trigger, is governed by the same laws of nature as those of the actual world, and is such that, in it, Pemba decides, at *t1*, not to squeeze the trigger. In this case, "Murder-1," a libertarian would presumably agree that, provided all other conditions of moral responsibility are met, Pemba would be morally responsible for his decision and for the state of affairs *Rubens being killed by t2*.[4]

3 One may worry that Bob's *indeterministically deciding* at *t2* to steal Ann's car raises a problem about luck. For if he so decides, there are worlds with the same laws as the actual world and that are just like the actual world up to *t2*, in which Bob is capable at *t2* of making a decision, Bob's own indeterministic decision-making process is not at *t2* pre-empted or otherwise disturbed by any event or process external to it, yet this decision-making process does not cause Bob's deciding at *t2* to steal Ann's car (Mele and Robb 2003, p. 128). In the actual world, then, this indeterministic process causes Bob to decide on his own at *t2* to steal the car; in some other world with the same laws and the same past as the actual world, though, it is false that this indeterministic process causes Bob to decide on his own at *t2* to steal the car (even though, in this world, Bob decides at *t2* to steal the car). If there is nothing about Bob's capacities, moral character, powers, states of mind, and the like in either world that accounts for this difference, then the cross-world difference seems to be just a matter of luck. How, then, can he be morally responsible for the decision that he makes in the actual world? I discuss this sort of concern with Frankfurt examples featuring relevant indeterminism further in Haji 2006, sec. 3. The problem of luck that appears to plague (pertinent) libertarian theories is discussed at length in Chapter 9.

4 Again, I set aside concerns of luck. See note 3 above.

Modifying Murder-1, assume that there is a device in Pemba's brain, the "mimic randomizer," that operates in the following fashion. When Pemba's decisions are indeterministically caused by desire/belief pairs of which he is conscious, the mimic randomizer is triggered. Once triggered, it initiates neural processes in Pemba's unconscious that mimic the actional sequence of events that Pemba initiates at the conscious level. So, for example, if Pemba's undetermined decision, *D*, to squeeze the trigger at the conscious level is caused by a certain desire/belief pair, *P*, the mimic randomizer, when triggered, initiates a sequence of events in Pemba's unconscious in which another desire/belief pair, *P**, of which Pemba is unconscious and which is type-identical to *P*, also leads, though deterministically, to the very same decision *D*.[5] So there are two independent routes, one indeterministic (Pemba's reasoning at the conscious level) and the other deterministic (the sequence of events initiated by the mimic randomizer in Pemba's unconscious), each causally producing the very same event—Pemba's deciding at *t1* to squeeze the trigger. (As a *rough* analogy, imagine that, each of two assassins operating independently of each other at *t1*, initiates, at *t1*, a sequence of events that leads to Ruben's death at some later time, *t2*: each fires a bullet into Rubens. If one of the assassins is "subtracted from the scene," Rubens would still be killed by *t2* as a result of the activities of the other assassin. Imagine, further, that the relevant sequence of events that Assassin-1 initiates is not deterministic, whereas the pertinent sequence of events that Assassin-2 initiates is deterministic.)

Should one not favor the mimic randomizer set-up, imagine, as in Mele's case, that there is a mechanism, totally independent of Pemba's own conscious practical reasoning, which will deterministically cause Pemba to arrive at the very decision that he does to squeeze the trigger at the precise time *t1* when he indeterministically decides on his own to squeeze the trigger. One might wonder what happens if the two pathways diverge; specifically, what happens if Pemba's own reasoning favors the decision not to squeeze the trigger when the deterministic pathway favors the contrary decision? Following Mele and Robb, this case stipulates that the deterministic pathway overrides the indeterministic one and causally produces Pemba's deadly decision.

It seems that Pemba (Pemba *qua* conscious reasoner) is morally responsible for his choice. Still, he could not have decided otherwise because of the parallel deterministic sequence of events that is an independent cause of this choice. Now, of course, a "dilemma defender" may be expected to

5 In this context, when we say that two things are type-identical, they are of the same sort in relevant respects. So, for instance, two different quarters of the same mint are type-identical; they have the same size, shape, monetary value, are made of the same material, etc. One desire/belief pair is, then, type-identical to another desire/belief pair if these pairs are of the same sort. Token-identity (again, in this context) would amount to "strict numerical identity"; each thing is strictly identical to one and only one thing: itself.

rejoin that Pemba's case succumbs to the first horn: since Pemba's deadly decision, *D*, is co-caused by a *deterministic* sequence of events, Pemba is not responsible for this decision. But this rejoinder is a bit too quick. For, presumably, the libertarian (or an interested party not already predisposed either to accepting or rejecting the **Principle of Alternative Possibilities**) would concede that if the deterministic sequence of events were "removed from the scenario," Pemba (given certain assumptions) would or may well be morally responsible for his deadly decision in this "one-sequence scenario." (It will be convenient to refer to this one-sequence scenario as "**Pemba-1**" and to the "two-sequence" original scenario in which Pemba's deadly decision is co-caused as "**Pemba-2**.") "Addition" of the parallel deterministic sequence of events to **Pemba-1** does not in any way influence how Pemba brings about his decision in **Pemba-1**: if Pemba is an ultimate originator of his decision in **Pemba-1**, he is so in **Pemba-2** as well; if, in **Pemba-1**, Pemba makes his decision in light of the belief that in so doing he is doing moral wrong, his decision in **Pemba-2** is based on this belief as well; if Pemba satisfies various agency requirements of responsibility in **Pemba-1**, he satisfies these very requirements in **Pemba-2** as well; if he exercises self-control in making his decision in **Pemba-1**, he also does so in **Pemba-2**, and so forth. So one might then well wonder how the removal of alternative possibilities, accomplished by the addition of the deterministic sequence of events to **Pemba-1**, "transfers" a case of responsibility to one of nonresponsibility.

An advocate of the **Principle of Alternative Possibilities** might claim that Pemba lacks a certain species of *control* in **Pemba-2**, the sort of control one can have in making a decision or in performing a nonmental action only if one has (pertinent) alternative possibilities. This is an interesting claim but, given the dialectical context, the partisan of this principle should tread carefully in her use of this claim to vindicate the proposal that alternative possibilities are required for responsibility-relevant control. To explain, in the last chapter we distinguished three different conceptions of control. Recapitulating briefly, *active control* is a species of causal control. *Negative ultimate control* is the sort of control one has in, for example, making a decision that is nondeviantly and indeterministically caused by the agent's apt springs of action. *Positive ultimate control* consists in an agent's agent-causing her decisions or actions.

We revert to the concern that Pemba in **Pemba-2** lacks freedom-relevant control in deciding to squeeze the trigger owing to his not being able to decide otherwise. The control in question could not be *active* control. Since active control is a species of causal control, the mere lack of alternatives (ensured by inclusion of the deterministic pathway in **Pemba-2**) cannot augment or diminish whatever (active) causal control Pemba exercised in deciding and acting as he did in **Pemba-2** (see, for e.g., Haji 2003; 2006).

What about negative ultimate control? When Pemba decides on his own to squeeze the trigger, his decision is indeterministically caused in so deciding. Given overdetermination, it is, of course, also deterministically caused. Suppose we were to "subtract" from **Pemba-2** the independent deterministic causal route to his decision. Then, presumably, we would agree that Pemba exercises negative ultimate control in making his decision. And let us simply suppose that such control suffices for freedom-relevant (responsibility-grounding) control. Now "add," again, to **Pemba-2** the independent deterministic causal route. Addition of this causal route does not in *any way* interfere with Pemba's bringing about his decision on his own (although it, too, brings about the decision). So it would be puzzling why, in the two-pathway overdetermination version of the story, Pemba is not responsible for his deadly decision.

A libertarian might rejoin that what negative ultimate control gives you is freedom from control by the past. If your choices are causally determined, then there are factors over which you have no control of any kind and which are causally sufficient for your choices. To be responsible, though, for your choices, these choices must be "up to you" in that you must be responsible, at least partly, for anything that is a sufficient cause of, or motive for your choices (Kane 1996, pp. 73–74; 2007, p. 22). Furthermore, having negative ultimate control in making your choices is a necessary condition, on this libertarian view, for your choices to be "up to you." This rejoinder, though, is suspect. For consider the very first free action of yours. Assume that this action is a mental action—some decision that you make. As it is a mental *action*, this decision is caused by antecedents such as your having a desire or belief (or your being in an appropriate motivational state). Either these antecedents are free in the sense that you have the control, whatever it precisely is, that moral responsibility requires regarding these antecedents, or they are not free. The first option is ruled out on the rejoinder that we are entertaining and on the hypothesis that your pertinent decision is your *first* free decision. This is because if these antecedents—your having of desires or beliefs—are free, they are *indirectly* free; they owe their freedom to the control that you have over (perhaps other) "basic actions," again, whatever these are, regarding which you are directly free or have direct control. (It would be highly unusual, to say the least, to suppose that you can have direct control in acquiring a desire or belief in the way in which, for example, you can have direct control in forming an intention.) But these basic actions (assuming there are some) that supposedly give rise to the causal antecedents of your decision cannot be free if this decision is the *first* free action of yours. On the second option, your decision is free despite its causal antecedents not being free. But if this decision can be free even if you have no control over any of its causal antecedents, then you have renounced the proposal, at the heart of the liberatarian rejoinder, that to be responsible for a choice, you must be partly responsible for anything that is a sufficient cause of, or motive for your choice. In addition, if you hold that your decision can be free even though you are not free with respect to any of its causal antecedents, then you might as well embrace compatibilism. You might as well embrace the compatibilist's tenet that the control that responsibility requires may arise from the natural workings of a deterministic world.

Lastly, as far as positive ultimate control is concerned, an agent is an ultimate originator of her free actions because she is an uncaused agent-cause of them. We previously mentioned that Clarke has developed an interesting "integrated agent-causal account" of free action according to which a free action is *both* agent-caused and non-deterministically caused by prior apt agent-involving events (Clarke 1996; 2003a). If an event can, in principle, be both agent-caused and indeterministically event-caused, as Clarke proposes, then it seems that it should also be the case that that event can, in principle, be both agent-caused and deterministically event caused, as Clarke concedes. Revert, again, to this sort of thought experiment: First, modify **Pemba-2** so that it is a one-path case in which Pemba agent-causes his deadly decision, and assume, this time around, that his agent-causing his decision suffices for this decision's being free. Then we would agree that Pemba exercises positive ultimate control in deciding as he does. Next, reintroduce in **Pemba-2** the independent deterministic causal route to Pemba's deadly decision. This addition has no influence whatsoever on Pemba's deciding on his own. Specifically, Pemba's lacking pertinent alternatives on re-addition of the independent deterministic pathway does not in any way undermine Pemba's being an uncaused agent-cause of his decision. So, once again, it would seem implausible to suppose that Pemba is not responsible for his decision to kill Reubens in the two-pathway overdetermination incarnation of the story.

We should, hence, conclude that the dilemma defender's claim that in the two-path case (**Pemba-2**), Pemba lacks freedom-level control *because* he lacks pertinent alternatives, ought to be taken with a grain of salt.

Finally, the dilemma defender might dig in her heels and insist that one *cannot* be responsible without having the control that comes with having alternative possibilities. But this simply amounts to refusing to entertain seriously Frankfurt-type thought experiments, one primary objective of which is to question whether having alternatives is a requirement of enjoying responsibility-relevant control. This sort of refusal to engage debate with the Frankfurt defender is especially suspect if one is not already committed to the view that responsibility requires alternative possibilities but is reflectively undecided over whether leeway is indeed essential to responsibility (Haji and McKenna 2004; 2006).

3.6 LUCK AND ALTERNATIVE POSSIBILITIES

In a recent, highly insightful paper, Zimmerman advances reasons having to do with luck that, if cogent, undermine the **Principle of Alternative Possibilities.** Zimmerman directs our attention to the general point that "the degree to which we are morally responsible cannot be affected by what is not in our control. Put more pithily: luck is irrelevant to moral responsibility" (M. Zimmerman 2002, p. 559). He says that pursuit of this point will show that the question whether freedom requires alternative possibilities, and even the question whether freedom is compatible with causal determinism, become considerably less significant than they are often taken to be.

Distinguish between two broad types of luck, *resultant* and *situational*. Resultant luck consists in luck with respect to the results of one's choices and actions; situational luck consists in luck with respect to the situations in which one finds oneself. Ponder this example involving resultant luck:

> Suppose that George shot at Henry and killed him. Suppose that Georg shot at Henrik in circumstances which were, to the extent possible, exactly like those of George (by which I mean to include what went on "inside" the protagonists' heads as well as what happened in the "outside" world), except for the fact that Georg's bullet was intercepted by a passing bird (a rather large and solid bird) and Henrik escaped injury. Inasmuch as the bird's flight was not in Georg's control, the thesis that luck is irrelevant to moral responsibility implies that George and Georg are equally morally responsible. (2002, p. 560)

Zimmerman explains that George may well be responsible *for more things* than Georg. After all, whereas George's attempt to kill was successful, Georg's was not; so George could well be responsible for murder whereas Georg is not. But Zimmerman denies that George is *any more responsible* than Georg. We must, he cautions, distinguish the *degree* of someone's responsibility from its *scope*. In Zimmerman's view, George and Georg bear responsibility to the same degree even though George's responsibility has greater scope—George is responsible for more things than is Georg. Each is responsible for his attempt on the life of someone but George (unlike) Georg is responsible for (let's suppose) murder as well.

If George and Georg are responsible for their respective attempts, this is partly because they freely made these attempts. Whether freedom requires alternative possibilities, though, is still a question whose significance is not diminished by the phenomenon of resultant luck.

Turning now to situational luck,

> Suppose, as before, that George shot at Henry and killed him. Suppose also, as before, that Georg did not kill Henrik; suppose, now, however, that his was not because he took a shot that was intercepted by some unfortunate bird, but rather because he took no shot at all. And suppose that this was

> because of something quite fortuitous: Georg sneezed just as he was about to shoot, for example; or a truck pulled up in front of Henrik, blocking Georg's line of fire; or Henrik turned suddenly into a doorway, just as Georg was about to squeeze the trigger. Whereas in the case involving the bird, luck intervened after the shot took place, thereby preventing Henrik's death, in this sort of case the intervention occurs earlier, before Georg has a chance to act at all. But the cases are united in that, in all of them, Georg would have freely killed Henrik but for some feature of the case over which he had no control. This being so, it seems that we must conclude here, as before, that Georg is as culpable as George. The circumstances that conspired to save Henrik afford Georg no excuse. (2002, p. 563)

Well, as Georg did not even make an attempt to kill, what is he responsible *for* this time around? Zimmerman's answer is intriguing:

> I think that there is nothing ... for which Georg might be said to be responsible. If so, this sort of case serves to emphasize, in even more dramatic fashion than before, the distinction between degree and scope of responsibility. The degree of Georg's responsibility remains the same as George's, but the scope of Georg's responsibility has dwindled to nothing. Georg is responsible; he is just not responsible for anything. He is, as I shall put it, "responsible tout court." Lest this appear unduly paradoxical, let me hasten to add that it is nonetheless the case that Georg is responsible *in virtue of* something, and this something just is his being such that he would have freely killed Henrik, had he had the cooperation of certain features of the case. All responsibility, including responsibility *tout court*, is fundamentally relational. It is precisely because George is responsible in virtue of the very same sort of fact (the fact that he would have freely killed someone, had he had the cooperation—as he did—of certain features of the case) in virtue of which Georg is responsible, that George and Georg are responsible to the same degree. (M. Zimmerman 2002, pp. 564–65, note omitted)

The sort of luck that is involved in this last example is *circumstantial*—it has to do with the external situation in which the major players find themselves. Turn, now, from circumstantial luck to luck having to do with one's internal situation or *constitutive luck*. Suppose the reason that Georg did not kill Henrik was that he was too timid, or that he was deaf and did not hear the insults that Henrik hurled his way. If it is, nonetheless, true that

Georg would have freely killed Henrik but for some such feature of the case over which he had no control, then, Zimmerman contends, Georg is just as responsible, in virtue of this fact, as George (M. Zimmerman 2002, p. 565).

Finally, introduce a Frankfurt-type case in which George, on his "own," kills Henry. Had George not killed on his own, Black—the counterfactual intervener—would have forced his hand. Some people might claim that George killed freely despite having no alternatives; others might protest that if it is really true that George could not but have killed Henry, then George is not responsible. The *luck thesis*—the thesis that degree of responsibility cannot be affected by what is not in one's control—yields an interesting result with respect to George's responsibility. We may assume that in the Frankfurt-type case, George has no control over whether or not Black is on the scene; nor does he have any control over the doings of Black. Assume, further, that regardless of whether George freely or did not freely kill Henry, he *would* have freely killed Henry in the absence of Black (or, more generally, he would have freely killed Henry in the absence of the ensuring mechanism). Then the luck thesis implies that George *is* morally responsible for the killing (even if, given his Frankfurtian predicament, he did not have any alternatives). As Zimmerman emphasizes, given the luck thesis, it does not matter whether George *could* have killed Henry. What matters is whether he *would* have freely killed Henry, *if* he had the cooperation of certain features of the case, and this is true despite freedom's being crucial to judgments of responsibility. Analogously, even if George was deterministically caused to shoot Henry, that he was deterministically (or, for that matter, indeterministically) caused to shoot Henry is largely irrelevant to whether George was responsible. Rather, what matters is whether George would have freely killed Henry had his causal history cooperated (M. Zimmerman 2002, p. 567).

More fully, Zimmerman summarizes his position as follows. He first lays out two inconsistent triads:

(A) (1) Moral responsibility requires freedom.
(2) Freedom requires alternative possibilities.
(3) Moral responsibility does not require alternative possibilities.

(B) (1) Moral responsibility requires freedom.
(2) Freedom requires causal indeterminism.
(3) Moral responsibility does not require causal indeterminism.

To resolve the inconsistency in (A) and (B), Zimmerman distinguishes between cases in which the scope of responsibility is greater than zero (these are cases in which one is responsible *for* something); and cases in which scope of responsibility has diminished to nothing (these are cases involving responsibility *tout court*, cases in which though one is responsible, one is not responsible *for* anything). Regarding the former cases, Zimmerman agrees that one cannot be responsible *for* something unless that thing is or was in one's control. So in such cases (1) of (A) and (B)—the member of each triad that says that moral responsibility requires freedom or control—must be granted. And if (2) is granted, (3) should be rejected. As for cases involving responsibility *tout court*, (1) of (A) and (B) should be rejected. Recall, Georg can be *just as responsible* as George even though Georg is not responsible *for* anything. So even if clause (2) is then accepted, (3) may also be accepted (2002, pp. 568–69). In brief, in cases in which one is responsible even though one is not responsible *for* anything, what is relevant is whether one would have freely done what one would have done had one been responsible for something, if one had had the cooperation of certain features of one's case.

To collect results: the intermediate conclusion of the original or **Basic Version** of the **Consequence Argument** says that if determinism is true, then no one could have done otherwise. Even if these versions sustain this conclusion, if the **Principle of Alternative Possibilities**, as Frankfurt examples or implications of the luck thesis suggest, is false, they fall short of establishing the incompatibility of determinism and moral responsibility.

Taking stock, some people reject versions of the **Consequence Argument** that rely on the **Principle of Alternative Possibilities** because they do not accept this principle (see, for example, Fischer and Ravizza 1998; and Stump 1996). Included in this class of critics are incompatibilists who believe that determinism undermines responsibility not because it subverts our having alternatives but because it precludes our being the ultimate originators or sources of our actions (for example, see Hunt 1999; Pereboom 2001; Stump 1999; and Zagzebski 2000). Others accept the **Principle of Alternative Possibilities** on a compatibilist reading of 'avoidability' (or 'can'). They then argue that on this reading, the conclusion or one or more of the premises, such as the premise concerning the fixity of the past or the premise concerning the fixity of the laws, of, for example, the **Original Consequence Argument** fails. I find the **Original Consequence Argument** captivating because, among other things, it calls upon us to pay close attention to control; and control is central to free action and moral responsibility. I argued, in the last chapter, that when we reformulate the **Consequence Argument** in a fashion that exposes its reliance on control, the resulting argument—the **Reformulated Consequence Argument**—loses some of its allure. Finally, some people have proposed that the principal weakness of *any* version of the **Consequence Argument** that relies on a β-like rule is that this rule is contentious. For this reason, β-evaders have attempted to defend a version of the **Consequence Argument**—the **Basic Version**—that bypasses such a rule altogether, and that is motivated principally by the thought that what it is in our power to do is or could be an extension of the actual past (holding fixed the natural laws). The **Basic Version** of the

Consequence Argument, though, must still invoke the **Principle of Alternative Possibilities** to secure the further conclusion that determinism and moral responsibility are incompatible. Frankfurt examples and considerations of luck, however, appear to speak against this principle. It would, consequently, be desirable to motivate incompatibilism independently of relying on the **Principle of Alternative Possibilities.** The **Direct Argument**, which is the topic of the next chapter, attempts to do so.

4 The Direct Argument

4.1 INTRODUCTION

The original version of the **Consequence Argument**, as we have seen, proceeds from the premises that no one can render false facts of the past and facts that express the natural laws, and that no one can render false the fact that, if determinism is true, the past and the laws entail a unique future, to the conclusion that no one can alter the future from its actual trajectory. If no agent is able, at a time, to render false a true proposition regarding what she does at that time, then, at that time, this agent could not have done otherwise. So the original version of the **Consequence Argument** evolves from premises concerning our powerlessness over the past and the laws to the upshot that no one can do otherwise than what one in fact does. In van Inwagen's version of this elegant argument, various premises appeal, among other things, to a set of principles about the *unavoidability* (or fixity) of the past and the laws of nature. We have remarked that different parties have come to loggerheads over the correct interpretation of 'can' in the premises and conclusion of this argument. Van Inwagen is perfectly aware that some opponents of the **Original Consequence Argument** might try to escape this argument by exploiting the disagreement over the relevant sense of 'can.' So van Inwagen has constructed a different argument—the **Direct Argument** (van Inwagen 1983, pp. 184–88)—that is meant to show that moral responsibility is incompatible with determinism for considerations *different* than those having to do with freedom to do otherwise. This argument is supposed to eschew *all* appeal to the concept of avoidability. The **Direct Argument** is the topic of this chapter.

4.2 THE DIRECT ARGUMENT

Once again, let '$\Box$' represent logical necessity, '$\vdash$' stand for 'therefore,' and '$p \supset q$' symbolize 'if *p* then *q*' (the material conditional). Take 'NR(*p*)' to abbreviate '*p* and no one is, or ever has been, even partly morally responsible for the fact that *p*.'[1] The **Direct Argument**, like the Original **Consequence Argument**, invokes two rules of inference:

(A) $\Box p \vdash \text{NR}(p)$.
(B) $\text{NR}(p \supset q), \text{NR}(p) \vdash \text{NR}(q)$.

Rule (A), just like **Rule α**, is straightforward; from *p*'s being necessarily true, infer that no one is or ever has been morally responsible for *p*. For instance, no one is now, or ever has been, even partly morally responsible for the fact that *all triangles have three sides*. **Rule (B)**, the principle of the "Transfer of Non-Responsibility" or simply "**Transfer NR**" says, roughly, that if an agent is not responsible for one thing, and she is not responsible for that thing's leading to a second, then she is not responsible for the second. If no one is ever even partly responsible for the flood's occurring, and no one is ever even partly responsible for the fact that if the flood occurs, then the bridge is washed away, then, it seems, no one is ever even partly responsible for the bridge's being washed away. Similarly, if nobody is ever responsible for the occurrence of the Big Bang, and if nobody is ever responsible for the fact that if the Big Bang occurs, then the largest explosion in history occurs, then it appears that no one is ever responsible for the occurrence of this largest explosion.

In roughly chiseled strokes, the **Direct Argument** works in this way: Suppose that, at some time, Hera in her deterministic world, buys some heroin despite believing that she morally ought not to do so. Clearly, no one is even partly responsible for what the state of the universe at a time close to the Big Bang was and for the laws being what they are. Further, assuming determinism, no one is even partly responsible for the fact that the combination of the distant past (the complete state of the universe at a time close to the Big Bang) and the laws entails that Hera buys the heroin (at the time when she buys the heroin). It follows from these premises and **Transfer NR** that Hera is not morally responsible for buying the heroin.

More carefully, again, let '**Past**' stand for a proposition expressing the complete state of the world at a time when no human being existed, '**Laws**' stand for a proposition expressing the laws of nature, and '**Action-Now**' stand for any true proposition about the state of the world now. The **Direct Argument** may be formulated in this way:

1 In 1983, p. 184, van Inwagen uses 'N' instead of 'NR,' taking 'N' to stand for 'no one is, or ever has been, even partly responsible for the fact that ... .'

THE DIRECT ARGUMENT

(1) The thesis of determinism is true. [assumption]
(2) $\Box$ (**Past** and **Laws** $\supset$ **Action-Now**) [from 1]
(3) $\Box$ (**Past** $\supset$ (**Laws** $\supset$ **Action-Now**)) [from 2, by logic]
(4) NR (**Past** $\supset$ (**Laws** $\supset$ **Action-Now**)) [from 3, by **Rule (A)**]
(5) NR (**Past**) [assumption]
(6) NR (**Laws** $\supset$ **Action-Now**) [from 4,5 by **Transfer NR**]
(7) NR (**Laws**) [assumption]
(8) NR (**Action-Now**) [from 6,7 by **Transfer NR**]
(9) Therefore, if determinism is true, no one is now, or ever has been, even partly morally responsible for **Action-Now** (or for any other event that occurs now).

In van Inwagen's estimation, the **Direct Argument** is at its weakest in its reliance on **Rule (B)**. He writes:

> If the compatibilist wishes to refute this argument ... here is what he will have to do: he will have to produce some set of propositions intuitively more plausible than the validity of (B) and show that these propositions entail the compatibility of moral responsibility and determinism, or else he will have to devise a counter-example to (B), a counter-example that can be evaluated independently of the question whether moral responsibility and determinism are compatible. (1983, p. 188)

4.3 TRANSFER NR AND TWO-PATH CASES

Fischer and Ravizza, picking up van Inwagen's gauntlet, produce alleged counterexamples to **Rule (B)** (see Ravizza 1994; Fischer and Ravizza 1998, ch. 6). These counterexamples are variations or modifications of Frankfurt-type examples. In each, an agent performs an action "on her own" for which, or for an outcome of which, she is supposedly morally responsible. But unbeknownst to the agent, her action or its pertinent outcome is inevitable in that, had she not performed the action or brought about the outcome "on her own," something would have ensured that she perform the action, or that she see to the occurrence of its germane outcome, or that the outcome occur. (In this respect, the examples are similar to the overdetermination example involving Pemba that we discussed in section 3.5.) Here is an illustration of such a "two-path" case:

> Imagine that Betty plants her explosives in the crevices of a glacier and detonates the charge at T1, causing an avalanche that crushes the enemy fortress at T3. Unbeknownst to Betty

> and her commanding officers, however, the glacier is gradually melting, shifting, and eroding. Had Betty not placed the dynamite in the crevices, some ice and rocks would have broken free and crushed the enemy base camp at T3. (Ravizza 1994, pp. 72–73)

This case, call it "**Erosion**," is supposed to show that **Transfer NR** is not valid because the following instantiation of this rule has true premises but a false conclusion.

> (1) The glacier was eroding, and no one is, or ever has been, even partly morally responsible for this fact.
> (2) If the glacier was eroding, then there is an avalanche that crushes the enemy's base at T3, and no one is, or ever has been, even partly morally responsible for this "conditional fact."
> (3) Therefore, there is an avalanche that crushes the enemy's base at T3, and no one is, or ever has been, even partly morally responsible for this fact.

We can readily grant (1) and (2). Nobody need be even partly morally responsible for the fact that the glacier was eroding, and that if it was eroding, the enemy's base would be destroyed at T3. But (3) seems false. Betty's acting on "her own" is causally sufficient for the destruction of the base at T3. Hence, had the other pathway involving the eroding glacier been "subtracted from the scene," Betty would still have succeeded in destroying the enemy camp. Since this other pathway does not in any way interfere with Betty's base-destroying activity, it appears that Betty *is* morally responsible for the destruction of the base.

These interesting "two-path" cases have generated controversy over whether they will, in the end, undermine the **Direct Argument**. We should be clear on the distinction between "one-path" and two-path cases. In one-path cases, in the actual sequence of events that unfold, there is only one pathway or causal sequence of events that culminates in the relevant outcome (such as the camp's being destroyed at T3). In two-path cases, there are two such *independent* pathways. In **Erosion**, for instance, there is the pathway involving Betty that is causally sufficient for *the base being destroyed at T3*, and the independent pathway involving the eroding glacier that is also causally sufficient for this same outcome. Conceding that **Erosion** is a counterexample to **Transfer NR**, some have proposed that it is *not* a counterexample to a suitably revised version of **Transfer NR** that is restricted to one-path cases and that may be called to do duty to sustain the **Direct Argument** (see McKenna n.d.; 2001; Stump 2000; 2002). Michael McKenna explains the primary motive for such restriction:

> If determinism is true, it is not as if there is one path to a certain result in virtue of which determinism is true, and then there is some other distinct path, unhinged from the former, that a morally responsible agent initiates so that he or she bears responsibility for the object of responsibility in question (be it an act, an omission, or a consequence). The facts settled by the truth of determinism include the facts pertaining to the "action path" in virtue of which the agent is alleged to be responsible. (McKenna 2008b, p. 365, note omitted)

McKenna's essential, interesting point is that the "way" in which determinism would lead to one unique future would seem to be distinctly unlike the way in which a person could be morally responsible for, say, a certain outcome (such as the enemy camp's being destroyed) in two-path proposed counterexamples to **Transfer NR**. In such counterexamples, there is one route to the germane outcome for the initiation of which the agent (like Betty) is responsible. There is also, though, another distinct route to this same outcome (in **Erosion**, this route involves the eroding glacier). But if determinism is true, there is solely *one* pathway into the future. McKenna supplies a version of **Transfer NR—Transfer*****—with the built-in one-path restriction, a version, he says, that both compatibilists and incompatibilists should find intuitively appealing. He proposes that this one-path principle may be captured in this way:

> **Transfer*****: If a person is not responsible for a fact, and this fact is at some particular time the sole causal antecedent of the path to the bringing about of a further fact, and if the person is not responsible for any part of the path between the two facts, then he or she is not responsible for the further fact either. (2008b, p. 368. See, also, McKenna 2001, p. 45)

Erosion, being a two-path case, is not a counterexample to **Transfer*****. On McKenna's view **Transfer***** "would do the requisite work for the proponent of the **Direct Argument** even if the 'bringing about' relation is weaker than a causally deterministic one" (2008b, p. 368). We may provisionally conclude that it is still an open question whether **Erosion** and relevantly analogous two-path cases decisively refute the **Direct Argument**. (Further discussion of these cases can be found in Fischer 2004a and 2005; Pereboom 2001; and Widerker 2002.) It would help move the debate along if we could uncover a case that undermined both **Transfer NR** and a restricted version of this principle such as McKenna's one-path candidate.

4.4 DAVID WIDERKER'S RESPONSE TO THE DIRECT ARGUMENT

The **Direct Argument**, recall, is meant to enjoy an edge over the **Consequence Argument** insofar as it evades delicate issues concerning avoidability, such as the precise sense of 'can' in one or more of the premises and the conclusion of the Original **Consequence Argument** in which this term appears. In this section, we consider Widerker's recent attempt to bid farewell to the **Direct Argument.**

4.4.1 Widerker's Concerns

Widerker proposes that even incarnations of the **Direct Argument** which draw on restricted versions of **Transfer NR**, like the version McKenna formulates, fall prey to the concerns that these incarnations either illicitly call upon the notion of avoidability (so they lose their alleged advantage over the Original **Consequence Argument**), or that the versions of **Transfer NR** upon which these formulations of the **Direct Argument** rely succumb to counterexample.[2]

Regarding the first of these concerns, Widerker suggests that premise (7) of the **Direct Argument**—the premise that *no one is now, or ever has been, even partly responsible for the laws of nature*—owes its credibility to the fact that no one could have prevented the laws from obtaining. Widerker's suggestion is that if we believe that the laws are fixed, it is because we think that there is nothing anybody can do to preclude the laws from being what they are. But if we can't preclude the laws from being what they are, we cannot avoid their "hold" on us. Thus, it seems, premise (7) that involves non-responsibility for the laws, covertly appeals to avoidability for its credentials. But calling on avoidability is something that the **Direct Argument**, in the first place, was meant to work around. So, Widerker concludes that premise (7) rests illicitly on the notion of avoidability.

With respect to the second concern, Widerker reasons that since van Inwagen submits that the **Direct Argument** does *not* rely on the notion of avoidability, the compatibilist is free to introduce a compatibilist account of this notion (such as, perhaps, the **Can-Hypothetical** notion) in proposed counterexamples to whatever version of **Transfer NR** is in question. Doing so would not, for example, beg any questions against the proponent of the **Direct Argument** (again, on the assumption that the **Direct Argument** resists any appeal to avoidability concepts). Widerker proposes that there are indeed credible counterexamples of this sort. These counterexamples are fueled by a principle—principle **(M)**—"which is explicative of the very notion of blameworthiness":

2 Widerker (in 2002) mentions revised versions advanced by Ginet 2003; McKenna 2001; and Stump 2002.

> **(M)**: Someone who knowingly acted in a morally wrong way, and believed correctly that he could have avoided acting as he did, is blameworthy for his act. (2002, p. 323)

In Widerker's illustration of this sort of counterexample, Jones lives in a deterministic world. He murders Smith for some selfish reason, knowing that in so acting he does moral wrong. We are to imagine, further, that Jones could have done otherwise than murder Smith, and believed that he could have done otherwise, in some compatibilist sense of 'could have done otherwise.' Since Jones satisfies **(M)**, Widerker recommends that the compatibilist need not shy away from holding that Jones is morally to blame for the murder (2002, pp. 322–23). Thus, the compatibilist whom Widerker envisions as the adversary of the **Direct Argument** is licensed to claim that we have the following falsifying instance of even restricted versions of **Transfer NR** (an instance with true premises but a false conclusion):

(1W) NR (if **Laws**, then Jones murders Smith). That is, if the laws are as they are, then Jones murders Smith, and no one is or ever has been morally responsible for this conditional fact. This premise is based on the determinist's assumption that the past and the laws entail that Jones murders Smith.

(2W) NR (**Laws**). Equivalently, no one is or ever has been morally responsible for the fact that the laws are as they are. This is an assumption.

(3W) Therefore, NR (Jones Murders Smith); alternatively, therefore, no one is or ever has been morally responsible for the fact that Jones murders Smith. (3W) follows from an application of the version of **Transfer NR** in question to (1W) and (2W).

The **Direct Argument**, as we have explained, appeals to **Transfer NR** to get us from the premises that no one is even partly morally responsible for the past being what it is, and that no one is even partly morally responsible for the laws being what they are, to the conclusion that no one is even partly morally responsible for any of their choices or actions. But if even restricted versions of **Transfer NR** are susceptible to counterexample, as Widerker argues, then the **Direct Argument** is in trouble.

4.4.2 Reply to Widerker

These subtle and probing criticisms of Widerker against the **Direct Argument**, however, are not beyond question. First, addressing the concern that premise (7) of this argument (*no one is or ever has been even partly morally responsible for the laws*) presupposes some notion of avoidability, and so assumes something that is dialectically improper, Widerker considers and rejects the fairly obvious rejoinder that no human being is responsible for the laws of nature because no human being could have brought them about in the first place (and *not* because, as proposed, no human being could have prevented them from obtaining). Widerker explains:

> This reply [that no human being is responsible for the laws because no human being could have brought them about] assumes that one's not being causally responsible for a fact is sufficient for one's not being morally responsible for that fact. But this assumption is false. We are often morally responsible for facts or events for which we bear *no* causal responsibility. I might be morally responsible for the event of Smith's being bitten by a cobra even if I did not bring about this event, given that I knew that it was about to happen and could have prevented it. (2002, p. 324)

In other words, against the proposal that we are not responsible for the laws because *we* could not have brought them about, Widerker responds that the proposal rests on the assumption that if one is not causally responsible for something, then one is not morally responsible for that thing (or, in short, causal nonresponsibility suffices for moral nonresponsibility). But examples such as the one involving Smith's being bitten by the cobra refute this assumption.

One can, though, strengthen this assumption without appeal to the notion of avoidability, so that the resulting, strengthened principle *does* do the required work of ruling out our being morally responsible for the laws. Consider, first, a necessary state of affairs such as *if something is a triangle, then it is three-sided.* Such a state of affairs obtains independently of whether anyone exists or fails to exist. Alternatively, we may capture this truism as follows: the "truth-makers" of such states of affairs obtain independently of the existence of anyone; that is, roughly, what "makes" such states of affairs true obtains independently of the existence of anyone. Even if the human race had not evolved, or there were no agents of any sort, necessary states of affairs would still obtain. No one is, of course, causally responsible for the obtaining of necessary states of affairs. It is reasonable to suppose, as well, that no one is morally responsible for the obtaining of such states of affairs, and this is because, again, such states of affairs obtain independently of the existence of anyone. Indeed, it is this sort of consideration that seems to be, or may well be, what underlies the undeniable attraction of **Rule (A)**, the rule that from a proposition's being necessary, we may infer that no one is, or ever has been, even partly morally responsible for what is expressed by this proposition. This rationale for non-responsibility for necessary states of affairs is relevantly *divorced* from considerations of avoidability. What bears emphasis is that it is crucial to guard against *this* rationale's being conflated with the *distinct* rationale that no one is responsible for a necessary state of affairs because, roughly, no one can "prevent" a necessary state of affairs from obtaining. If some state of affairs obtains independently of whether one exists or one does not exist, then it may follow that there is a sense in which one cannot prevent this state of affairs. Similarly, if the "truth-makers" of such a state of affairs obtain prior to the existence of one—what "makes" this state of affairs obtain, does not in any way depend upon the existence of anyone—then perhaps it is true that there is a sense in which one cannot prevent this state of affairs. But one's not being able to prevent this state of affairs need *not* be the rationale of why one is not morally responsible for the obtaining of this state of affairs. Again, one might plausibly insist that one is not responsible for this state of affairs because irrespective of whether one exists or fails to exist, this state of affairs obtains.

What I have said about the "truth-makers" of necessary states of affairs is reminiscent of what Warfield proposes about the "truth-makers" of the laws of nature. Warfield submits that the "truth-makers" of the laws "obtained prior to the existence of any human agent" (1996, p. 218). So, with respect to their "truth-makers," a proposition that states a law is just like a proposition that expresses a necessary truth. This similarity suggests that the assumption in question (causal nonresponsibility for something does not entail moral nonresponsibility for that thing) may be reinforced, when it is the laws that are at issue, by supplementing the clause that no one is causally responsible for a natural law with the proposition that the "truth-makers" of a law obtain independently of the existence of any individual person. Should such talk of "truth-makers" strike one as somewhat elusive, the augmented assumption may simply be parsed as follows:

> *A1*: If one is not causally responsible for a fact (or event), and this fact obtains (or this event occurs) regardless of whether one exists or fails to exist, then one is not morally responsible for this fact (or this event).

It is not implausible to suppose that it is *A1* (or a related cousin that appeals to the "truth-makers" of the laws) that underwrites (or that may be used to underwrite) the intuitively plausible claim that the laws are "beyond us" and, thus, that no human being is morally responsible for them.[3]

What of the clever counterexample that Widerker constructs on behalf of the compatibilist adversary? One concern with it is that it is unclear what compatibilist sense of "avoidability" is at issue and so it is unclear whether, given this construal of "avoidability," (3W) is false but (2W) is

3 Helen Beebee and Alfred R. Mele (2002) argue that on a Humean conception of the laws, there is a robust sense in which the laws *are* "up to us."

true. Reflect again, for example, on this gloss of 'could have done otherwise' that some compatibilists have favored:

> **Can-Hypothetical**: *S* can, at time *t*, do *A* at time *t** (*t* may be identical to or later than *t**) =df. *S* would, at *t*, do *A* at *t** if *S* were, at *t*, to choose, or want, or try to do *A*, at *t**.

This hypothetical account supports the compatibilist's claim that while Jones could have avoided murdering Smith, Jones could not have avoided its being the case that the laws are as they are. But it is well known that this account is susceptible to counterexample itself. In one of J.L. Austin's examples (Austin 1961), we are to imagine that a person needs to hole an easy three-foot putt to win a golf tournament. Owing to a nervous twitch in his arm, he misses the putt. It's true that he could have holed the putt; it's false, though, that he would have holed the putt had he tried to do so. In the sort of case that Keith Lehrer (1964) gives, you are presented with a jar of red sweets. Nothing would prevent you from eating one of the sweets if you chose to do so. But you have a pathological fear of blood and of eating anything the color of blood. So you cannot choose to eat the sweets. Thus, you can't eat them contrary to the verdict delivered by **Can-Hypothetical**, the analysis of 'can' that is at issue. The proof, then, lies in the pudding: the compatibilist, or the advocate of the sort of counterexample that Widerker has in mind against **Transfer NR**, must cough up and defend an analysis of 'could have done otherwise' that is both independently plausible and that entails (in conjunction with the facts of Jones' case) that premises (1W) and (2W) are true but the conclusion, (3W), is false.

We have taken note that a number of disputants of the Original **Consequence Argument** have come to an impasse over the proper analysis of 'can,' 'powerlessness,' and 'ability.'[4] It would be something of an irony if central disagreements concerning the **Direct Argument** were to end in a similar dialectical stalemate over the analysis of such terms, given that one of the driving motives to transition from the Original **Consequence Argument** to the **Direct Argument** is to sidestep disputes of this sort. Such a stalemate would, of course, play directly into Widerker's hands. Still, this does not get around the problem of settling on a compatibilist sense of 'avoidability' that discharges the burden it is supposed to in Widerker's counterexample.

A second worry is that, first, some of the most promising *compatibilist* accounts of moral responsibility reject appeal to any avoidability condition as a necessary condition for responsibility (examples include the accounts advanced by Frankfurt in 1971, Fischer and Ravizza in 1998, and Mele in 1995). Compatibilists who champion such accounts may well be persuaded that Frankfurt-type examples, or considerations having to do with luck, do

4 For an excellent overview of the pertinent literature, see Kane 1996, ch. 4.

in fact show that responsibility does not require alternative possibilities. We have mentioned that Fischer is a semicompatibilist: A champion of the **Basic Version** of the **Consequence Argument**, he believes that determinism precludes us from having genuine pathways into the future. But he also argues, largely on the basis of Frankfurt examples, that moral *responsibility* does not require that we have such genuine pathways or alternative possibilities. Further, Fischer (as we sketched in section 2.4.2.3.), defends a set of compatibilist conditions on responsibility. Second, "*source incompatibilists*," like Pereboom, also reject the view that moral responsibility requires alternative possibilities (again, largely by appealing to Frankfurt examples), though they affirm that responsibility requires that we be the ultimate sources of our actions, something that they argue is not possible if determinism is true. Thus, since theorists of this sort believe that responsibility does *not* require alternative possibilities, they will not regard a Widerker-style putative counterexample, such as the Jones case which does appeal to the notion of avoidability, to any restricted version of **Transfer NR** as effective. Even if such theorists are suspicious of **Transfer NR**, given their theoretical commitment to the view that responsibility does not require our having access to alternative possibilities, they cannot help themselves to an alleged counterexample to **Transfer NR** that *does* appeal to avoidability. Thus, Widerker's sort of counterexample to **Transfer NR** will not command wide acceptance.

A final worry concerns Widerker's principle **(M)**—the principle that if an agent knowingly acted in a morally wrong way, and believed correctly that he could have avoided acting as he did, then he is blameworthy for his act. The first conjunct of this principle captures an epistemic (or knowledge) condition (or a constituent of such a condition) on responsibility, and the second a freedom or control condition. In addition, Widerker regards this principle as *sufficient* for moral blameworthiness and, thus, it appears he must regard the proposed epistemic and control conditions as sufficient for blameworthiness: if they are satisfied, the agent is blameworthy. But it is far from evident that these dual conditions suffice for moral blameworthiness. As we recorded in the previous chapter, various free will theorists—compatibilists and incompatibilists included—have argued for an additional authenticity condition on responsibility. The root thought underlying this condition is that to be responsible for an action, the action must causally derive nondeviantly from agent-involving events, such as desires, beliefs, and best judgments that are "truly the agent's own." We have already introduced Mele's example that inspires this sort of condition: **Ann/Beth-1**. A slight modification in the tale as we presented it will adapt it to our concerns. To test principle **(M)**, we present an example that features a character who has been manipulated into arriving at the decision that she does. The manipulation is crafty enough to ensure that the character knowingly acts in a morally wrong way, and believes correctly that she could have avoided acting as she did (so **(M)** is satisfied). But owing to the nature of the manipulation, this character is not morally responsible for the relevant deed.

Suppose that Widerker's demon, murderer Jones, also turns out to be a diligent philosophy professor and that new-wave manipulation results in some character, Trish, being, in pertinent respects, the psychological twin of Jones. (So, for example, if Jones kills the chancellor, and in so doing, knowingly acts in a morally wrong way, and believes correctly that he could have avoided acting as he did, post-manipulated Trish, when she kills, also acts in light of the belief that she is doing wrong and that she could have avoided acting as she did.) Suppose, then, that post-manipulated Trish does indeed murder the dean and this gruesome deed of hers expresses an unsheddable engineered-in value. This sort of case convinces Mele (1995, 2006) and others (Kane 1996; Pereboom 2001) that the verdict that Beth is morally blameworthy for her murderous deed, despite its being true that in acting as she did, she knowingly did moral wrong in light of the correct belief that she could have avoided doing what she did, is mistaken (see, for e.g., Haji and Cuypers 2004; 2006; 2008).

Now, of course, it is one thing to appeal to some authenticity condition that is allegedly necessary for responsibility and quite another to deliver the goods: producing a viable analysis of authenticity and defending this analysis. (I shall say much more on such an analysis in Chapter 7.) Be that as it may, cases such as the Trish/Jones case cast at least a dark shadow, which cannot be ignored, over principle **(M)**.

It is open to Widerker, however, to strengthen principle **(M)** with an authenticity or any *other* proposed plausible condition on responsibility. Simply add these other conditions, whatever they turn out to be, to the epistemic and freedom condition of **(M)** so that the result is a "full package." Such a move would not be obviously dialectically illicit on the assumption that even credible *libertarian* accounts of responsibility feature such conditions; a libertarian, for example, might well welcome an authenticity condition.

Imagine, then, that Jones satisfies a rich set of compatibilist requirements of responsibility—a full package of requirements—including some requirement of authenticity and some requirement of avoidability where, again, the notion of 'avoidability' is a compatibilist one. One could not, consequently, complain that **(M)** is inadequate because it leaves out some important condition on responsibility. Would Jones's case (in which Jones murders Smith), so refined now not turn the trick? Would it not be a potent counterexample to **Transfer NR** and its one-path cousins when the compatibilist in question is allowed to appeal to a full package of conditions on responsibility and to a (compatibilist) notion of avoidability in an attempt to refute the inference rule (**Transfer NR**) in dispute?

To appreciate a shortcoming of this maneuver, bear in mind van Inwagen's challenge to a compatibilist who wishes to evade the **Direct Argument**: produce a set of propositions intuitively more plausible than the validity of **Transfer NR** and show that these propositions entail the compatibility of moral responsibility and determinism, or else devise a counterexample to **Transfer NR** that can be evaluated *independently* of the question whether moral responsibility and determinism are compatible. If principle **(M)** is strengthened to include a rich set of compatibilist conditions on responsibility, then it is false that the proposed counterexample to **Transfer NR**, such as Jones's case, can be assessed *independently* of the issue of the compatibility of responsibility and determinism. This is because, first, the strategy to defend the Widerker-style counterexample to **Transfer NR**, which appeals to a principle such as **(M)**, will not succeed if **(M)** fails to rope in a plausible condition, such as the authenticity condition, on responsibility (as we have explained). But, second, when principle **(M)** has been enriched to include all such conditions, whether the resulting enriched principle is credible rests on whether the set of compatibilist conditions that the enriched principle incorporates is a compelling set of sufficient conditions for moral responsibility. How plausible is the full package? Whether the full package is compelling, though, will rely partly but importantly on assessing how its members measure up to pressures from determinism. In brief, it seems that the full package cannot be evaluated *independently* of the question whether moral responsibility and determinism are compatible.

I conclude that Widerker's attempt to bid farewell to the **Direct Argument**, though instructive, leaves something to be desired.

4.5 A NEW COUNTEREXAMPLE

In the remaining sections of this chapter, I work toward a counterexample that, if persuasive, should tell against both the original version of **Transfer NR** and restricted one-path variations such as McKenna's **Transfer*****. To construct the counterexample, some preliminary background on the epistemic condition of responsibility and freedom presuppositions of moral obligation will be useful.

4.5.1 On the Epistemic Condition of Moral Responsibility

Among the requirements of moral responsibility, as we have mentioned, are a freedom or control requirement and an epistemic (or knowledge) requirement. An implausibly strong epistemic requirement is the following:

> **Econdition-1**: Agent, *S*, is morally blameworthy for action, *A*, only if *S* knows that *A* is morally wrong; and *S* is praiseworthy for *A* only if *S* knows that *A* is morally obligatory or permissible.

Surely, you can be blameworthy for an action even though you did not *know* that it was wrong, had good reason, though, to believe that it was wrong, and intentionally performed the act despite your (nonculpable) belief that you would be doing intentional wrong in performing it.

A necessary condition of propositional knowledge—a required condition of knowing any proposition—is that you believe that proposition. For example, necessarily, if you know that *the cat ate the mouse*, you believe that the cat ate the mouse; or, necessarily, if you know that *some act is wrong*, you believe that that act is wrong. As knowledge entails belief, **Econdition-1** entails **Action-Status** which many do take to be a plausible condition, concerning the moral status of actions—whether the action is right or wrong—on responsibility:

> **Action-Status**: Agent, *S*, is morally blameworthy for action, *A*, only if *A* is morally wrong; and *S* is morally praiseworthy for *A* only if *A* is morally obligatory or morally permissible.

Action-Status says, in a nutshell, that moral blameworthiness requires or presupposes moral wrongness; it is only wrongdoings for which you can be blameworthy; necessarily, if you are morally to blame for an action, it is wrong for you to perform that action. Similarly, **Action-Status** implies that moral praiseworthiness requires or presupposes moral obligatoriness or moral permissibility; necessarily, for you to be morally praiseworthy for an action, it is morally obligatory or morally permissible for you to perform that action.

Econdition-1 has the following weaker rival:

> **Econdition-2**: Agent, *S*, is morally blameworthy for action, *A*, only if *S* does *A* in light of believing that *A* is morally wrong; and *S* is praiseworthy for *A* only if *S* does *A* at least partly on the basis of the belief that *A* is morally obligatory or permissible.

According to **Econdition-2**, at least if this condition is taken to be a competitor to **Econdition-1**, moral blameworthiness requires, loosely, only belief in what is wrong and not the stronger condition that the object for which one is blameworthy—an intentional action, for instance—is in fact wrong. So, for example, suppose you believe that eating the cake which you mistakenly think has been prepared for special guests is morally wrong. But despite this belief, you gobble up the cake. Suppose it turns out that mother baked the cake for you (but did not tell you ahead of time that it was for you because she wanted to surprise you). It could, then, turn out that your eating the cake is not in fact wrong for you, though, from *your perspective*, you *are* doing wrong in eating it. You satisfy the knowledge condition for blameworthiness that is laid down in **Econdition-2**: you eat the cake while (mistakenly) believing that you're doing moral wrong in eating the cake. But the condition specified by stronger **Econdition-1** is not met; your eating the cake is not in fact morally wrong despite your believing it to be so. Analogously, **Econdition-2** implies that praiseworthiness requires only belief in what is obligatory or permissible; it does not require that the act that you perform be morally obligatory or morally permissible for you.

Assuming that **Econdition-1** is not in the running because it is too demanding, one *may* endorse both **Action-Status** and **Econdition-2**. On this view, to be blameworthy for an action, it must be that both the action is wrong *and* one performs it in light of the belief that one is doing wrong. Or one might accept **Econdition-2** and renounce **Action-Status** or, perhaps, accept the latter but not the former. This matter need not be settled here. For in the context of interest, the dispute between those who accept one or the other but not both of **Econdition-2** and **Action-Status**, as we shall see, is of no consequence.

In summary, we have a pair of options for an epistemic principle concerning blame. The stronger says that an agent is morally blameworthy for an action only if she knows that it is morally wrong. The weaker (when taken to be a rival of the stronger) says that an agent is morally blameworthy for an action only if she believes that it is morally wrong. We also have a principle about the moral status of an action (whether it is right or wrong) as required for blame.

4.5.2 A Requirement of Alternative Possibilities for Obligation

We can show that there is a requirement of alternative possibilities for the truth of judgments of moral right, wrong, and obligation; or in short, there is such a requirement for the truth of judgments of (overall) obligation. No agent, for instance, can perform an act that is morally wrong (or morally obligatory) unless she could have refrained from performing that act. Two principles of obligation that command widespread intuitive appeal as well as support from promising analyses of the concept of obligation (or if we want, "theory-backed" support) are the "ought" implies "can" principle (principle **K**) and the principle that it is obligatory to do something just in case it is wrong not to do it (principle **OW**).[5] The "ought" implies "can" principle can be put in this way:

5 By way of "theory-based" support, see, for example Feldman 1986; Haji 2002; and M. Zimmerman 1996.

> **(K)**: If it is overall obligatory for one to do something, then one can do it, and if it is (overall) obligatory for one to refrain from doing something, then one can refrain from doing it.[6]

Moral obligation expresses a kind of necessity or requirement. If morality *requires* that you do something, then you can do it. If you can't, for example, save the drowning child because you have been tethered to your seat, or because you have been overcome by paralysis, the "ought" implies "can" principle indicates that you don't have a moral obligation to save the child; morality can't require you to do what it is not in your power to do.

We have emphasized that moral *responsibility* requires control; if you are morally praiseworthy or blameworthy for an action, then you have responsibility-relevant control in performing this action. Similarly, think of the "ought" implies "can" principle as a control principle for moral *obligation*; if you have a moral obligation to perform an action, then you have obligation-relevant control in performing it. If you can't perform an action, then, you can't have control in performing it; so you can't be morally obligated to perform it.[7]

Turning, next, to **(OW)**, **(OW)** may be stated in this way:

> **(OW)**: It is (overall) obligatory for one to do something if and only if it is (overall) wrong for one to refrain from doing it.

One would think that to say that some action is morally wrong (that is, morally forbidden) for you is just to say that you morally ought—you have a moral obligation not to do it (or there is a moral requirement that you not do it). But then it would seem that an act is morally obligatory for you—morality *requires* that you do it—if and only if your not doing it is morally wrong; this is just what **(OW)** says.

If we accept **(K)** and **(OW)**, we may confirm that there is a requirement of alternative possibilities for the truth of judgments of obligation. First, we register that **(K)** and **(OW)** entail that an agent can do moral wrong only if the agent had an alternative; that is to say, from **(K)** and **(OW)**, we may infer:

> **(WAP)**: If it is wrong for one to do something, then one can refrain from doing it.

Barring cogent reasons to believe otherwise, if we assume that "ought" implies "can," there is little reason not to assume, too, that "wrong" (and "right") imply "can." Again, think of the "ought" implies "can" principle

6 With temporal indices included, part of the principle says: If, at t, one ought to do a at t^* (t^* may be identical to, or later than, t^*), then, at t, one can do a at t^*.

7 The "ought" implies "can" principle is discussed further in the next chapter.

as a control principle for obligation. Just as praiseworthiness and blameworthiness require control, so does obligation and wrongness. The control requirements of blameworthiness, unless we have sound reason to believe the contrary, mirror those of praiseworthiness: both have the same freedom requirements. Similarly, it would seem that the control or freedom requirements of obligation, unless we have strong reason to think otherwise, should also be the very ones of wrong and right (see Haji 2002).

If we grant that just as "ought" implies "can," "wrong," too, implies "can," there is a straightforward argument for the conclusion that obligation requires alternative possibilities:

(1*) If it is obligatory for one to refrain from doing *A*, then it is wrong for one to do *A*. [From **(OW)**]

(2*) If it is wrong for one to do *A*, then one can do *A*. [From the "wrong" implies "can" analogue of **(K)**: *if it is wrong for one to do A, then one can do A*.]

(3*) Therefore, if it is obligatory for one to refrain from doing *A*, then one can do *A*.

There is no similar way to derive the proposition that rightness, likewise, requires alternatives. This is because even if it is agreed that "right" implies "can," there is no principle like **(OW)** that will allow us to infer that "right" implies "can refrain." Nevertheless, it is very plausible that "right" does imply "can refrain." For suppose an agent, Jones, is in a situation, perhaps a Frankfurt-type situation, in which Jones cannot refrain from pushing an innocent child off the pier to her death. It is neither wrong nor obligatory for Jones to perform this act in his circumstances because there is a requirement of alternative possibilities for wrongness and obligation. It seems, then, that there are two principal options. An act has a *primary moral status* only if it is morally right, wrong, or obligatory. Either pushing the child off the pier is permissible for Jones or this act lacks a primary morally deontic property altogether, not being morally right, morally wrong, or morally obligatory; it is, we can say, "amoral" for Jones. The latter is more plausible than the former. After all, Jones's act is the cold-blooded killing of an innocent child; for that matter, his act could have been any other heinous deed. In Jones's circumstances, if pushing the child to her death were not amoral for Jones, this act would be morally *right* (that is, a good thing, but not obligatory) for Jones, a result that resists acceptance. Insisting, again, that in the absence of persuasive reason to think otherwise, the freedom requirements of "right" parallel those of "wrong" and "obligation," enables us to circumvent this unpalatable result. Hence, "right," too, implies "can refrain."

We conclude that the truth of judgments of obligation requires alternative possibilities: one has a moral obligation to do something only if one could have done otherwise (see Haji 2002 for further defense of the view that moral obligation requires alternatives).

4.5.3 An Informal Presentation of the Counterexample to Transfer NR

In this section, I give a simplified sketch of a "one-path" counterexample against **Transfer NR** (or **Transfer*****). (For those who are interested, I fill in the details in the next section.)

The counterexample involves creation of a best world. So let's first say something about *best worlds* and their *creation*. We suppose that each possible world can be ranked in terms of how intrinsically good—how good in itself—it is. Presumably, some worlds are intrinsically better than others; some are just as good as others. A *world is best* if and only if no world is intrinsically better than it is. Possible worlds have parts that are creatable and parts that are not creatable. The creatable parts are states of affairs that it is possible for a suitably empowered being to make obtain or to bring about. So, for example, it would seem that God could bring about the state of affairs, *Everest being the highest mountain on earth*, or *Al's being six feet tall*, or *Sue's eating a chocolate bar*. The non-creatable parts are non-contingent states of affairs, such as *2 + 2's being 4* or *some square's being round*.

Consider the following creation story involving God-like Hal who creates a best world. Hal cannot do otherwise than create this world, W1, owing to an unknown (to Hal) condition of his brain—his other neural pathways are closed down. He has no alternative possibilities to his actual conduct. Hence, given the principle that moral obligation, right, and wrong require alternative possibilities, Hal's act of creating W1 does not violate a moral obligation of his; nor is this creative act morally right, or morally obligatory. Suppose, also, that Hal is an amoral agent as he lacks any understanding of moral right, wrong, and obligation. Note that he thus would violate either the strong or weak epistemic requirements on praise (or blame). If praiseworthiness requires obligatoriness or rightness (as the strong epistemic requirement implies), Hal is not praiseworthy for his creative act because this act is not right or obligatory. If praiseworthiness requires only belief in what is obligatory or right (as the weak epistemic requirement implies), then again Hal is not praiseworthy for his creative act because Hal is amoral: being amoral, he does not create W1 on the basis of the belief that he is doing something that is morally obligatory or right.

Imagine that Hal creates a deterministic world in which a person, Michael, performs an act to please his gracious host—Michael eats noodles (which he does not like eating). And suppose that Michael's doing so is morally praiseworthy. Under various scenarios normal agents would be deserving of praise for such an act.

Hal is not responsible for creating W1 (he is neither praiseworthy nor blameworthy for creating W1). Nor is he responsible, it seems, for the fact that, if he creates W1, then Michael eats noodles. And of course, Michael is not responsible for Hal's creating W1, nor for the causal chain that will lead to his eating noodles. But unless the advocate of the **Direct Argument** wants to presuppose the falsity of compatibilism, which (it appears) would be question begging, it is open to the compatibilist to claim that, at W1, when Michael eats noodles, Michael *is* praiseworthy and so morally responsible for doing so. Assume, also, that there are no other agential candidates for praise (or blame) regarding Michael's act of noodle-eating at W1. Hence, we have:

> NRp [No one is or ever has been morally responsible for *Hal creates W1.*]
> NR(p ⊃ q) [No one is or ever has been morally responsible for the fact that *if Hal creates W1, then Michael eats noodles.*]
> ~NRq [It's false that no one is or ever has been morally responsible for *Michael eats noodles*; Michael *is* praiseworthy for eating noodles.]

Essentially, all the counterexample really requires is the creation of a (putatively) morally responsible agent (in this case Michael) by an amoral god-like being (Hal), which is certainly a conceptual possibility.

ON RESPONSIBILITY FOR CONDITIONALS

One might well be somewhat puzzled about the second premise: No one is or ever has been morally responsible for the fact that *if Hal creates W1, then Michael eats noodles*. And the puzzle has to do with the nature of responsibility for the truth of conditionals. If someone is responsible for the truth of a conditional, in virtue of what is that so? This is a difficult issue. Without delving into a full account of responsibility for conditionals, we can make do with the following. First, the conditionals of concern are of a certain sort: their antecedents record someone's doing something or bringing about some state of affairs (e.g., Hal's creating a world). Their consequents, roughly, specify something that results from what the relevant agent who is mentioned in the antecedent does. Reflect on a conditional of this variety:

> **C**: If Hal injects Michael with the drug, then Michael dies.

Suppose Hal fatally stabs Michael. And suppose, first, that Hal is blameworthy for killing Michael (as a result of stabbing him). It does not, of course, follow that Hal is, in virtue of being responsible for killing Michael, blameworthy for conditional C. He is not blameworthy for this conditional, roughly, because there is no appropriate connection between Hal's injecting Michael with the drug, and Michael's death or Hal's killing Michael. Suppose, next, that Hal is blameworthy for injecting Michael with the drug. Again, it doesn't follow from the *mere* fact that he is blameworthy for injecting Michael that he is thereby responsible for Michael's death. Maybe Hal is, in this scenario, blameworthy primarily because he believes that the drug will cause minor discomfort to Michael. Let's alter the case somewhat. Hal is well aware that if he injects Michael with the drug, a drug that he knows to be fatal, the drug will kill Michael. And suppose, third, that Hal does kill Michael as a result of injecting him with the drug. Then it is plausible to think that Hal *is* responsible for conditional C. In this case, Hal rightly believes that he will bring about an outcome (Michael's death) by doing something (injecting Michael with the toxic drug); he intentionally brings about the deadly outcome. Suppose that, in another variation of the case, Hal has no reason whatsoever to believe that the drug will kill Michael; indeed, Hal has every reason to think that he will be helping Michael to fight a deadly disease by injecting him with the drug. If Hal injects Michael partly on the basis of the nonculpable belief that he will be helping Michael, then, again, Hal won't be responsible for killing Michael. After all, he has no intention to bring about the deadly outcome. And further, he won't, in this case, be responsible for conditional **C** either.

We may now revert to the conditional of interest:

> **CW**: If Hal creates W1, then Michael eats noodles.

As Hal's case has been described, there is no reason at all to think that there is an appropriate "responsibility-grounding connection" between Michael's eating noodles and Hal's creating W1. It isn't as though Hal intentionally creates W1 for the purpose of ensuring that Michael eats noodles at the time at which he does. So we have no reason to believe that Hal is responsible for **CW**. Nor, given what we have said about responsibility for the truth of conditionals, do we have reason to think that Michael is praiseworthy for **CW** even though he is praiseworthy for eating noodles.

Developing further the counterexample, suppose one *is* concerned about the supposition that both W1 is *deterministic* and that Michael is morally *praiseworthy* for eating noodles in this world. Specifically, one might worry that this supposition begs the question against the *incompatibilist*. Well, then, simply modify the example in this way: Imagine that W1 is not deterministic and that some events in this world—at least some human actions—are free in a libertarian sense of 'free.' Suppose that Michael's eating noodles is one of these libertarian free acts. Nothing in this imagined case prevents us from hypothesizing that it is true that Michael's decision to eat noodles is free in this libertarian's sense of 'free'; and that Michael may well be morally praiseworthy (on some suitable libertarian account of praiseworthiness) for this decision. Then once again we have this falsifying instance of **Transfer NR**: No one is or ever has been morally responsible for *Hal creates* W1; no one is or ever has been morally responsible for the fact that *if Hal creates W1, then Michael eats noodles*; yet, it's false that no one is or ever has been morally responsible for *Michael eats noodles.*

4.5.4 Filling in the Details of the Counterexample

(Some readers may want to skip this sub-section.) To supply the details of the counterexample to **Transfer NR** (call the counterexample "**Hal's Creation**"), we note, first, that there are strong reasons to believe that if there is a best world, there are indefinitely many bests (see, for instance, Rosenkrantz and Hoffman 2002, p. 159). Only one such world can be created owing to the worlds being incompatible. Assume that Hal can, at time, *t*, create a best world, W1. Hal believes, at *t*, that, at *t*, he can instead create an alternative world, W2, that is also best or that he can, at *t*, refrain from creating any world at all. But this belief is mistaken. A cosmic anomaly "neutralizes" all of Hal's neurological pathways (or simply, "actional pathways") that are required to be operational in order for Hal to create a world other than W1, or to refrain from creating any world. At *t*, then, Hal can create W1, does create W1, and has no alternative to creating W1. As there is a requirement of alternative possibilities for the truth of judgments of obligation, Hal's act of creation is neither right, nor wrong, nor obligatory. Not having any primary moral status, Hal's creative act is amoral. Add the embellishment that Hal is an *amoral agent* in that he lacks any conception of moral right, wrong, or obligation. Thus, none of his acts is such that he performs them on the basis of the belief that he is doing something that is morally obligatory, right, or wrong. Suppose that in W1 Michael decides, at *ts*, to eat noodles. So it is true that if Hal creates W1, then Michael decides, at *ts*, to eat noodles. Now consider this line of reasoning:

HAL'S ARGUMENT
(1H): NR (Hal creates W1).
(2H): NR (Hal creates W1 ⊃ Michael decides, at *ts*, to eat noodles).
(3H): Therefore, NR (Michael decides, at *ts*, to eat noodles).

Hal's Argument impugns **Transfer NR.** To rehearse that it does, we record, first, that **Hal's Creation** is a one-path case. Premise (1H) is true for the following reason. Suppose, on the one hand, that **Action-Status** is true—to be blameworthy for an act, that act must be wrong; to be praiseworthy for an act, that act must be obligatory or permissible. Then **Action-Status,** in conjunction with the proposition that Hal's creative act is amoral, entails that Hal is not morally responsible for this act. Suppose, on the other hand, that one renounces **Action-Status** but endorses **Econdition-2** (to be praiseworthy for an act, for instance, one must perform the act in light of the belief that one is doing something that is right or obligatory). Then, once again, Hal is not morally responsible for his creative act in virtue of its being false that Hal performs this act on the basis of the belief that the act has some primary moral status; bear in mind that Hal is an amoral agent. So we may conclude that Hal is not morally responsible for creating W1. As there is no reason to believe that anybody else is morally responsible for creating W1, (1H) is true.

Before arguing for the possibility that (2H) is true even if (3H) is false (and (1H) is true), let's first address (3H). Suppose W1 is a deterministic world. There is nothing in **Hal's Creation** to preclude its being true that Michael's decision, at *ts*, to eat noodles is free in a compatibilist's sense of 'free'; and that Michael may well be morally praiseworthy (on some compatibilist account of praiseworthiness) for this decision. Unless the proponent of the **Direct Argument** assumes the falsity of compatibilism, something seemingly question-begging in the context, compatibilists are well within their rights to claim that, at W1, when Michael eats noodles, he is praiseworthy for doing so.

Suppose, alternatively, that W1 is not deterministic and that some events in this world—at least some human actions—are free in a libertarian sense of 'free.' Such actions satisfy the following (strong libertarian) condition. Let *d* stand for Michael's decision to eat noodles, one that he makes at *ts*. Let *c* be a proposition that expresses all the causal conditions which obtain in the world up to *ts*. Michael's decision, *d*, that he makes at *ts* is a libertarian free (mental) action only if, possibly, (i) Michael is in *c* and Michael freely refrains, at *ts*, from making *d*, and (ii) if *d* is caused by agent-involving events, such as Michael's having of reasons, *d* is indeterministically caused by these events.[8] Again, nothing in **Hal's Creation** forecloses the possibility of its being true that Michael's decision to eat noodles is free in this libertarian sense of 'free'; and that Michael may well be morally praiseworthy (on some apt libertarian account of praiseworthiness) for this decision.

But now one may well wonder how (2H) could be true if Michael is indeed praiseworthy for the decision that he makes at *ts*. The state of affairs for which one might insist that Michael is also praiseworthy *if* he is praiseworthy for the decision that he makes at *ts* is:

> **MC**: If Hal creates W1, then Michael decides, at *ts*, to eat noodles.

8 Not all libertarians accept conditions (i) and (ii). Non-traditional libertarians reject the requirement that a decision is free only if one could have refrained from performing it. Libertarians who are traditional agent-causalists endorse the alternative possibilities requirement, and insist that a free decision has no event as its cause but has, instead a substance—its agent—as its cause.

If you are responsible for something, then you must satisfy the epistemic condition of responsibility in bringing about that thing, or in seeing to its occurrence. Thus, if Michael is responsible—praiseworthy, for instance—in seeing to the occurrence of **MC**, then Michael must satisfy the epistemic condition in seeing to **MC**'s occurrence. **Econdition-2** implies that to be morally praiseworthy for seeing to the occurrence of some state of affairs, you must see to its occurrence partly on the basis of the moral belief that your seeing to its occurrence is morally obligatory or morally permissible. But if this is true, Michael is *not* morally praiseworthy for seeing to the occurrence of **MC**. For he does not see to **MC**'s occurrence on the basis of the belief that **MC** is morally obligatory or morally permissible. As I have explained, it is implausible to suppose that Michael is responsible for conditional **MC** merely in virtue of being responsible for deciding at *ts* to eat noodles. Some may reject **Econdition-2** and opt, instead, for some still weaker epistemic constraint. Perhaps it might be a condition to the effect that to be praiseworthy for some state of affairs *p*, at least the agent morally ought to have known or believed that *p* is obligatory or (as some might prefer) morally good (in some specified sense of 'good'). With respect, though, to **MC**, there are no compelling grounds *to require* that in **Hal's Creation**, Michael ought to have known or believed that **MC** is obligatory or morally good. My general suggestion is that whatever the doxastic (that is, belief) constituent of the epistemic constraint on responsibility, there is no reason to insist that Michael has (or meets) this constituent in **Hal's Creation**. Others might resist any sort of doxastic or awareness constraint on praiseworthiness (or on responsibility in general). I find this implausible. I know of no discussion on the epistemic requirements of moral responsibility in which it is maintained that *no* sort of belief or awareness constituent is any part of the epistemic constraint.

If Michael is not morally responsible for **MC**, no one need be responsible for **MC**. We need simply assume that there are no other candidates for praise regarding Michael's act of eating noodles at W1.Thus, (2H) can be true consistently with its being the case that (1H) is true and (3H) is false. So **Hal's Argument** is a falsifying instance of even one-path **Transfer NR**-like principles.

Some people will be disturbed by the heavy reliance of **Hal's Creation** on the view that there is a requirement of alternative possibilities for the truth of judgments of obligation. To pacify these skeptics, I end with a minor variation on **Hal's Creation** that bypasses this view altogether. It seems highly plausible that an amoral agent, like Hal, who has no conception whatever of moral right, wrong, or obligation (and perhaps who has no conception of morality whatsoever) cannot be *morally* praiseworthy or blameworthy for any of his actions. Suppose, now, that in "**Amoral-Hal**," Hal does have an alternative to creating W1. Still, he opts for W1. We may even assume that *Hal's creating W1* has some primary moral status. However, in virtue of being an amoral agent, Hal is not morally responsible for *any* of the acts that he performs. Again, in this variation of Hal's case, (2H) may be true for the same reason that it is in the original, and (3H) may be false for the very reason that it is in the original.

Transfer NR concerns responsibility whereas **Rule β** concerns *one* condition of responsibility, namely, control. The counterexamples to **Transfer NR** that I have proposed all exploit the fact that responsibility has *other* requirements besides the freedom or control requirement; responsibility, for instance, also has an epistemic requirement.

I conclude that the **Direct Argument**, resting as it may on perhaps restricted one-path versions of **Transfer NR**, is not sound because even such restricted versions of this principle fall to counterexample. In the next chapter, we turn to another indirect argument for incompatibilism—indirect in that it avoids direct appeal to the **Principle of Alternative Possibilities.** The argument first attempts *to show* that a person can be neither blameworthy nor praiseworthy for performing an action unless that person could have refrained from performing that action. Then, together with the premise that determinism expunges all alternatives, it proceeds to the conclusion that determinism and moral responsibility are incompatible.

5 The Deontic Argument

5.1 INTRODUCTION

Of the versions of the **Consequence Argument** that we have examined, in my estimation it is the **Basic Argument** that is the most promising. Working around the premise that no one has the power to alter the past or the laws, this argument relies on the *extension principle*: an agent can do *X* only if his doing *X* can be an extension of the actual past, holding fixed the laws of nature; we are free only to add to the past consistent with the laws of nature. Suppose, then, that you won't do *X* at time, *t*, because, among other things, in your deterministic world your failing to do *X* at this time is deterministically caused by apt antecedents. The extension principle generates the result that you could not have done *X* at *t*. For, supposing otherwise, supposing that you could have done *X* at *t*, your doing *X* at *t* would have to have been an extension of the past, holding fixed the laws. But given that your world is deterministic, with the past fixed, your doing *X* at *t* could not have been an extension of the actual past. This is because any extension of the actual past, holding fixed the laws, and assuming that your not doing *X* at *t* is deterministically caused, would have been one in which you do not do *X* at *t*. Thus, if determinism is true, you could not have done otherwise than refrain from doing *X* at *t*.

Assume that this argument does succeed in establishing the incompatibility of determinism and freedom to do otherwise. We have observed that if this conclusion is taken in tandem with the **Principle of Alternative Possibilities**, we derive the further skeptical result that determinism is incompatible with moral responsibility. But we have also observed that many theorists—compatibilists and incompatibilists included—are inclined to reject this principle by invoking, for example, Frankfurt-type examples.

Fischer, for instance, says that he is a *semicompatibilist*. The semicompatibilist takes determinism to be incompatible with freedom to do otherwise but compatible with responsibility. How might an incompatibilist attempt to convince the semicompatibilist (and others) that even if we reject the **Principle of Alternative Possibilities**, determinism and responsibility cannot co-exist? One option would be to defend the **Direct Argument**. As I have explained, there are reasons to be less than optimistic about the prospects of this argument. The argument relies on an inference rule that is suspect: if you are not even partly responsible for one thing, and you are not even partly responsible for the fact that this thing "leads to" a second, then you are not even partly responsible for the second.

Another option would be to pay close attention to other moral dimensions of responsibility and to argue that these dimensions can be secured only if we have alternatives. Since determinism rules out our having alternatives (as we are now assuming), incompatibilism may be sustained. In this chapter, I develop this second option. I discuss the **Deontic Argument** which draws on the view that there is a requirement of alternative possibilities for moral right, wrong, and obligation, and the view that moral praiseworthiness presupposes obligation and that moral blameworthiness presupposes wrongness.

5.2 THE DEONTIC ARGUMENT

Assume that determinism precludes our being able to do otherwise. Assume, further, that if you are morally blameworthy for performing an action, then that action is morally wrong; and that if you are morally praiseworthy for performing an action, that action is either morally obligatory or permissible (we have dubbed this principle **Action-Status**). In section 4.5.2, we produced an argument for the conclusion that there is a requirement of alternative possibilities for the truth of morally deontic judgments (judgments of moral right, wrong, and obligation). To recapitulate, I said that a highly plausible morally deontic principle is the "ought" implies "can" principle: if you morally ought to do something, then you can do it. But if "ought" implies "can," "wrong" and "right" imply "can" as well. Further, the principle, if it is obligatory for one to refrain from doing something, then it is wrong for one to do that thing, is true as well. This principle, in turn, in conjunction with the "wrong" implies "can" principle, yields the result that if it is obligatory for one to refrain from doing something, then one can do that thing. I concluded that the truth of judgments of obligation requires alternative possibilities: one has a moral obligation to do something only if one could have done otherwise and, similarly, it is wrong for one to do something only if one could have done otherwise. Assume that regarding the requirement of alternative possibilities for the truth of obligation judgments, the alternative possibilities are strong or categorical: given the past and the laws, you could have done other than what you in fact did. But if blameworthiness does require wrongness, and if there is a requirement of (strong) alternative possibilities for wrongness, then determinism undermines blameworthiness (supposing that determinism precludes our having alternatives). An analogous line of reasoning would establish that determinism undermines praiseworthiness as well. Let's formulate this argument—the **Deontic Argument**—somewhat more formally. In the interests of simplicity, when I construct the argument, I appeal only to blameworthiness.

Let '*S*' range over any person and '*A*' range over any action. (Again, construe 'action' broadly to include intentional omissions as well as mental actions such as decisions.)

THE DEONTIC ARGUMENT

1. If *S* is morally blameworthy for doing *A*, then *A* is morally wrong for *S*. Line (1) is based on the part of **Action-Status** that says that an agent is morally blameworthy for performing an action only if it is morally wrong for the agent to perform this action.
2. If *A* is morally wrong for *S*, then *S* can refrain from doing *A*. (2) rests on the view that there is a requirement of alternative possibilities for the truth of judgments of right, wrong, and obligation.
3. Therefore, if *S* is morally blameworthy for doing *A*, then *S* can refrain from doing *A*.
4. If determinism is true, and *S* does *A*, then *S* cannot refrain from doing *A*. This premise may be predicated on the **Basic Consequence Argument.**
5. If *S* cannot refrain from doing *A*, then *S* is not morally blameworthy for doing *A* (from (3)).
6. Therefore, if determinism is true and *S* does *A*, then *S* is not morally blameworthy for doing *A*.

A similar argument with minor changes may be developed to show that determinism is incompatible with moral praiseworthiness. So, for instance, in this parallel argument, the first premise would say that if *S* is morally praiseworthy for doing *A*, then it is morally obligatory or permissible for *S* to do *A*; the second would state that if *A* is morally obligatory (or permissible) for *S*, then *S* can refrain from doing *A*; and the fifth would affirm that if *S* cannot refrain from doing *A*, then *S* is not morally praiseworthy for doing *A*.

The **Deontic Argument** is a kind of indirect argument: it attempts to establish that determinism is incompatible with responsibility by assuming, first, that determinism is incompatible with freedom to do otherwise, and showing that obligation or wrong require such freedom, and then invoking the principle that in order to be morally responsible (praiseworthy or blameworthy) for something, that thing must be obligatory or wrong.

5.3 PROBLEMS WITH THE DEONTIC ARGUMENT

The argument may be challenged at a number of places. So, for instance, some reject the "ought" implies "can" principle (principle **(K)**). Since this principle plays an essential role in establishing that there is requirement of alternative possibilities for obligation and wrongness, these people will reject line (2) of this argument. Let's rehearse what perhaps some would take to be three of the most telling sorts of argument against this principle.

5.3.1 Genuine Moral Dilemmas and "Ought" Implies "Can"

Various people have claimed that the existence or possibility of genuine moral dilemmas undermines principle **(K)**. Genuine moral dilemmas, or as some may prefer to say, "basic moral dilemmas" or "conflicts of overall moral obligation," involve there being two or more (overall or all-in) obligations which cannot all be satisfied, though each can be. More precisely, the following constitute such dilemmas: Agent *S* ought to do *A* (and *S* can do *A*); *S* ought to do *B* (and *S* can do *B*); but *S* cannot do *A* and *B*.[1] Suppose that, for instance, your twins are both drowning, and you are the only person who can help. If you are in a genuine moral dilemma, then you ought to save one (Tom), you ought to save the other (Tim), but you can't save both; you cannot do the conjunctive act: your saving Tom and Tim. Moral dilemmas, then, involve inevitable wrongdoing. If one fails to perform an obligation, one does wrong. In your dilemmatic situation, if you save Tom, you cannot save Tim. Hence, if you save Tom, you fail to do something that is obligatory (save Tim), and thus do wrong. Similarly, if you save Tim, you thwart an obligation (the obligation to save Tom), and so do wrong again. Sartre's case of what many take to be a basic dilemma is famous. A student in France, during the second World War, must choose between joining the Free French Forces and taking care of his mother (Sartre 1975, pp. 354-57). Proponents of genuine moral dilemmas might propose that the student ought to join the resistance *and* he ought to take care of his mother, but he cannot do both.

To see why such dilemmas, if they are indeed possible, undercut the "ought" implies "can" principle, we introduce the **Agglomeration Principle**. This principle says that if one ought, at some time, to do one thing, *A*, and one ought, at that time, to do another thing, *B*, then one ought, at that time, to do the conjunctive act, *A* and *B*:

> **Agglomeration (AG)**: If O(*A*) and O(*B*), then O(*A* and *B*).

---

1 With temporal indices added, at *t*, *S* ought to do *A* at *t1* (and *S* can, at *t*, do *A* at *t1*); at *t*, *S* ought to do *B* at *t2* (and *S* can, at *t*, do *B* at *t2*); but *S* cannot, at *t*, do both *A* at *t1* and *B* at *t2*.

Reverting to the twin case, suppose that you ought, at *t*, to save Tom at *t**, and you ought, at *t*, to save Tim at *t** (*t** may be identical to, or later than *t*). Then according to the **Agglomeration Principle**, you ought at *t*, to do the conjunctive act, (save Tom at *t** and save Tim at *t**). If the "ought" implies "can" principle, **(K)**, is true, then you can, at *t*, do this conjunctive act. However, since you cannot, at *t*, do this conjunctive act—you cannot save both Tom and Tim—despite the alleged claim that you ought to, **(K)** is false.[2]

One rebuttal of this case for dilemmas involves jettisoning the **Agglomeration Principle** (see, for example, Hudson 1986; pp. 16–18; van Fraassen 1987, p. 146; and Williams 1987, pp. 132–33). But this is controversial. Indeed, many who reject the possibility of moral dilemmas *accept* the **Agglomeration Principle**. Appealing to this principle, one can argue that genuine moral dilemmas can't occur: Suppose (for *reductio*) that the case involving Tim and Tom is one in which you are in a genuine moral dilemma. Then, you ought to save Tom and you ought to save Tim, but *you cannot do the conjunctive act: your saving Tom and Tim.* The **Agglomeration Principle** entails that you ought to do this conjunctive act. If you ought to do this conjunctive act, principle **(K)**, in turn, implies that *you can do this conjunctive act.* Since it cannot be both that you can do this conjunctive act and that you cannot do this act, it is false that your situation is genuinely dilemmatic.

So we arrive at the following standoff. The argument (in question) against **(K)** appeals to the **Agglomeration Principle** and the alleged existence of genuine moral dilemmas. The argument (in question) against the possibility of genuine moral dilemmas also invokes the **Agglomeration Principle**, but it makes use of the "ought" implies "can" principle as well. Assuming that the **Agglomeration Principle** is not in question, some might claim that it is more evident that there are, or that there can be genuine moral dilemmas than that **(K)** is true.[3] Others will claim that the reverse is true.[4] We may conclude that the argument from genuine moral dilemmas against **(K)** is far from knock-down. I suggest that one way in which this debate may be moved is by turning to what we think is the most plausible analysis of the concept of moral obligation, and seeing whether this analysis bears fruitfully on whether the "ought" implies "can" principle is true or false, or whether there can indeed be genuine conflicts of obligation.

---

2 This species of argument is carefully laid out by Gowans 1987, pp. 20–22 and McConnell 1987, pp. 155-57. It is invoked by Lemmon 1987 to discard principle *K*.

3 For arguments in favor of genuine moral dilemmas, see, for example, Marcus 1987; Sinnott-Armstrong 1988; Stocker 1990; and Williams 1987.

4 For arguments against such dilemmas, see, for instance, Conee 1987; Donagan 1987; Feldman 1986, sec. 9.1; McConnell 1987; and M. Zimmerman 1996, pp. 217–25.

5.3.2 Self-Imposed Impossibility and "Ought" Implies "Can"

Some think that examples of self-imposed impossibility in which a person (freely) takes deliberate steps to cause herself to be unable to do something later present a serious challenge to **(K)**.[5] Suppose, for instance, that Lottie's spouse-to-be refuses to marry Lottie unless she gets rid of "Lottie's little pest," her baby. Lottie believes that it is wrong to kill her baby but still settles on the decision to do so. To help with the execution of this vile decision, Lottie imbibes a pill, in the full realization that having taken it, she won't be able to refrain from squeezing the trigger. Still, one might insist, Lottie ought not to squeeze the trigger (or kill the baby) when she does *even though* she cannot, at the time, refrain from squeezing the trigger. Further, surely, it might be claimed, Lottie is blameworthy for her monstrous deed; she cannot get off the hook so easily by disabling herself in the relevant way. But if she ought to refrain from her deed at the time of its performance, it follows that **(K)** is false. This is because **(K)** implies that if Lottie ought not to squeeze the trigger when she does, she can then refrain from squeezing the trigger.

I agree, though, with Zimmerman's proposal that careful attention to the distinctions between immediate and remote control, and immediate and remote obligation enables us to meet this objection. As Zimmerman explains, regarding the former distinction, it is common to ascribe a double time-index to "can" contexts, one to the "can" itself and one to the action on which the "can" operates. So I may say that I can now be in Chicago tomorrow, but if I leave for Zanzibar this afternoon, I won't be able to make the Windy City tomorrow. In the phrase-form, '*S* can at *t* do *A* at time *t**,' Zimmerman proposes, what 'can' denotes is immediate if *t* is identical with *t** but remote otherwise. Thus, we should understand the claim that "ought" implies "can" as the claim that if *S* ought at *t* to do *A* at *t**, then *S* can at *t* do *A* at *t**. And just as control can be remote or immediate, so, too, can obligation. I may now have an obligation to lecture now, or I may now have an obligation to lecture this afternoon (M. Zimmerman 1987, pp. 199–200; 1996, pp. 96–97).

5.3.2.1 Changing Obligations with Passing Time

The distinction between immediate and remote control, and immediate and remote obligation, is justified partly on the basis that it helps to shed light on a number of puzzling moral issues. For instance, it appears that our obligations can change with the passage of time, and that "time-relativizing" "ought" statements by ascribing a double temporal index to them can explain how this can be so without paradox. To illustrate, I use an example that Feldman (1986, pp. 52–57) develops. Suppose a patient

5 Such cases are discussed in Henderson 1966, p. 106; Richman 1983, p. 85; Robinson 1971, p. 252; Sinnot-Armstrong 1988, pp. 116–17; and M. Zimmerman 1996, pp. 95–96.

is ill, and that his doctor can choose between two main courses of treatment. He can either give the patient medicine *A* today, and then give him *A* again tomorrow, or he can give him medicine *B* today and again tomorrow. Suppose the course of treatment with *B* would cure the patient but would produce some nasty side effects, while the course of treatment with *A* would cure the patient with no nasty repercussions. Suppose, finally, that mixing the treatments would kill the patient. Assume, plausibly, that prior to the time at which he gives any medicine, it is obligatory for the doctor to give *A* on the first day, and obligatory for the doctor to give *A* on the second day. Suppose, however, that the doctor fails to do what is best. For whatever reason, he gives the patient *B* on the first day. It seems clear that it is no longer right for him to give *A* on the second day—that would kill the patient. Once the doctor has failed to do his duty, and has given *B* on the first day, the rights and wrongs of the case seem to change.

One may wonder how obligations may change with passing time in the way in which the example illustrates. Time-relativization illuminates what is going on. Suppose that *t0* is a time before the treatment is begun, *t1* the time at which the first dose is to be given, and *t2* the time at which the second dose is to be administered. Feldman's claims can then be summarized in this fashion:

(1) At *t0* it is obligatory to give medicine *A* at *t1*.
(2) At *t0* it is obligatory to give medicine *A* at *t2*.
(3) At *t2* it is not right to give medicine *A* at *t2*.

(2) and (3) entail that the moral status of an action changes between *t0* and *t2*. There is an air of paradox here because it appears that giving *A* at *t2* is both obligatory and wrong, something that is impossible. Time-relativization, again, enables us to see why the moral status of the action changes, and so dissipates the semblance of incoherence. Suppose, again, that, for whatever reason, at *t0*, the doctor fails to do the best for the patient by giving the first dose of *B*. As of the time this dose of *B* is given, it would be wrong to give *A* to the patient (because doing so would kill her). So as of this time, what is best for the doctor to do is *different from* what was best for him to do earlier on when no medicine had been administered.

5.3.2.2. Reply to the Objection

These distinctions between immediate and remote control, and immediate and remote obligation, pave the way for responding to the objection that Lottie ought, at the time she takes the pill, and then again when she squeezes the trigger, to refrain from shooting the baby even though, as of the relevant times, she *cannot* refrain from shooting the baby. What is in fact true is that prior to taking the pill, Lottie ought to refrain from shooting the baby (in part, because she can, prior to taking the pill, refrain from shooting the baby). After taking the pill, though, and so no longer being able to refrain from the shooting, it is no longer true that Lottie ought to refrain, and that it is wrong for her to shoot the baby. Of course, we can maintain that Lottie ought, up to the time of taking the pill, to refrain from shooting her baby later, and as this (remote) obligation is *not* satisfied, a wrong *is* done. But this is consistent with holding that as of the time she takes the pill, Lottie's not shooting her baby is not obligatory for her. (See, for e.g., M. Zimmerman 1996, pp. 98–100; Haji 2002, pp. 47–52.)

That part of the objection that Lottie is *blameworthy* for her gruesome deed even though she cannot refrain from performing it at the time that she performs it is correct. It is important to see that the proponent of **(K)** need not deny this. For the control or freedom-relevant requirements of blameworthiness are quite reasonably taken to be satisfied by Lottie. Regarding this requirement, a "tracing" principle of the following sort is plausible: an agent, *S*, is blameworthy for *A*-ing only if *S* exerts "responsibility-grounding control" in *A*-ing; or *S* intentionally takes deliberate steps, over which she has responsibility-grounding control, to see to it that, when she performs *A*, she will lack such control in *A*-ing; or *S* intentionally does something, *B*, over which she has such control, and is aware that, if she then performs *A*, she will lack this sort of control in *A*-ing. We think this sort of tracing principle is reasonable, in part, because the agent intentionally executes a plan in the belief that by carrying through with the elements in her plan, she will achieve her end, a component of which is her not being able to refrain from doing something. Lottie's goal, for instance, is to kill her baby by shooting him. If we assume, simply for illustration, that freedom to do otherwise is the pertinent sort of control required for responsibility, and Lottie cannot refrain from squeezing the trigger, the tracing principle allows us to conclude that Lottie is blameworthy for squeezing the trigger. She is blameworthy as her action traces to earlier steps over which she has control—she could have done otherwise at these earlier times—and she takes these steps in the belief that their execution will eventually lead to attainment of her goal; their execution will do so by ensuring that she won't be able to refrain from squeezing the trigger.

In sum, Lottie is blameworthy for squeezing the trigger even though it is false that, as of the time she takes the pill, she ought not to squeeze it. Thus, given that one ought not to do something if and only if it is wrong for one to do that thing, although Lottie is blameworthy for squeezing the trigger, her squeezing of the trigger is not something that she ought not to do. It is not in the least obvious, then, that this second argument against **(K)** succeeds either.

5.3.3 Negative Duties and "Ought Not" Implies "Can Refrain From"

Some people (for example, Gideon Yaffee 2005) have proposed that it is false that "ought not" implies "can refrain from." If correct, then their strategy of reasoning for the falsity of this part of principle **(K)** also imperils the part that says that "ought" implies "can." In very simple terms, the argument that it is false that "ought not" implies "can refrain from" is this: Suppose (again, for *reductio*) that:

(**KC**): *S* ought not to do *A* only if *S* can do other than *A*.

It might be proposed, however, that we can be subject to a moral duty (or requirement) at a time at which we cannot act. For instance, surely you can discharge a "negative" obligation not to steal when you are asleep without performing any action at all (Yaffee 2005, p. 312). (Similarly, you can be subject to a "positive" obligation to feed your dog, Bowser, even while you are asleep.) If you ought not to steal even when you cannot act at all, then **KC** is false. (Analogously, if you ought to care for Bowser even when you are asleep, and so can't then act at all, it is false that "ought" implies "can.")

One of the chief defects in this argument, though, is its failure to pay attention to the fact, to which we have already called attention, that we should ascribe a double time index to "ought" statements (as, for example, M. Zimmerman 1996 and Feldman 1986 propose): one is the time at which a person is subject, or acquires a moral obligation, to do something, and the other is the time at which the person does this thing. In the terminology we have adopted, control (as well as obligation) can be immediate or remote.

Addressing, now, Yaffee's proposal that "ought not" does not imply "can refrain from," Yaffee claims that you can discharge your obligation not to steal at a time when you are asleep and so when you perform no action at all. It, thus, follows that it is false that "ought not" implies "can refrain from." When we claim, though, that you have a negative duty or obligation not to steal, the background presupposition is that, given that you can steal, you ought not to do so. If you are anesthetized, it would be far-fetched to suppose that as of the time you are lying unconscious on the table, you ought *then* not to steal. Rather, when the anesthetic has taken effect, and we say that you ought not to steal, we mean, roughly, to be saying something of this sort: as of various times when you have the ability and opportunity to steal, you ought not to steal then. We can, in consequence, acknowledge that you have a negative moral duty not to steal while you are asleep if we pay judicious attention to the temporal indexing of the obligation; we need to pay attention to whether the obligation is immediate or remote. So, for example, your (remote) time-relativized obligation not to steal while you are asleep may be construed in this fashion: as of the time you are asleep, you ought not to steal at some later times; further, if you ought not to steal at these later times, when you are up and kicking, presumably, as of the time you are asleep, you ought to do something other than steal at these later times. So **(KC)**—*S* ought not to do *A* only if *S* can do other than *A*—is not in jeopardy.

In summary, none of these three arguments against principle **(K)** is decisive. Needless to say, there are other considerations against **(K)** but let me record, somewhat dogmatically, that I have not come across a single one that refutes this principle; more cautiously, I have not come across a single one that lives up to what it is cracked up to be: a knock-down argument against **(K)**. So it would be worthwhile to examine whether the **Deontic Argument** has other deficiencies.

5.4 DOES BLAMEWORTHINESS REQUIRE WRONGNESS AND DOES PRAISEWORTHINESS REQUIRE OBLIGATORINESS?

In this section, I argue that principle **Action-Status** is false. This is the principle that blameworthiness requires wrongness and praiseworthiness requires rightness or obligatoriness. Thus, line (1) of the **Deontic Argument** is false. A number of considerations speak against this principle. Here, I restrict attention to four of them.

5.4.1 A Counterexample to the Principle that Blameworthiness Requires Wrongness

First, regarding the part of the principle that says that blameworthiness requires wrongness:

> **Action-Status-Blame:** One is blameworthy for an action only if it is wrong for one to perform that action,

it appears that we can construct plausible cases in which one can be blameworthy for something despite its not being wrong for one. Here's one. Suppose that, through no fault of anyone, Ernie is incorrectly diagnosed as suffering from disease *D*. Deadly, who wants Ernie dead, gets wind of the mistaken diagnosis and discovers that injecting medicine *A* into a person afflicted with *D* kills the person. Deadly, though, is squeamish about needles and under normal circumstances is psychologically incapable of thrusting a needle into anyone. It is only under the special circumstances in which he has the purpose or intention of killing his bitter foe, Ernie, that he can force the contents of the injection containing *A* into Ernie. Suppose Deadly executes his intention to inject Ernie with *A* while believing that he is doing wrong. But it so happens that had he not thrust the needle into Ernie just when he did, Ernie would have died. Unbeknownst to Deadly, and luckily for Ernie, Deadly's deed actually prevents Ernie's death. Under these circumstances, it appears that Deadly is blameworthy for this state of affairs:

> **(P*):** Deadly's injecting Ernie with *A* for the purpose (or with the intention of) killing Ernie.

It seems, though, that any plausible account of what makes right acts right, wrong acts wrong, and obligatory acts obligatory will allow for moderate consequentialist considerations; the account will accommodate the view that the consequences of an action do matter, or can make a difference, to the moral status of that action. If we take into consideration the relevant weighty consequence of **P*** (Ernie's surviving), then it would seem that **P*** is *obligatory* for Deadly (under the circumstances). Bear in mind that without the relevant purpose or intention, Deadly could not have thrust the needle into Ernie.

Notice that **P*** *entails* the following:

> **(Q*)**: Deadly's injecting Ernie with *A*.

In other words, **Q*** is simply a logical consequence of **P***; or if you want **Q*** is a necessary prerequisite of **P*** (because it is true that **P*** obtains only if **Q*** obtains). But now, if you ought to do something, *p*, and if *q* is a logical or causal consequence of *p*, then you ought to do *q* as well. We, then, have this principle:

> **DP**: If *S* ought to do *p*, and *q* is a logical or causal consequence of *p*, then *S* ought to do *q*, too.[6]

As Deadly ought to do **P***, and as **Q*** is a logical consequence of **P***, he ought to do **Q***, too. So Deadly's case is one in which Deadly is blameworthy for injecting Ernie with *A*—he is blameworthy for **Q***—even though it is *obligatory* for Deadly to inject Ernie with *A*.

Perhaps it will be objected that Deadly is blameworthy for *his attempting to kill Ernie*, as attempting to kill Ernie is wrong. But Deadly is not blameworthy for *his injecting Ernie with A*, as this latter state of affairs is, in the circumstances and unbeknownst to Deadly, obligatory for Deadly (and not wrong for Deadly). But why think that attempting to kill (in such circumstances) is always wrong? Surely not because of some such view as that, generally, attempting to kill an innocent person is wrong; hence, Deadly's attempt to kill Ernie must also be wrong. For whereas it might *generally* be wrong to kill an innocent person, it doesn't follow from this that it is *always* wrong to kill an innocent person. I think those who believe that attempting to kill in such circumstances is wrong rely on the principle that *it is wrong to attempt to do wrong*. There are different versions of this principle. The more plausible version says that if an agent's doing something is (or would be) wrong, and that agent attempts to do that thing, then the agent's attempt to do that thing is also wrong.

---

6 **DP**, really, needs to be understood in this way: if *S* cannot do *p* without doing *q* (perhaps because *q* is a logical consequence of *p*), and if *S* can refrain from doing *q*, then, if *S* ought to do *p*, *S* ought also to do *q*. **DP** is discussed, among other places, in M. Zimmerman 1996, sec. 2.3, and in Feldman 1990.

But this version is, to say the least, controversial. Suppose that it would be wrong for Hera to become an addict. But faced with pressure from her associates and tensions in her unhappy home, she attempts to become an addict; she acts on the counsel of her peers that addiction to the psychoactive drug will "solve all worries." However, in her attempts, she comes to realize that becoming addicted would be a grave mistake. Her experiences give her the fortitude to seek alternative aid for her ailments, and they also prompt her to help other unfortunate youths from becoming addicts. Here, again permitting for modest consequentialist considerations, it is not clear that Hera's attempt to become an addict is wrong for Hera.

In other instances, an attempt to do something that is wrong may lead to the discovery that that thing is wrong. Suppose you invite a colleague over to your lab to discuss some results over a coffee. Unbeknownst to either of you, the sugar cubes have been laced with poison. As you attempt to spoon a cube into your colleague's mug, the cube accidentally falls into a beaker containing a chemical. It reacts in a distinct fashion. As a chemist, you know that it would only react in that fashion if it were coated with the poison. Here, placing the lethal sugar into the coffee is (or would be) wrong for you, but your attempt to do so is not, as this attempt, among other things, leads to the discovery that it would be wrong for you to dissolve the cube in the coffee.

In the first case Hera does not (at least not initially) believe that becoming an addict is wrong; and in the second case you do not (initially) believe that sweetening the coffee with the sugar is wrong. The first version of the "attempt principle" says that if an agent's doing something is (or would be) wrong, and that agent attempts to do that thing, then the agent's attempt to do that thing is also wrong. Zimmerman (M. Zimmerman 1997, pp. 236–37) has suggested that the general problem with this version is that if one lacks the belief that doing something is wrong, and is not to be blamed for not believing that this thing is wrong, then it is implausible to suppose that one's attempt to do that thing is wrong, even if one's doing it is or would be wrong.

Others might protest that, in Deadly's case, Deadly deliberately does what he believes is wrong. But it is always wrong, it might be proposed, for a person to do what he or she thinks or believes is wrong. This suggests an alternative version of the attempt principle: it's always wrong to attempt to do what one believes is wrong. We have supposed that Deadly does believe that he is doing wrong by injecting Ernie with *A* (but he still goes ahead and injects Ernie with *A*). However, if Deadly injects Ernie with *A*, it is also true that Deadly attempts (and successfully) to inject Ernie with *A*; he can't inject Ernie with *A* without successfully attempting to do so. So Deadly attempts (and successfully) to do what he believes is wrong: he injects Ernie with *A*. It may, thus, be claimed that the second version of the attempt principle yields the result that Deadly does do wrong by injecting Ernie with *A*. And if Deadly is blameworthy for injecting Ernie with *A*, we have no violation of principle **Action-status-Blame**, the principle that one is blameworthy for doing something only if it is wrong for one to do that thing.

If this line of reasoning is to be commissioned successfully to defend the view that *Deadly's injecting Ernie with A* is wrong, it must allow us to infer:

> Premise-2: Deadly's injecting Ernie with *A* is wrong.

from this premise:

> Premise-1: Deadly (mistakenly) believes that injecting Ernie with *A* is wrong, but still injects Ernie with *A*.

But beliefs can, of course, be mistaken, and when they are Premise-2 need not follow from Premise-1. If Deadly's belief is false, we can still fault *Deadly* for what he does consistently with maintaining that his *deed* is not in fact wrong. Deadly may, for example, be condemnable in that he does not act out of virtue, and as I have proposed, he may well be blameworthy. But these agent-focused evaluations should not be conflated with the act-focused one that Deadly's injecting Ernie with *A* is not (in the relevant circumstances) wrong. Recall that agent-focused evaluations are targeted at *agents*; act-focused ones are targeted at acts.

Finally, suppose we grant that Deadly is blameworthy for *attempting to kill* Ernie. Even then we can reason to the conclusion that attempting to kill Ernie is not wrong for Deadly. For it seems that the following state of affairs:

> **A***: Deadly's attempts to kill Ernie (by injecting Ernie with *A*),

entails:

> **P***: Deadly's injecting Ernie with *A* for the purpose, or with the intention of, killing Ernie.

Indeed, one might plausibly claim that Deadly's attempt to kill Ernie just is his injecting Ernie with *A* for the purpose or with the intention of killing Ernie. So **P*** entails **A***. As **P*** is obligatory for Deadly, and **P*** entails **A***, then, given the deontic principle **DP**,

> **DP**: If *S* ought to do *p*, and *q* is a logical or causal consequence of *p*, then *S* ought to do *q*, too,

A* is obligatory for Deadly. This gives us sufficient reason to reject the second version of the attempt principle. Deadly attempts to do what he takes to be wrong (his killing Ernie by injecting Ernie with *A*), but it is not the case that his attempting to kill Ernie (by injecting Ernie with *A*) is wrong for Deadly.[7]

5.4.2 Supererogatory and Suberogatory Actions

Second, against the principle that blameworthiness requires wrongness and praiseworthiness requires obligatoriness or rightness, in addition to the normative statuses of moral right, wrong, and obligation, commonsense morality presupposes that actions can be supererogatory and suberogatory. Roughly, a supererogatory action is a morally permissible action that is beyond the call of duty. More fully, a supererogatory action is morally optional (morally permissible) in that it is not morally wrong or obligatory; it is not morally indifferent and so is morally significant, being especially valuable in some way; and it goes beyond duty's call. Stock illustrations of supererogatory behavior include the mailperson's rescuing the child from the building that is engulfed in flames at considerable risk to her own well-being, or the soldier's sacrificing his life by throwing himself on the grenade to save his comrades. Many would want to say that though it is not foolhardy to rescue the child, doing so is over and above the call of duty; similarly, the soldier's sacrifice is beyond duty's call. These two examples involve heroic action. A number of advocates of the supererogatory concede that the supererogatory is not confined to the saintly or heroic; unmomentous action, the doing of small favors, for example, can also qualify as going beyond duty (see, for example, Heyd 1982, p. 142). So, for instance, holding open a door for a person who has both arms around grocery bags may qualify as supererogatory.

Suberogatory actions, the roughly symmetric counterparts of supererogatory ones, are morally optional, morally significant, and are offensive or fall short of decency. In one of Julia Driver's proposed examples of a suberogatory act, a man—call him "Grumpy"—boards a train just at the time when two lovers board as well. It is obvious to anyone—certainly to Grumpy—that the two want to sit together. Despite availability of another single seat, Grumpy takes the only remaining unoccupied bench that accommodates two, thereby intentionally preventing the love birds from sitting together. Arguably, Grumpy does no wrong, but he falls short of decency (1992, pp. 286–87). Roderick Chisholm and Ernest Sosa propose that minor discourtesy (such as taking too long in a restaurant when others are waiting, and you are aware that they are waiting) may also be suberogatory (1966, p. 326).

Commonsense morality also sanctions ascriptions of praiseworthiness and blameworthiness, respectively, to those who supererogate and to those who suberogate. There may well be conditions under which we think that

7 I believe that it is fairly easy to think of cases in which a person is morally praiseworthy for something even if it is not morally obligatory or permissible for the person to do that thing. See, for example, Haji 2002.

the mailperson is praiseworthy for saving the child. If she is, and her action is supererogatory, then moral praiseworthiness does not require obligation. Similarly, assume that although he (mistakenly) believes that he is doing wrong by preventing the lovers from sitting together despite availability of another seat, Grumpy fails to give up his seat. Grumpy does wrong from his own perspective. Thus, he may well be blameworthy for not giving up his seat even though, let's assume, his not giving up his seat is suberogatory and, hence, is not morally wrong but is in fact morally permissible. If Grumpy is blameworthy, then it follows that moral blameworthiness does not require moral wrongness.[8]

5.4.3 The Coming Apart of Blameworthiness and Wrongness

Third, against **Action-Status-Blame** (the principle that blameworthiness requires wrongness), it is widely acknowledged that a person may do moral wrong but may not be morally blameworthy for doing wrong. In cases of this sort, the person has a legitimate excuse, blameworthiness and wrongness come apart. In **Sweet Deception**, you do wrong by placing the poisoned sugar-looking-like cubes into your friend's coffee but you are not blameworthy for so doing because you had no reason whatsoever to suspect that the original cubes had been replaced by deadly surrogates. But if a person can do wrong and not be blameworthy for the wrongdoing—if wrongness and blameworthiness may come apart in one direction—one wonders why a person cannot be blameworthy for an act that turns out not be wrong, especially if the person takes himself to be doing wrong in performing the act. One wonders, that is, why wrongness and blameworthiness cannot come apart in the other direction. Zimmerman, reflecting on some of the adventures of Mark Twain's character, Huck Finn, says that Huck, moved by sympathy, refrains from thwarting Jim's bid to freedom as he thinks (and let's suppose correctly) he (Huck) morally ought. Zimmerman remarks that some may venture that blaming Huck is inappropriate because Huck's act is not wrong. But Zimmerman insists that we should not lose sight of the fact that, in such cases, the agent is indeed doing wrong from his perspective even if not in fact. He explains that Huck is to blame as long as it is accepted that he acted on the basis of the belief that he was doing wrong and that Huck satisfied other conditions of blameworthiness such as acting freely (M. Zimmerman 1997, pp. 235–36).[9] In short, we may assume that Huck's helping Jim to escape, or that Huck's not preventing Jim from escaping is *not* morally wrong for

8 For further discussion on being praiseworthy or blameworthy for supererogating or suberogating, see Haji 2002, ch. 10.

9 See, also, M. Zimmerman 1988, especially, pp. 38–54. Other partisans of the view that praise- or blameworthiness requires action on the basis of suitable beliefs of right and wrong include Brandt 1958, pp. 38–39; Milo 1984, ch. 1; Parfit 1984, p. 24; Parfit n.d.; and Thomson 1991, p. 295.

Huck (indeed, it may be morally obligatory). But since Huck takes himself to be doing wrong in helping Jim to escape, he may well be blameworthy for this act that is not wrong.

It goes without saying that similar considerations impugn the principle that praiseworthiness requires obligation (or permissibility). One can do what is obligatory for one but not be praiseworthy for doing this thing. Equally, praiseworthiness and obligation can come asunder in the other direction: one can be praiseworthy for something that it is not obligatory (or permissible) for one to do.

5.4.4 Blameworthiness and Frankfurt Examples

Finally, Frankfurt-type examples give us additional reason to reject premise (1) of the **Deontic Argument**, the premise that one is blameworthy for doing something only if it is wrong for one to do that thing. (Just as surely, such examples give us reason to renounce the principle that praiseworthiness requires obligation or permissibility.) In one of the Frankfurt examples that we previously presented (sec. 3.2.), although Jones lies on his own, he could not have done otherwise because of Black's presence. Many are inclined to judge that Jones is blameworthy for lying even though he could not have refrained from doing so. But if Jones could not have done other than lie, his lying was not morally wrong (or right or obligatory) because, as we have seen, an agent cannot do something that is wrong (or right or obligatory) unless he could have refrained from doing that thing.

It might be rejoined that if Frankfurt examples cast doubt on the **Principle of Alternative Possibilities**—that persons are morally responsible for having done something only if they could have done otherwise—such examples also call into question the "ought" implies "can" principle. But this principle plays a fundamental role in establishing that right, wrong, and obligation require alternative possibilities. Thus, we should not draw on Frankfurt examples to impugn the principle that blameworthiness requires wrongness.

My reply to this rejoinder turns on the view that responsibility judgments and obligation judgments have different objects of evaluation; the first assess persons, the second actions. To elucidate: appraisals of moral responsibility are, first and foremost, appraisals of the *person*—they are, as I have said, *agent-focused*. Such appraisals disclose the moral worth of an agent with respect to some episode in her life—a person "expresses what she morally stands for" when she is morally responsible for some deed. To elaborate, metaphorically speaking, when a person does something for which she is morally blameworthy, a negative mark that is a measure of a person's moral worth with respect to that deed is entered in her "moral ledger of life." When blameworthy, one expresses ill will (typically) toward another, and it is the expression of such ill will that (in part) sanctions the judgment that one's moral worth with respect to the relevant action has been diminished. On the view that I defend, an expression of such ill will is manifested when one nonculpably believes that some act is wrong, and despite this belief, performs the act; in short, when blameworthy, one acts in light of the belief that one is doing moral wrong.

Similarly, when a person is morally praiseworthy, a positive mark is registered in her ledger. When one is praiseworthy, one expresses good will (typically) toward another, and it is the expression of such good will that (in part) validates the judgment that one's moral worth *vis-à-vis* the relevant deed has been augmented. When praiseworthy, one acts on the basis of the nonculpable belief that one is doing what is obligatory or permissible.

An agent can manifest ill will or good will by an action that she performs even when she lacks, as she would in a Frankfurt-type situation, alternative possibilities. This is because such expression does not presuppose the availability of alternative options. Since an agent, in a Frankfurt-type case, discerns her situation and subsequently acts in just the way in which she would discern her situation and then act if there were no counterfactual intervener in the wings, in such cases agent-focused appraisals of responsibility should not be affected merely because the agent lacks alternatives. Or, coming at this point from another direction, if an act from your perspective is wrong—if you take yourself to be doing intentional wrong—then even if you lack alternatives (and, thus, your act is not in fact wrong), you can still express ill will in your conduct; and, similarly, if you take yourself to be doing something that is obligatory, even without alternatives, you can still express good will in your conduct.

In contrast, moral appraisals of rightness, wrongness, and obligatoriness—deontic appraisals—are pronouncedly *act-focused*. They are *not* connected, in any necessary fashion, with how the agent perceives the situation or with germane motivations or beliefs. An agent, for instance, may act "from" virtue on a certain occasion and (assuming the act is not virtue-deficient or not significantly so), be commendable for so acting, consistently with doing (moral) wrong on that occasion. Whether an agent's act has a primary deontic property—whether it has the property of *being right*, or *being wrong*, or *being obligatory*—then, is *not* essentially connected with, for example, whether the agent performs that action in the belief that it is wrong, or more generally, with the agent's "moral perception" of her act. Act-focused morally deontic appraisals turn primarily on conditions that the act itself must satisfy. And these conditions may not be met despite the agent's believing otherwise or failing to believe that the conditions are not met.

Some might dispute the claim that morally deontic appraisals of right, wrong, and obligation are act-focused. For though we say things like "Elf did what was wrong," and this appraisal seems to be act-focused, we also say things like "Elf was wrong to do what he did," and this appraisal seems to be agent-focused. Still, there is a significant difference in the two sorts of appraisal. We can readily agree that it can be the case that, though Elf did wrong (or right), he was not blameworthy (or praiseworthy) for what he did. It can also be the case that an agent can be blameworthy (or praiseworthy) for doing something that is not wrong (or right).

If responsibility appraisals (appraisals of moral blameworthiness and praiseworthiness) are different, in kind, from morally deontic appraisals (appraisals of moral right, wrong, and obligation), there is no reason to assume that the conditions requiring satisfaction for one to be apt must be the very conditions requiring satisfaction for the other to be apt. For instance, freedom to do otherwise may well be necessary for the latter sorts of moral appraisal but not for the former sorts. In light of this, there is little preliminary reason to believe that a counterexample against a proposed condition for the appropriateness of one sort of moral appraisal (for instance, Frankfurt-type examples as proposed counterexamples against the **Principle of Alternative Possibilities**) will also be a counterexample against an analogous condition for the other. Hence, even though Frankfurt-type examples cast doubt on the **Principle of Alternative Possibilities**, it is not clear that they cast doubt on the "ought" implies "can" principle.

In conclusion, the **Deontic Argument** as presented in this chapter relies on the principle that blameworthiness requires wrongness: if one is blameworthy for doing something, then it is wrong for one to do that thing. I said toward the outset of this chapter that a slight revision in the argument transforms it into an argument for the view that if determinism is true, then no one is praiseworthy for anything. I mentioned that this revised argument relies on the principle that praiseworthiness requires rightness or obligatoriness: if one is praiseworthy for doing something, then it is right or obligatory for one to do that thing. I believe that we have good reason to reject both the principle involving blameworthiness and wrongness, and the principle involving praiseworthiness and rightness or obligatoriness. Thus, we have good reason to reject the **Deontic Argument**.

We are, then, back to this question: if one has reservations about both the **Direct Argument** and the **Principle of Alternative Possibilities**, and, we might now add, if one has doubts about the **Deontic Argument**, to what other resources might an incompatibilist appeal to seek to persuade us that determinism rules out responsibility? Some incompatibilists—source incompatibilists—believe that determinism threatens responsibility in virtue of threatening ultimate sourcehood. On one development of this view, just as manipulated-Beth's actions that express implanted springs have their final source in the manipulator, so a deterministically caused action has its final source in the far distant past and the laws, things over which we have no control. Hence, it is proposed, a causally determined action is relevantly similar to an action performed "out of" manipulation: both undermine responsibility. We examine this sort of argument in the next chapter.

6 The Manipulation Argument

6.1 THE BASIC CONTOURS OF THE ARGUMENT

Some people have offered the view that the best type of challenge to compatibilism is that determinism "is in principle as much of a threat to moral responsibility as is covert manipulation" (Pereboom 2001, p. 89; see, also, Kane 1996; Kane 2007, pp. 16–19). In this chapter, we discuss the **Manipulation Argument.** The basic contours of this argument are simple enough: Covert manipulation of the sort we find in the **Ann/Beth** cases, because of certain of its characteristics, undermines moral responsibility. (Call to mind that in these cases, unbeknownst to her, new-wave psychosurgeons transform Beth, in relevant respects, into a psychological twin of Ann, the diligent philosophy professor.) But any deterministic causal history—a deterministic causal pathway to any action—shares these very responsibility-subverting characteristics as well. Hence, determinism, too, undermines responsibility. A compatibilist view of free action and responsibility that features determinism will, thus, just like a causal trajectory to action that features responsibility-threatening manipulation, also undermine responsibility. So the **Manipulation Argument**, it is claimed, undercuts every compatibilist view. If it can indeed be shown that any compatibilist view is false, then since compatibilism is the denial of incompatibilism, incompatibilism is on secure footing. The **Manipulation Argument** is, thus, of commanding interest to us.

6.1.1 The Manipulation Argument

Exposing more fully the structure of this argument: a case is introduced involving manipulation, such as **Ann/Beth-1** or **Ann/Beth-2**, in which the victim of manipulation, *S*, performs some action, *A*, only because of covert manipulation. (*A* may be an overt action or a mental action such as Beth's making a decision.) The carefully selected case is one in which it is *highly credible* that *S* does not perform *A* freely and so is not responsible for doing *A* *owing* to *S*'s being manipulated. The argument then evolves in this way:

THE MANIPULATION ARGUMENT

1. Manipulated *S* does not freely *A* and is not morally responsible for *A*-ing. (In **Ann/Beth-1**, for instance, manipulated Beth is not morally responsible for her first post-transformation act that expresses engineered-in desires, beliefs, and values. Perhaps this act is Beth's decision to referee a paper.)
2. Regarding free action and moral responsibility, there is no relevant difference between manipulated *S*'s *A*-ing and any action deemed to be free and for which its agent is morally responsible on any compatibilist account of free action and moral responsibility.
3. If (1) and (2), then no compatibilist account of free action and moral responsibility is true.
4. Therefore, no compatibilist account of free action and moral responsibility is true.

Among the most interesting rationales for the primary premises (lines (1) and (2)) are the ones that Derk Pereboom (2001) supplies. Pereboom suggests that a victim of global manipulation, such as Beth in **Ann/Beth-1**, is not morally responsible for *A*-ing because her *A*-ing ultimately stems from sources beyond her control. More specifically, line (1) rests on the following principle of ultimate origination:

> **Principle O**: If an agent is morally responsible for her deciding to perform an action, then the production of this decision must be something over which the agent has control, and an agent is not morally responsible for the decision if it is produced by a source over which she has no control. (Pereboom, 2001: pp. 4, 43)

Line (2) is predicated on what Pereboom calls his "**Four-Case Argument**" (2001, p. 117). To understand this argument, some background will be useful.

6.1.2 Hard Incompatibilism and the Four-Case Argument

Take the phrase 'free will' to refer to the freedom that moral responsibility requires. *Hard incompatibilism*, a position that Pereboom defends, says that we would lack free will if determinism were true, and we would also lack free will if our world were indeterministic and the causes of our actions were exclusively states or events (and not agent-causes) (Pereboom 2007, p. 85). This is a hard position because it implies that any libertarian account of free action that is not wedded to agent-causation, and any compatibilist account of such action, is false. To support this view, Pereboom explains why determinism and non-agent causal libertarian views cannot accommodate free action.

First, with respect to determinism, Pereboom agrees that a causal history involving apt manipulation, a "manipulated causal history," undermines free action and, therefore, responsibility. (This is simply premise (1) of the **Manipulation Argument**.) Responsibility-subverting manipulation or, alternatively, *menacing manipulation*, is manipulation that undermines responsibility. We have already registered that the pertinent principle to which Pereboom appeals to support his verdict of unfreedom and non-responsibility in scenarios involving menacing manipulation is **Principle O**. We may conceive of this principle as a principle of ultimate origination. Post-surgery Beth's actions that she performs as a result of manipulation have their sources in the manipulator, a source over whom Beth has no control. It follows from **Principle O** that post-surgery Beth is not morally responsible for these actions. (Theorists who disagree that an agent, such as manipulated Beth, is not morally responsible despite the manipulation regard the manipulation as *benign*: this sort of manipulation does not undermine free action or responsibility.)

Moving on to premise (2): a deterministic causal history, Pereboom contends, is pertinently like a manipulated one in that in both, an action that is causally determined issues from sources—the distant past and the natural laws—over which the agent lacks any control. Pereboom submits that no relevant and principled difference can distinguish an action that results from menacing manipulation from an action that has a more ordinary deterministic causal history. (Pereboom 2002, p. 478. See, also, Kane 1996, pp. 64–68.) It is in support of this submission that Pereboom invokes what he characterizes as a combined counterexample and generalization strategy—the **Four-Case Argument**. The strategy unfolds in this way: A case is presented in which the star character meets all of the prominent compatibilist conditions on moral responsibility. (It doesn't matter which compatibilist contenders are at issue; pick your favorites.) But owing to this character's being a victim of manipulation, the case elicits, or is meant to elicit, the intuition that this character is *not* responsible for his pertinent deed; he is not the ultimate originator of this deed. Pereboom describes his favored case—**Case 1**—as follows:

> **Case 1.** Professor Plum was created by neuroscientists, who can manipulate him directly through the use of radio-like technology.... The neuroscientists manipulate him by, among other things, pushing a series of buttons just before he begins

> to reason about his situation, thereby causing his reasoning process to be rationally egoistic. Plum is not constrained to act in the sense that he does not act because of an irresistible desire ... and he does not think and act contrary to character since he is often manipulated to be rationally egoistic. His effective first-order desire to kill Ms. White conforms to his second-order desires. Plum's reasoning process exemplifies the various components of moderate reasons-responsiveness. He is receptive to the relevant patterns of reasons, and his reasoning process would have resulted in different choices in some situations in which the egoistic reasons were otherwise. At the same time, he is not exclusively rationally egoistic since he will typically regulate his behavior by moral reasons when the egoistic reasons are relatively weak—weaker than they are in the current situation. (Pereboom, 2001, pp. 112–13)

A second case is then advanced, also involving allegedly menacing manipulation, though manipulation of a different variety than the variety found in the first. We are supposed to judge that if the agent is not responsible in the first case, the agent is not responsible in the second either because there are no salient differences between the two cases. Here is the second case:

> **Case 2.** Plum is like an ordinary human being, except that he was created by neuroscientists who, although they cannot control him directly, have programmed him to weigh reasons for action so that he is often but not exclusively egoistic, with the result that in the circumstances in which he now finds himself, he is causally determined to undertake the ... process ... that results in his killing Ms. White. (Pereboom, 2001, pp. 113–14)

Case 2 is very much like **Ann/Beth-1**. In a third case, the role that the manipulation plays in the first two cases is replaced by the rigorous training practices of the agent's home and community.

> **Case 3.** Plum is an ordinary human being, except that he was determined by the rigorous training practices of his home and community so that he is often but not exclusively rationally egoistic (exactly as egoistic as in Cases 1 and 2). His training took place at too early an age for him to have had the ability to prevent or alter the practices that determined his character. In his current circumstances, Plum is thereby caused to undertake the moderately-reasons-responsive process and to possess the first-and second-order desires that result in his killing

> White. He has the general ability to grasp, apply, and regulate his behavior by moral reasons, but in these circumstances, the egoistic reasons are very powerful, and hence the rigorous training practices of his upbringing deterministically result in his act of murder. Nevertheless, he does not act because of an irresistible desire. (2001, p. 114)

Again, it is proposed that this replacement should have no bearing on our judgment of non-responsibility.

Finally, in a fourth case, the agent is deterministically caused to act in a way in which any compatibilist would deem to be unproblematic insofar as free agency is concerned. Yet the case appears to be one in which the agent does not differ in any relevant manner from the agent in the preceding case.

> **Case 4**. Physicalist determinism is true, and Plum is an ordinary human being, generated and raised under normal circumstances, who is often but not exclusively rationally egoistic (exactly as egoistic as in Cases 1-3). Plum's killing of White comes about as a result of his undertaking the moderately reasons-responsive process of deliberation, he exhibits the specified organization of first- and second-order desires, and he does not act because of an irresistible desire. He has the general ability to grasp, apply, and regulate his behavior by moral reasons, but in these circumstances the egoistic reasons are very powerful, and together with background circumstances they deterministically result in his act of murder. (p. 115)

Pereboom challenges the compatibilist to expose a difference between the fourth case and the others that explains why the agent can be morally responsible in this case but not morally responsible in one or more of the manipulation cases. He contends that there is no such difference (Pereboom 1995, pp. 21–45; 2001, pp. 110–17; 2005, pp. 228–47). If there is no such difference, then line (2) of the **Manipulation Argument**,

> Regarding free action and moral responsibility, there is no germane difference between an action resulting from menacing manipulation, and any action that the compatibilist account of free action at issue implies is free and is one for which its agent is morally responsible,

seems to be true.

Now let's turn to the second half of hard incompatibilism, the half concerning indeterminism. Regarding, second, why non-agent-causal libertarian accounts cannot accommodate free action, Pereboom ventures that an indeterministic event causal history (the sort of history that we find in Claude's case in which Claude indeterministically decides to buy a Coke)—a history not including agent-causation and in which various antecedents of an action, such as the agent's having of reasons, indeterministically cause elements in the action's causal history or the action itself—is not relevantly different from a manipulated one: this sort of history, also, undermines responsibility. This is because in scenarios involving indeterminism, just as in those involving determinism, the causal antecedents that produce the relevant action have their ultimate home in sources beyond the agent's reach. After all, even if Claude indeterministically decides to buy the Coke, this decision arises from some of Claude's desires, beliefs, values, etc. Tracing the causal ancestry of these actional antecedents, we will invariably find that they owe their origin to "sources," such as the culture in which Claude was born and perhaps in some of Claude's genetic constitution, over which Claude has no control. Again, Pereboom's position is that the four-case **Manipulation Argument**, suitably adapted to appraise such libertarian accounts of free action, shows that no relevant and principled difference can distinguish an action that results from menacing manipulation from an action that has an indeterministic causal history. If a manipulated causal history undermines responsibility because in cases involving such a history the agent is not the ultimate originator of her actions, so, too, will an indeterministic causal history. This is because in cases involving pertinent indeterminism, the agent is, again, not the ultimate originator of her actions (Pereboom 2002, p. 478). Pereboom concludes that these libertarian theories are doomed to go the way of compatibilist ones.

Pereboom argues that only agent-causation can accommodate free action. But he thinks that our best scientific theories give us no reason to believe that we are agent-causes. He concludes that no one ever acts freely and so no one is ever morally responsible for anything that one does.

6.2 MCKENNA'S HARD-LINE RESPONSE TO THE ARGUMENT

Prior to assessing this argument, it will be instructive to discuss Michael McKenna's recent, illuminating response to the **Four-Case Argument** because, among other things, his response helps to expose two different interpretations of this argument. On the first interpretation (as we will see), the argument need not perturb compatibilists; they seem to have a good response to the argument. On the second interpretation, the argument seems to have greater clout.

Questioning the four-case strategy, like Pereboom, McKenna starts with a case in which an agent is covertly manipulated in some manner ("manner X," he says) into satisfying "all of the conditions sufficient for the Compatibilist-friendly Agential Structure (CAS) ... [that exhausts] the freedom relevant condition for moral responsibility" (McKenna 2008a, p. 142). Paraphrasing: responsibility requires control. Imagine some account of control that is compatible with determinism—perhaps it is Fischer and Ravizza's or Frankfurt's account. McKenna's agent is manipulated in such a way (in "manner X") that the manipulation leaves untouched this sort of compatibilist control, whatever it turns out to be; the manipulated agent, despite being manipulated, can still exercise this species of control in performing her actions, actions she would not have performed but for the manipulation.

McKenna calls a compatibilist reply that rejects premise 1 of the basic argument a "*hard-line reply*." (Premise 1 says that *S does not freely A and is not morally responsible for A-ing*.) The hard-liner affirms that the manipulated agent, like Beth, *is* morally responsible despite the manipulation. McKenna refers to a compatibilist reply that rejects premise 2 of this argument as a "*soft-line reply*." (Premise 2 says that *regarding free action and moral responsibility, there is no relevant difference between S's A-ing and any action deemed to be free and for which its agent is morally responsible on any compatibilist account of free action and moral responsibility*.) The soft-liner denies that the manipulated agent, like Beth, is morally responsible but claims that there is a relevant difference between a manipulated causal history and an ordinary, garden-variety deterministic causal history, a difference that a well-worked out compatibilist theory can recognize and explain. McKenna is a hard-liner.

6.2.1 The Hard-Line Reply

The crux of McKenna's hard-line reply is his proposal that we should help make the first two cases involving manipulation in Pereboom's four-case sequence better. McKenna claims that we should improve the first two cases in a fashion in which it becomes transparent that the victims of manipulation satisfy the proposed compatibilist sufficient conditions of freedom in question. The more confident we are that the manipulated agent does satisfy these conditions, the more the compatibilist who is a hard-liner would be inclined to hold that the agent *is* responsible despite the manipulation. McKenna writes:

> I propose a four-step [hard-line] reply to any instance of [the **Manipulation Argument**]. *Step One: Reject all non-starters.* Consider the example. See if it is in the running for CAS. If not, the jig is up. Reject premise 2 and be done. *Step Two: Help make the manipulation cases better.* If the example gets past step one, if it comes close to getting CAS right but falls shy, amend the example. Help out your "good friend" the incompatibilist so that the example does get CAS right. This calls into relief that manipulation can be "just like" determin-

> ism. *Step Three: Fix attention on salient agential and moral properties.* Illustrate how the agent manipulated in manner X to satisfy CAS lives up to a rich sort of agency and genuinely satisfies certain moral properties (for example, does moral wrong). *Step four: Make clear that "manipulation" is not all that uncommon.* Lessen the intuitive uneasiness of the claim that an agent manipulated in manner X is free and responsible by calling attention to mundane causal factors that have a similar result, but are not thought to be freedom or responsibility undermining. (McKenna 2008a, pp. 144-45)

Commenting on Step Two, suppose that what we simply dub "**CC**" is the compatibilist contender at issue, and that it is a plausible contender (it may, for example, be Fischer and Ravizza's reasons-responsiveness account). The step enjoins us to help out the incompatibilist by ensuring that the manipulation case that is fabricated to test **CC** be one in which it is plain that the victim, who is manipulated into performing some action, does indeed satisfy the demands of control specified by **CC** in performing this action. The thought is that if **CC** is independently plausible, then the victim should be regarded as responsible for the relevant action despite her being manipulated into performing the action: when all is said and done, the manipulation leaves intact the sort of control that **CC** requires for free action. So if you really buy into **CC**, you will not regard the manipulation as menacing.

6.2.2 Concerns with the Hard-Line Reply

There are concerns, though, with this way of interpreting the four-case strategy; it is not dialectically the most charitable way to understand Pereboom's argument. In particular, McKenna's second step, the "embellishing" or "bolstering" step, is troubling. As McKenna is well aware, the **Four-Case Argument** is selective in that it proceeds by targeting, severally, specific compatibilist (or libertarian) candidates. Limiting attention to compatibilist candidates, there is no consensus among compatibilists regarding when manipulation is menacing and when it is benign. Reconsider Pereboom's **Case 2** which may well be an instance of global manipulation akin to the **Ann/Beth** scenarios. Free will theorists differ over whether the agent in question (Plum or post-surgery Beth, for instance) is morally responsible for actions that express the agent's engineered-in pro-attitudes, values, deliberative principles, and so forth. Kane, Mele, and I, for instance, think that the agent is not morally responsible for these actions; Frankfurt and McKenna believe otherwise.

I submit that if Pereboom's generalization strategy is to be regarded as even prima facie tenable, the first two cases involving manipulation in the four-sequence progression must command the allegiance of targeted compatibilists and libertarians: the targeted audience must *agree* that the manipulation in question in these cases is of the variety that, on the face of it, *does* threaten free action or responsibility. For if the manipulation were of the sort that a targeted party deemed benign, *right from the outset*, the four-case sequence would have *no purchase at all* on this compatibilist; this compatibilist would not regard the **Four-Case Argument** as a threat to her account of control. If anything is clear, the literature reveals that targeted compatibilists have, generally, *not* taken the **Four-Case Argument** to be toothless, something that would be difficult to appreciate if the first two cases were to be bolstered in the way in which McKenna suggests. To bring out this point, contrast two approaches to the **Four-Case Argument** by theorists who defend different compatibilist conditions on free action.

Imagine, first, that the **Four-Case Argument** has its sights on Frankfurt and take **Case 2** to be a case in which Plum is globally manipulated; he is subjected to a similar sort of manipulation as Beth. So the test case against Frankfurt's compatibilist conditions of free action is one in which Plum is manipulated into performing some action, but in performing this action, Plum satisfies the control conditions laid down by Frankfurt's account. Frankfurt has persisted in maintaining that as long as the agent's action nondeviantly arises from a first-order desire with which the agent *identifies*, the agent is responsible for the action no matter what the origins of the agent's psychological repertoire. On one of Frankfurt's earlier views of identification, an agent identifies with a first-order desire of hers if she has an unopposed second-order volition concerning this first-order desire. (Again, a second-order volition is a second-order desire that some first-order desire move one all the way to action.) Regarding the origins of our springs of action, Frankfurt writes:

> A manipulator may succeed, through his interventions, in providing a person not merely with particular feelings and thoughts but with a new character. That person is then morally responsible for the choices and the conduct to which having this character leads. We are inevitably fashioned and sustained, after all, by circumstances over which we have no control. The causes to which we are subject may also change us radically, without thereby bringing it about that we are not morally responsible agents. It is irrelevant whether those causes are operating by virtue of the natural forces that shape our environment or whether they operate through the deliberate manipulative designs of other human agents. (Frankfurt 2002, pp. 27–28)

> [T]o the extent that a person identifies with the springs of his actions, he takes responsibility for those actions and acquires moral responsibility for them; moreover, the questions of

> how the actions and his identifications with their springs are caused are irrelevant to the questions of whether he performs them freely or is morally responsible for performing them. (Frankfurt 1975, p. 54)

In Frankfurt's assessment, it would seem, the manipulation in the first two cases is benign. Regarding responsibility, Frankfurt affirms that it is immaterial what the sources of our desires are. It doesn't matter whether our desires are caused by the "natural forces that shape our environment" or whether "they operate through the deliberate manipulative designs of other human agents." We are responsible for actions that causally issue from our first-order desires as long as (other conditions of responsibility satisfied) we identify with these desires. The relevant moral, then, is this: imagine that Frankfurt's account is the compatibilist account that is to be tested by seeing how it fares in connection with a fabricated manipulation case. In the proposed case, Plum is manipulated into performing some action but the manipulation leaves intact the sort of control that Frankfurt demands for responsibility: Plum identifies with the first-order desire from which the action that he is manipulated into performing causally arises. Frankfurt would simply regard this sort of manipulation as benign; so he wouldn't take this sort of test case to undermine his compatibilist account of control.

Imagine, next, that the **Four-Case Argument** is launched against Mele. Unlike Frankfurt, Mele does *not* take globally manipulated agents to be morally responsible for their germane actions. Commenting on the **Ann/Beth Case**, Mele says:

> Ann, by hypothesis, freely does her philosophical work, but what about Beth? In important respects, she is a clone of Ann—and by design, not accident. Her own considered values were erased and replaced in the brainwashing process. Beth did not consent to the process. Nor was she even aware of it; she had no opportunity to resist. By instilling new values in Beth and eliminating old ones, the brainwashers gave her life a new direction, one that clashes with the considered principles and values she had before she was manipulated. Beth's autonomy was violated. And it is difficult not to see her now, in light of all this, as heteronomous—and unfree—to a significant extent in an important sphere of her life. (Mele 2006, pp. 165–66, note omitted. See, also, Mele 1995, p. 159)

It is, thus, not surprising that, with certain amendments to **Case 2**, Mele *accepts* the judgment that Plum is not morally responsible for killing White in this case. He argues, though, that this judgment can be endorsed consistently with maintaining that Plum may well be responsible for his murderous deed in **Case 4**. In other words, Mele argues for a soft-line reply. He theorizes that if various historical considerations regarding the acquisition of actional antecedents, such as desires or beliefs, are not met, then the agent is not responsible for behavior to which these antecedents give rise. If, for instance, an agent acquires a pro-attitude, such as a desire, via a process (such as new-wave psychosurgery) that totally bypasses the agent's normal capacities of deliberative control, the agent is practically unable to shed this pro-attitude, and the bypassing was not itself arranged (or performed) by the agent, then the agent is not responsible for acquiring that pro-attitude and is not responsible for actions that express that pro-attitude (Mele 1995, pp. 171–72; 2006, pp. 164–73). We may say that a "bypassing condition" on free action is a condition that is not satisfied when an agent acquires a pro-attitude (or other actional elements) in a manner described in the last sentence. Assuming Mele is the quarry, if we were to try to amend **Case 2** (and **Case 1**) so that all the historical conditions including the bypassing condition that Mele deems relevant to free action were satisfied, **Case 2** would (in the eyes of Mele) *no longer qualify as a case of global manipulation featuring menacing manipulation*. It would then, once again, be puzzling why Mele should expend any energy on the **Four-Case Argument** if the first two cases were to appeal to manipulation that Mele regards as *benign*.[1]

Reverting to the supposition that it is Frankfurt's theory that is the prey of the **Four-Case Argument**: would this argument not minimally show that since Frankfurt's account of freedom generates the result that manipulated Plum and Beth *are* responsible for their actions despite the manipulation, the account is therefore mistaken? In other words, we are to imagine someone as responding to Frankfurt in this way: "In the fabricated test case against your conception of control, Plum is manipulated into performing the action in question—killing White. So what if Plum identifies with the first-order desire that causes him to kill White? *Because* he kills as a result of *manipulation*, Plum is *not* responsible for this murderous deed. If your account of control implies otherwise, so much the worse for your account." However, the **Four-Case Argument**, *on its own*, does not support this sort of retort to Frankfurt. This is because when the argument is tar-

1 I do not, of course, deny that some compatibilists, as Mele notes, may reject the **Four-Case Argument** for reasons other than that **Case 2** is a case of global manipulation. Here is a revealing passage from Mele's 2005. Addressing **Case 3**, Mele writes: "When Plum grew older, was he able, on a compatibilist reading of 'able,' to alter his 'character'? More specifically, was he able—perhaps partly through reflection on his values and experiences—to make himself less egoistic and more sensitive to moral reasons or to act in ways that have this result? Pereboom does not say. If the rigorous training practices did not render Plum unable to do these things, and if he was able—in a compatibilist sense—to do them, typical compatibilists have no good reason to agree that Plum is not morally responsible for the killing. If, however, the manipulation was such as to render Plum unable to attenuate its effects, some compatibilists can agree that Plum is not morally responsible for the killing." (p. 79)

geted at Frankfurt's compatibilism, its first two cases *assume* that Plum is not morally responsible despite Plum's satisfying Frankfurt's conditions on free action. In other words, the first two cases simply assume, contrary to Frankfurt, that the manipulation is *not* benign. So we have this sort of dialectical situation: Frankfurt insists that Plum, despite the manipulation, *is* morally responsible for killing White because Plum identifies with the relevant first-order desires; the proponent of the **Four-Case Argument** *denies* that Plum is morally responsible for the killing because Plum is manipulated into performing this action. Digging one's heels in this manner is not the way of progress. What is required to challenge Frankfurt are *independent* reasons that call into question his account of freedom or control or his account of when manipulation is benign as opposed to menacing.

But now we have a puzzle. What we have just said of how Frankfurt should react to the **Four-Case Argument** is equally true of how other targeted compatibilists or libertarians should react to this argument if the first two cases are *bolstered to accommodate their conditions on freedom.* If it is made plain that, despite the manipulation, the manipulated agent in the fabricated test cases satisfies the conditions of control of the compatibilist accounts in question, the proponents of these accounts, like Frankfurt, should first simply deny that the manipulation in the initial two cases is menacing. They should then indicate that the **Four-Case Argument** itself cannot impugn their account of freedom or their account of when manipulation is menacing and when benign. If the **Four-Case Argument** can be stopped in its tracks, in this fashion, at the first two cases in connection with *any* compatibilist account, where then is its bite?[2] Why do compatibilists have anything to fear from this argument?

Compatibilists (and libertarians) agree that whereas some forms of manipulation are menacing others are not. They may disagree, of course, on which forms are benign and which menacing. We have already noted a case over which there is disagreement: some take **Ann/Beth** style cases to feature manipulation that is responsibility-undermining, others do not. On the presumption that all cases of manipulation are not equal—they do not all subvert freedom or responsibility—these theorists must have some basis for distinguishing the benign cases from the menacing ones. Assume that there is a set of conditions—refer to this set as "**Benign-M**"—that is such that if an agent, despite being manipulated, satisfies all the members of this set, her free agency is not compromised; she is still morally responsible for actions that she may be manipulated into performing. And assume, further, that any well-worked out compatibilist or libertarian account of free action includes, as a component, its candidate of what **Benign-M** is. I suggest that the undeniable allure of Pereboom's four-step argument is that, among interested parties in the free will debate, *there is no consensus*

2 Interestingly, John Fischer (2004b, p. 158) holds that Plum is responsible in the first two cases (though he is not blameworthy).

*on what **Benign-M** is*; so, it is not transparent at the outset whether Plum in the first two cases involving manipulation does satisfy **Benign-M**. It is, therefore, prima facie credible that Plum, in these cases, may well not be morally responsible.

I said, previously, that it is worthwhile examining McKenna's hard-line response because, among its other virtues, it reveals two different interpretations of the **Four-Case Argument**. We can now appreciate what these two interpretations are. I suggest that it is misleading to construe the **Four-Case Argument** as unfolding in this fashion (this is the first interpretation): Let **Best-Freedom-Theory** refer to a targeted compatibilist or libertarian theory (such as Frankfurt's or Kane's) that has as a constituent its **Benign-M** account (its account of when manipulation is benign). Imagine that Plum in the first two cases satisfies the conditions of this account. Should Plum fail to satisfy these conditions, tweak the case so that it is obvious that he does satisfy these conditions. (This is simply McKenna's bolstering Step Two.) Then, the argument continues, the progression from **Case 1** to **Case 4** impugns **Best-Freedom-Theory** (the compatibilist or libertarian contender). The easy (and astute) response to this way of interpreting the argument would be McKenna's hard-line response: the compatibilist or libertarian at issue should simply reject the claim that Plum in the first two cases is not responsible for his germane actions despite being manipulated. They should claim that as the manipulated agent satisfies what *they* take to be the correct account of control that responsibility demands, the **Four-Case Argument** does not give them decisive reason to give up on their account of control.

Rather (and this is the second interpretation), I suggest that to appreciate why some compatibilists *should* be worried by this argument, Pereboom be taken to be saying something of this sort: "You, the compatibilist, agree that there are manipulation cases in which the agent, Plum, is *not* responsible *because* he is manipulated. After all, all you compatibilists agree that some cases of manipulation are cases in which the manipulation is benign whereas others are cases in which the manipulation is menacing. Understand the first two cases in the four-sequence argument as featuring manipulation which, *given your compatibilist account of control*, you think is menacing. Then I don't see how you can claim that Plum is also responsible in the fourth case. Since this is so, your compatibilist account goes down the drain. But what's true of your account is true of *any* plausible compatibilist contender, a contender that should imply that Plum is not responsible in the carefully-selected first two cases. So any compatibilist account fails."

Understood in this way, the four-sequence argument prompts the following challenge: what *is* the relevant account of manipulation (or free action) that generates the prima facie plausible verdict that Plum is not morally responsible in the first two cases? If we can uncover this account, we will subsequently be in a position to ascertain whether Plum in the fourth case is also not responsible. I propose (whether or not this was his original intention) to take Pereboom to be recommending that no libertarian account divorced from agent-causation or that no compatibilist account that takes seriously the view that Plum is not responsible in the first two cases delivers a contrary verdict in the fourth case. Thus, every compatibilist account fails. And if every compatibilist account fails, incompatibilism is victorious. Further, not only does every compatibilist account fail, but as Pereboom himself thinks, if this argument is sound, every non-agent-causal libertarian account fails as well.

6.3 ON PEREBOOM'S PRINCIPLE O OF ULTIMATE ORIGINATION

Well, how strong is the **Manipulation Argument** even on its charitable (second) interpretation that I have just outlined? I begin with some preliminary remarks on *Principle 0*. In the next chapter, having adumbrated an account of authentic springs of action, I respond directly to Pereboom's challenge. This is the challenge to expose a pertinent difference between cases 1 and 2 (in the sequence of the four cases featuring Plum) in either of which it is clear that Plum is a victim of menacing manipulation, and the fourth case involving ordinary deterministic causation without the sort of manipulation found in the first two cases.

If we begin with the presumption, as the charitable interpretation of the argument recommends, that the manipulation in the first two cases *is* menacing, why precisely is this so? Limiting attention in this subsection to Pereboom's own response, this response not surprisingly invokes **Principle O**. This principle implies that an agent is not morally responsible for an action if sources over which the agent has no control produce this action. Presumably, with the sort of manipulation involved in the first two cases, this implicate of **O** is satisfied as it supposedly is when more mundane deterministic causes (or, for that matter, indeterministic causes) culminate in an agent's performing an action. On pain of begging the question against compatibilists, caution needs to be exercised in not taking **Principle O** simply to be a disguised rendition of the doctrine of incompatibilism. (The **Manipulation Argument**, with the four-sequence argument as a component, is meant, among other things, to *establish* incompatibilism. It cannot, then, on route to establishing incompatibilism, assume the truth of incompatibilism.) So the credibility of **Principle O** must be assessed on independent grounds; really, the credentials of **Principle O**'s pertinent implicate that Plum is not morally responsible in the first two cases in the four-sequence argument must be assessed on independent grounds.

A cautionary note is in order. It would be dialectically unfruitful to understand the four-sequence argument as unfolding in, roughly, this way: (1) **Principle O** is true. (2) Plum is not responsible in the first two cases because the "origination conditions" laid down in **O** are not satisfied in these cases. (3) But if Plum isn't responsible in the first two cases, then (for the reasons Pereboom advances), he isn't responsible in the others as well. (4) Therefore, Plum isn't responsible in the fourth case that features mundane deterministic causation. As I see it, if a compatibilist or libertarian doesn't buy **O**, then, once again, she won't regard the **Four-Case Argument**, so interpreted, as compelling. Rather, as I have explained, my suggestion is to settle on manipulation cases that the compatibilist (or libertarian) *under scrutiny does* regard as responsibility-subverting and then challenge *this* theorist to expose a relevant difference between these cases and **Case 4** that involves deterministic (or indeterministic) causation minus manipulation.

I agree that manipulation cases may help to provide at least prima facie support for **Principle O**. There is nothing amiss with initially appealing to various cases—some involving manipulation—in order to support **O** and then, having gained confidence in **O**, invoking **O** to explain why manipulation, in the pertinent cases, undermines responsibility. This sort of methodology is standard practice when it is metaphysical principles or ethical principles that are at issue.

Again, in keeping with the second interpretation of the four-sequence argument, start with the presumption that the manipulation in (at least the first two cases) is responsibility-undermining. Now we ask, why, precisely, is it so? Different theorists will supply different answers. Fischer has his "ownership" or "taking responsibility" view; Mele defends a different "bypassing" reply; Galen Strawson has another comeback, etc. In this section, I'm interested in Pereboom's intriguing response, a response that, I gather invokes **Principle O**. I advance three initial concerns with this principle.

6.3.1 Principle O, Magical Agents, and God

First, we introduce the idea of "magical agents." These are individuals who spring into existence in an unusual fashion, but who are otherwise very much like normal, healthy, adult human beings. Perhaps these instantaneous agents are the product of other agents; maybe they are chance accidents of conspiring natural forces. The feature of these agents of interest to us is that they can be morally praiseworthy or blameworthy for even their very first decisions, choices, or actions. These agents are free, or morally responsible, or autonomous agents right from the time when they spring into existence. In assuming that it is possible that there are such agents, we are assuming that the concept of *instantaneous autonomous agency* is coherent; and, hence, we are assuming that an agent *could* have been created an instant ago, fully equipped with the compilation of responsibility-grounding psychological elements together with other features that free, responsible, or autonomous agency requires.[3]

Imagine that Rosa is such a magical agent: she was "born" an instant ago, and with the exception of her unconventional entrance into life, she enjoys the full complement of features that morally responsible agency demands. She hears about the plight of the children in Niger. Whipping out her "magical wallet," full of large denomination bills, she makes a bountiful donation to a well-reputed, pertinent charity. Assume, in addition, that Rosa has acted in the very fashion, down to minute details, in which Roselle, a conventional, morally sensitive, adult human being with a "normal" upbringing, has just done: Roselle, just like Rosa, has contributed to this well-reputed charity. Bracketing special pressures from the direction of determinism or indeterminism, assume that Roselle is morally praiseworthy for having made this donation. If Roselle is praiseworthy for this deed, then it seems that Rosa, too, should be praiseworthy for her similar deed. This is because Rosa is relevantly just like Roselle; she is Rosa's twin in the pertinent respects.

If Pereboom insists that in an ordinary case of deterministic causation, Plum's murderous activities derive from springs of action that, in turn, ultimately issue from sources—the distant past and the laws—over which Plum has no control, then I see no reason to deny that Rosa's first action also ultimately derives from sources over which she has no control. As Rosa enters life with her mature psychological inventory fully in place, she has no control over the sources of her springs of action. **Principle O**, it would seem, generates the result that Rosa is not responsible for her act of charity. However, intuitively, this action of Rosa's *may* well be free and *may* well be one for which Rosa is responsible *because* Rosa is relevantly just like Roselle. In brief, the possibility of magical agents motivates this argument against **Principle O**: If this principle is true, then Rosa is not responsible for donating to charity. But it is not clear that she is not responsible for this action because she is pertinently just like Roselle; if Roselle is praiseworthy for her donation, it seems that Rosa should be praiseworthy as well. So perhaps **Principle O** is the culprit.

Analogously, supposing that God exists, God is in germane respects just like Rosa. God is supposed to be a necessary existent (if he exists, he exists in every possible world); accordingly, he is not responsible for his agential features; he isn't responsible for his nature. It is, in fact, hard to see how *any* agent can be "ultimately responsible" for his nature, should ultimate responsibility require that one's "self-forming" or "nature-forming" actions not derive from sources over which one lacks control. For if one's actions are, in the end, not to derive from such sources, it would seem that one would have to be a *causa sui*, a cause of oneself. This is because if one

3 Externalist positions in the philosophy of mind pose a challenge to the notion of instantaneous agency.

were not a *causa sui*, it would appear that the way one is, one's nature, would ultimately derive from sources over which one did not have control. Further, one's choices, decisions, actions, etc. are, essentially, a function of the way one is. So if one were not a cause of oneself, one would not be ultimately responsible for any of one's choices or actions, again, on the proviso that ultimate responsibility requires that one's "nature-forming" actions not issue from sources over which one does not have control. (Indeed, God is often supposed to be, somehow, responsible for his own existence and actions, because a *causa sui*.)

However, Galen Strawson presents powerful considerations for the view that no agent can be a cause of oneself. We shall (in Chapter 8) look closely at Strawson's argument. Here, it suffices to recapitulate his line of reasoning that we summarized in the first chapter. Strawson proposes that if you are to be truly responsible (or ultimately responsible) for what you do, you must be ultimately responsible for the way you are; your nature or character must not derive from sources over which you lack control. But to be ultimately responsible for the way you are, you must have done something in the past, for which you were also ultimately responsible, that contributed to making yourself the way you are. However, if you were ultimately responsible for doing this thing (or things) in the past that contributed to your being the way you are now, you must have been ultimately responsible for the way you were then. But to be ultimately responsible for the way you were then, you must have been ultimately responsible for still earlier actions that contributed to your being the way you were then. So ultimate responsibility requires completion of a series of infinitely regressive choices; this is something that is impossible for any being—God, too, it would seem. Thus, even God, if he exists, is not ultimately responsible for his nature (contrary to the tradition). It would then follow, given the Strawsonian considerations just outlined, that God is not ultimately responsible for any of his actions. Again, though, contrary to what **Principle O** implies, it is not *obvious* that God (if he exists) is not responsible for any of his actions owing to his not satisfying responsibility's control requirements. Once again, **Principle O** might be the bad apple.

6.3.2 Principle O and Indoctrination

Second, there is a different sort of concern with **Principle O**. We distinguish between children whose indoctrinative upbringing renders them not responsible for actions that are expressive of pro-attitudes, values, deliberative principles, and so forth that have been acquired as a result of indoctrination, and children who have had what is deemed to be a normal upbringing. Intuitively, at least, we believe that an indoctrinative history may threaten responsibility in at least some spheres of the child's life whereas a normal history does not.[4] **Principle O**, in the fashion in which Pereboom understands it, cannot discriminate between these cases (granting that we are not agent-causes). For in either, the child's springs of action ultimately derive from sources over which the child has no control. Needless to say, various sorts of incompatibilist might not find anything amiss with this result. But we remind ourselves that **Principle O** is to be assessed independently of whether it finds favor with incompatibilists (or compatibilists).

6.3.3 Principle O and Control

Recall, **Principle O** says that if an agent is morally responsible for her deciding to perform an action, then the production of this decision must be something over which she has control, and an agent is not morally responsible for the decision if it is produced by a source over which she has no control. As a prelude to the third concern, distinguish between complete and fractional (or partial) control. One has complete control over something only if its occurrence is not dependent on anything that is beyond one's control. It is obvious that no one has complete control over anything. At best, any control that we ever have over something is fractional or partial.[5] No one, for example, has control over one's being born but one's being born is a necessary condition of one's performing any action. It is, thus, difficult to see why anyone, agent causalists included, would demand that our having complete control over our decisions is a requirement of responsibility for these decisions; or, alternatively, why anyone would claim that our lacking control over, for instance, some agent-external condition, such as being born, that is necessary for our being responsible for our behavior suffices to undermine responsibility for this behavior. **Principle O**, then, should not be construed as being wedded to any such demand. (Needless to say, I do not take Pereboom or agent causalists to be committed to any such demand.) One might then, though, wonder about **Principle O**'s precise commitments.

Suppose, upon awakening from transformation surgery, Beth agent-causes an action that expresses engineered-in beliefs, desires, values, and so forth. As long as the agent causalist insists that, minimally, reasons influence one's actions, and that one's reasons can be engineered into one, I cannot see how including agent-causation as a constituent of the control an agent must exercise in performing an action if that action is to be free escapes the manipulation problem. But if this is so, the third concern with **Principle O** acquires further urgency: what, exactly, is its content? To kindle this concern, we remind ourselves that 'control' is ambiguous. 'Control'

4 I (and my co-author, Stefaan Cuypers) argue for such a distinction between indoctrinative and normal upbringing in Haji and Cuypers, 2006; 2008.

5 See, for instance, M. Zimmerman 2006, p. 591.

may, for instance, refer to active control or ultimate control. If it refers to the latter, there are yet further problems of interpretation because there are different conceptions of ultimate control. Focusing on the second conjunct of **Principle O**—*an agent is not morally responsible for some decision if it is produced by a source over which she has no control*—and ignoring, initially, complications concerning the precise construal of 'source,' consider these candidates:

> **Principle O-1**: If *S* has no active control in making a decision *D*, then *S* is not responsible for making *D*.

This principle is plausible. If an agent does not exercise, roughly, causal control in forming a decision, then, it seems, she is not responsible for this decision. How can she be responsible for the decision if it is false that this decision nondeviantly causally arises from her desires, beliefs, values, and the like? But as we have already explained, determinism does *not* preclude an agent's exercising active control in making some decision.

> **Principle O-2**: If *S* has no agent-causal (ultimate) control in making decision *D*, then *S* is not responsible for making *D*.

Even some libertarians, such as Kane, who have various strong reservations about agent-causation, would reject **O-2**. So if 'control' in **Principle O** denotes agent-causal ultimate control, **Principle O**, even among various libertarians, will be too controversial to serve as an essential plank in an argument, such as the **Manipulation Argument**, for incompatibilism.

> **Principle O-3**: If *S* has no indeterministic event causal (ultimate) control in making decision *D*, then *S* is not responsible for making *D*.

Claude exercises indeterministic event causal (ultimate) control in arriving at his decision to buy a Coke. Given exactly the same past and the laws right up to or just prior to the time at which he makes his decision, there is a chance that he will decide to buy a Coke and there is a chance that he will decide to buy a Pepsi. He actually decides to buy a Coke. This decision of his is indeterministically caused by prior events (his having of desires, beliefs, etc.). He, thus, exercises indeterministic event causal control in making his decision.

The problem with **Principle O-3** is that this principle straightforwardly begs the question against compatibilists: it assumes that no agent can have the control that responsibility requires in a deterministic universe. So this principle can't, with propriety, be invoked in the **Manipulation Argument** when this argument has its sights on compatibilism.

> **Principle O-4**: If *S* has no control of any sort in making decision *D*, then *S* is not responsible for making *D*.

It's hard to understand **O-4**. If *D* is a bona fide *decision* of *S*, then, it seems, *S* exercises *some* control in making *D*. This would be a species of causal control. The making of a decision is a mental *action*. On the causal theory of action, any event that is an action (mental or otherwise) is appropriately caused by prior states of the agent or prior events involving the agent. This being so, there is a question about the very coherence of **O-4**.

Maybe some might insist that we should regard **Principle O** as attempting to capture the idea that if *S* has no control of *any sort* over the "sources" which produce a decision *D*, of *S*, then *S* is not responsible for *D*. (It may be affirmed that we have no control of any sort over the state of the universe in the distant past and the laws, "sources" of any of our actions if determinism is true.) But, again, this reading of **Principle O** merely begs the question against the compatibilist.

In sum, if we disambiguate 'control' in the second conjunct of **Principle O**—the conjunct that one is not responsible for an action if that action is produced by a source over which one has no control—it is not clear whether this principle will do the work that it is meant to in the **Manipulation Argument**.

6.4 A PROPOSAL

I conclude with the proposal that, despite initial appearances, the **Reformulated Consequence Argument** and the **Manipulation Argument** may not be so far apart; they may share a common kernel. That kernel concerns control. Although some people might find **Principle O** intuitively attractive, one may well wonder whether something more can be said in its support. Revisit the suggestion that responsibility-thwarting manipulation lends credence to **Principle O**. The thought is that the explanation of why manipulation undermines responsibility, when it undermines responsibility, is an explanation that essentially appeals to **Principle O**: the victim of manipulation is not responsible *because*, her behavior having been produced by a source over which she lacks control, she would not have engaged in the behavior in question *but for* the manipulation. But this partial justification for **Principle O** is contentious. Suppose that, unbeknownst to you, a "manipulator" implants a desire in you that is not irresistible. After some reflection on this desire, this desire in conjunction with apt beliefs and values causes you to form an intention. Assume that you would not have formed this intention but for the manipulation: had the desire not been implanted in you, you would not have acquired it and you would not, subsequently, have formed the intention that you did. In such a case, presumably we would regard the manipulation as benign; barring unusual circumstances, we would not want to say that you are *not* responsible for forming the intention that you did. Our judgment would be markedly different in an otherwise similar case save for the implanted desire's being irresistible. The manipulation in this second case is menacing: it undermines responsibility. The explanation of why you are not responsible in this second case could not be that your mental action of intention formation is produced by a source (the manipulator) over which you have no control and that you would not have formed this intention but for the manipulation. For if this is why you are not responsible in the second case, then it should also be true that you are not responsible in the first case involving benign manipulation; in the first case, just as in the second, your mental action also derives from a source over which you lack control and you wouldn't have formed the intention that you did had you not been manipulated.

Reflecting on the second case of menacing manipulation, it is, however, at least preliminarily attractive to argue in this way: "You have no control in acquiring the irresistible desire; further, you have no control in its being true that if you acquire the irresistible desire, then you form the intention in question; so you have no control in forming the intention in question. But if you have no such control, then you are not responsible for forming this intention." It should be evident that this line of reasoning invokes **Rule β (Control)**. The suggestion under consideration, then, is that when you are not responsible for a decision that is produced by a source over which you have no control, this is ultimately because the manipulation ensures that you lack control in the acquisition of necessary prerequisites of your decision and, moreover, you lack control in its being the case that if you acquire these prerequisites, then you make the decision. But if this is the route to securing the second conjunct of **Principle O**, why not get to the heart of the matter and focus directly on **Rule β (Control)** in one of its incarnations as a principle concerning control? I have already argued in Chapter 2, however, that there are serious doubts about whether any of the pertinent control variations of **Rule β (Control)** can sustain incompatibilism.

I close on this note: an account of manipulation that tells us when manipulation is benign and when menacing should be neutral between compatibilist and libertarian accounts—even agent-causal libertarian accounts—of free action. Further, the account should shed light on why a magical agent, such as Rosa, may well be morally responsible for her actions even in face of the presumption that a victim of global psychological finagling, such as Beth, bears no responsibility for her germane actions. Is there an account that meets these constraints? I believe that there is. It is outlined in the next chapter.

7 Authentic Springs of Action

7.1 TOWARD A SOFT-LINE REPLY TO THE MANIPULATION ARGUMENT

In this chapter, I work toward a soft-line reply to the **Manipulation Argument**. I have proposed that in the **Ann/Beth** cases, manipulated Beth is not morally responsible for those post-surgery actions that express her unsheddable engineered-in desires, values, etc. And she is not responsible because these springs of action are inauthentic or not "truly her own." Developing the soft-line reply requires getting clear on the distinction between authentic and inauthentic springs of action.

I undertake the task of constructing an account of authentic springs somewhat indirectly. I begin with an important debate—the internalism/externalism debate—in the literature on free action and moral responsibility. Roughly, externalists (some may prefer the label "historicists") believe that freedom and responsibility are essentially historical phenomena: whether agents are free or responsible vitally depends on *how* agents come to have the psychological features central to responsibility, such as desires, that they have. Internalists (some may prefer the label "structuralists") deny that the way in which such features are acquired plays any pivotal role in correct ascriptions of freedom or responsibility. An example will help to flesh out the difference between these two camps. Suppose, for instance, that you are Frankfurtian with respect to the freedom that responsibility requires: concerning control, you believe that if your action (say, intentionally refraining from smoking) arises from a first-order desire with which you identify, you exercise the freedom that responsibility requires in performing this action. (You "identify with" a first-order desire if you want this desire to move you all the way to action and you have no opposed second-order desire.) Internalists would claim that as far as ascriptions of responsibility are concerned, it really doesn't matter how this "mesh" between your first-order desires and higher-order desires is established. When, on a particular occasion, you are torn between smoking the first cigarette in the morning or refraining from doing so because you want to quit, you may form a second-order volition that your desire to refrain be the one that moves you all the way to action on the basis of your own deliberation. Or some manipulators may succeed in engineering the mesh or "fit" between this second-order volition of yours and the first-order desire to refrain. As long as there is an appropriate fit between higher- and lower-order desires, internalists will claim that you are responsible for performing the pertinent action. Against internalists, externalists insist that the manner in which you acquire your springs of action *does* matter when it comes to free action and responsibility. Externalists may well deny that you are responsible for refraining from smoking if your action issues from a mesh between your higher- and lower-order desires that is itself the product of apt manipulation. The thought here, loosely, is that you are not in control of establishing the mesh; so how can you be morally responsible for actions that issue from a fabricated mesh? Similarly, global manipulation cases typically signal a divide between internalists and externalists. The internalist who is Frankfurtian may well accept the view that post-surgery Beth (or for that matter Plum in Pereboom's **Case 1** and **Case 2**) is responsible for actions that express engineered-in springs as long as the engineering results in a psychological structure in manipulated Beth that the Frankfurtian deems adequate for free action. The externalist, in contrast, will probably deny that manipulated Beth (or Plum) is responsible.

It would appear, then, that if internalism can be defended, one might regard with suspicion the alleged distinction between authentic and inauthentic springs of action for the following forthright reason. Suppose manipulated Beth *can* be responsible for actions that express implanted, unsheddable springs. Then, it seems, it would be a mistake to claim that Beth is not responsible *owing* to her springs being inauthentic, roughly, because they are implanted in her against her will.

I proceed by introducing an engaging, powerful line of argument for internalism. The reasoning appeals to magical agents. In the last chapter, we defined such agents as just like normal, healthy, adult human beings, save for their unconventional entry into life. We stressed that, allegedly, such agents can be morally praiseworthy or blameworthy for at least some of their conduct, including their very first choices or actions. It is further alleged that if this is so, then it is also true that agents, such as maltreated Beth, may be morally responsible for behavior stemming from their engineered-in antecedents of action. If magical agents can be responsible for their pertinent behavior, then this seems to give internalism considerable leverage: the magical agent has no past; so how can facts about the past have any bearing, as the externalist insists, on responsibility—facts, for example in the external world concerning how such an agent acquired her springs of action? And if a magical agent *can* be responsible, shouldn't victimized Beth also, possibly, be responsible for her germane deeds? For, she need be no different with respect to the features that are salient for responsibility than the magical agent. So internalism, it is concluded, has much going for it.

But if internalism has a lot going for it and, hence, if it is credible that manipulated Beth is morally responsible for even her first few actions that express engineered-in springs, there is little theoretical motivation to differentiate between springs of action that are authentic or truly one's own, and those that are alien or foreign. I will rejoin, however, that the line of reasoning outlined in the last paragraph for internalism is not persuasive. An essential part of my reply draws on an account of authenticity. Differentiating between authentic and inauthentic springs helps to underpin a soft-line reply to the **Manipulation Argument**: manipulation victims, such as Beth or Plum (at least Plum as he is featured in the first two of Pereboom's cases), are not responsible for their actions that express engineered-in springs. And they are not responsible *because* these springs are inauthentic. In contrast, the springs of action of an agent (who is not also a victim of manipulation), such as Plum in Pereboom's fourth case featuring determinism, need not be inauthentic; so such agents may well be responsible for their actions that causally derive from authentic springs.

7.2 INTERNALISM VERSUS EXTERNALISM

We begin by formulating more precisely the distinction between internalism and externalism. It is safe to assume that at least certain elements of a person's psychology play an essential role in responsibility ascriptions. Specifically, we may assume that various conditions of moral responsibility, such as the freedom condition, cannot be specified independently of invoking these elements; these conditions essentially appeal to these elements. Frankfurt's condition of freedom invokes our desires; Fischer and Ravizza's appeals to our being appropriately responsive to reasons; Kane's builds on our decisions being indeterministically caused by our reason states. Call such psychological elements "responsibility-grounding psychological elements" and call the conditions of responsibility that essentially appeal to these elements "psychology implicating conditions of responsibility." Externalists hold that the psychology implicating conditions of moral responsibility cannot be specified independently of facts about how the person acquired her responsibility-grounding psychological elements. The focal idea is that facts about one's history or past in the external world that bear on the acquisition of one's responsibility-grounding psychological elements are relevant to whether one's actions are free. Hence, such facts are relevant to whether one can be morally responsible for them. Internalists claim that the psychology implicating conditions of moral responsibility can be specified independently of facts about how the person acquired her responsibility-grounding psychological elements. As David Zimmerman (2003, p. 642) comments, according to internalists, "the conditions of autonomous [or responsible] agency are limited to features internal to a person's attitude-system during the period of deliberation that proximally precedes action."

Mele takes global manipulation cases to support externalism:

> Ann, by hypothesis, is autonomous; but what about Beth?.... By instilling new values in Beth and eliminating old ones, the brainwashers gave her life a new direction, one that clashes with the considered principles and values she possessed prior to manipulation. Beth's autonomy was violated, we naturally say. And it is difficult not to see her now, in light of all this, as heteronomous to a significant extent. If that perception is correct, then given the psychological similarities between the two agents, the difference in their current status regarding autonomy would seem to lie in how they *came* to have certain psychological features that they have, hence in something *external* to their here-and-now psychological constitutions. That is, the crucial difference is *historical*; autonomy is in some way history-bound. (Mele, 1995, pp. 145–46, footnote omitted)

Frankfurt, though, plumps for internalism. We reintroduce salient passages (first cited in the last chapter) in which Frankfurt expresses commitment to internalism:

> A manipulator may succeed, through his interventions, in providing a person not merely with particular feelings and thoughts but with a new character. That person is then morally responsible for the choices and the conduct to which having this character leads. We are inevitably fashioned and sustained, after all, by circumstances over which we have no control. The causes to which we are subject may also change us radically, without thereby bringing it about that we are not morally responsible agents. It is irrelevant whether those causes are operating by virtue of the natural forces that shape our environment or whether they operate through the deliberate manipulative designs of other human agents. (Frankfurt, 2002, pp. 27–28)

> [T]o the extent that a person identifies with the springs of his actions, he takes responsibility for those actions and acquires

> moral responsibility for them; moreover, the questions of how the actions and his identifications with their springs are caused are irrelevant to the questions of whether he performs them freely or is morally responsible for performing them. (Frankfurt, 1975, p. 54)

As these passages make clear, on Frankfurt's internalism, it is irrelevant to free action or moral responsibility whether we acquire our actional springs through conventional upbringing or "through the deliberate manipulative designs of other human agents." As long as our resulting psychologies have a hierarchical organization that confers responsibility, we can be free and responsible agents.

7.3 MAGICAL AGENTS AND GLOBAL MANIPULATION: AN ARGUMENT FOR INTERNALISM

We reintroduce our magical agent, Rosa. Just at the time when she is "born"—an instant ago—Rosa makes a large donation to an appropriate charity to help the children in Niger. Is she morally praiseworthy for this deed?

Once again, we assume that the concept of instantaneous autonomous agency is coherent; so Rosa could have entered life as she did, with all the features that responsibility requires.[1] The possibility of instantaneous autonomous agents may be conscripted in an argument against the verdict that manipulated Beth in either **Ann/Beth** case is morally responsible for her behavior that expresses engineered-in springs. If sound, this argument provides support for internalism insofar as it removes what many have taken to be a major card in favor of externalism: individuals manipulated in the fashion in which Beth is are not responsible for their relevant behavior, and they are not responsible *because* of the way in which they acquire their actional springs.

A clear and instructive version of such an argument is McKenna's. McKenna's chief exhibit is magical agent Suzie Instant who comes into existence at an instant as a psychologically healthy woman much like "any other normally functioning thirty-year old person." (McKenna, 2004, p. 180) The handiwork of a god, Suzie has a complement of false beliefs "according to which she has lived a normal human life for thirty years" and a range of "values and principles that are unsheddable" (McKenna, 2004, p. 180). Suzie (falsely) believes that she has acquired her values through sustained effort over years leading up to what she thinks is her thirtieth birthday. She takes pride in this belief, all the while thinking that

1 On the coherence of instantaneous agency and the implications of such agency for the internalism/externalism debate, see D. Zimmerman 1999.

she is responsible for her efforts which she has freely exerted. We are to assume, in addition, that Suzie is a richly self-controlled person who is able to resist the inclination to act from weakness of will. Further, she "satisfies something like Frankfurt's hierarchical account of freely willed conduct ... [and] is reasons-responsive.... In short, Suzie satisfies the juiciest nonhistorical demands [a compatibilist might venture]" (McKenna, 2004, p. 180). Finally, we are to suppose that Suzie has a robust and relatively consistent range of (false) beliefs about her history similar to those that any psychologically healthy person would have. McKenna invites us to ponder the following:

> [S]uppose ... Suzie is presented with the option to do ... A or B.... [B] involves a violation of a value that is unsheddable for her.... [A] involves acting from one of her unsheddable values. Suzie A-s, acting as her unsheddable value counsels. Supposing that compatibilism is true, it is not clear to me that Suzie did not act freely or responsibly. I can't see how a causal history that zeroed in on this Suzie all in an instance ... renders ... [her] unfree in a way that she would not be if instead some causal history or other unfolded over the course of thirty years. Note that ... when Suzie A-ed from her unsheddable value, she was *not* compelled to do so. Her doing so was *nothing like* acting upon an irresistible desire. It would be natural to say that she A-ed freely—in at least some non-question begging, restricted sense of freely.... To press the point, suppose that every now and then this same god who created Suzie Instant visits another possible world and there creates another thirty year old Suzie, Suzie Normal, in the normal zygote manner. Other times she creates a (seemingly) thirty year old Suzie, Suzie Instant, at an instant. Now suppose that Suzie Normal at the age of thirty arrives at the precise point where she comes to be a nonhistorical duplicate of Suzie Instant. Suzie Normal faces the exact same choice between options A and B as Suzie Instant faces. Just like Suzie Instant, Suzie Normal opts to do A.... The crunch is now upon us: How is it that Suzie Instant is rendered not free and morally responsible when she A-s at the relevant time merely by virtue of the fact that the causal history giving rise to her action came compressed in a momentary package where Suzie Normal's history chugged along over the course of thirty years? A difference here seems arbitrary. (McKenna, 2004, pp. 180–81)

To secure the conclusion that victimized Beth (in **Ann/Beth-1**) may well be morally responsible, McKenna continues:

> Suppose that it is arbitrary to claim that Suzie Instant is not free and responsible but Suzie Normal is. Here we have a case and some attendant intuitions speaking on behalf of a nonhistorical [internalist] conclusion as regards the case of Suzie Instant. But of course, intuitions about varying cases can compete. So it is time for Suzie Instant, Suzie Normal, Ann, and Beth to meet. Let's start with Suzie Instant and Ann, and let us stick with a case in which each A-s as opposed to B-s in such a way that their respective acts of A-ing issue from their respective unsheddable values. Recall, unlike Beth, Ann acquired her wonderful professorial values under her own steam, with the sort of history that Mele finds to be freedom and responsibility conferring. Suppose that by mere cosmic accident, not even by the intentional design of the god who brought Suzie Instant into existence, Suzie Instant is a nonhistorical qualitative duplicate of Ann. She is so right down to her (false) beliefs about her history. If Ann recalls the hours of labor she spent knocking out her last article, Suzie Instant (falsely) recalls the hours of labor that she thinks she spent. Her psychic life, her memory of how she came to be is just as Ann's is. I submit that if Ann and Suzie Instant behaved in the same ways in the same circumstances, Suzie Instant's conduct should be regarded as free and responsible if Ann's is. If this result seems dubious, just start one step away from this. Make the cosmic accident that this god created Suzie Normal to be a qualitative duplicate of Ann, living out the very same life and history as Ann right up to the moment when Ann A-s instead of B-s.... But now, as I have argued above, we should treat the case of Suzie Instant no differently than we treat the case of Suzie Normal. Hence, we should treat Suzie Instant's no differently than we treat Ann's. (McKenna, 2004, pp. 181–82)

McKenna proposes that Beth is not relevantly different than Suzie Instant. So if Suzie Instant is responsible for *A*-ing, Beth should be responsible for *A*-ing as well. We summarize the argument in this way:

(1) Suzie Instant is morally responsible for *A*-ing. (This is because Suzie Normal is morally responsible for *A*-ing, and Suzie Instant is not pertinently different in the constellation of features required for moral responsibility from Suzie Normal. So if Suzie Normal is morally responsible for *A*-ing, so, too, is Suzie Instant.)

(2) If (1), then globally manipulated Beth is morally responsible for *A*-ing. (This premise rests on the view that Beth

is not relevantly different in possessing the features that responsibility requires from Suzie Instant.)

(3) Therefore, globally manipulated Beth is morally responsible for *A*-ing.

7.4 WHY THE ARGUMENT FAILS

I accept the rationale for the first but not the second premise. In this section I explain why. I shall attend, first, to a possible problem that infects McKenna's test case: barring special reasons to believe otherwise, internalists have no reason to resist the standard view that ignorance, when one is not blameworthy for it (nonculpable ignorance) is (or may well be) an excusing condition. In **Sweet Deception**, you are not blameworthy for poisoning your friend because you were unaware that the sugar cubes had been switched with deadly surrogates. This saddles Suzie Instant's tale with an instant glitch: though the lion's share of her beliefs are false, Suzie is *not* culpably ignorant regarding these beliefs. So if some of Suzie's false beliefs for which she is not culpable are among the actional antecedents that lead her to do *A*, then, presumably, she would have an excuse for *A*-ing. To handle this concern, perhaps the case can be suitably modified so that when Suzie *A*-s, her *A*-ing does not implicate false beliefs; thus, her *A*-ing evades worries concerning satisfaction of epistemic constraints on responsibility. Assume that the case can be so modified.

To understand why premise (2) is on slippery footing, it is important to distinguish two stages in an individual's development (in the case of individuals, like us, who acquire responsibility-grounding psychological elements over time). These are, roughly, the stage prior to which one is an agent who is a suitable candidate for responsibility ascriptions, and the stage when or after one satisfies the agency requirements of responsibility. Some spade work is in order.

7.4.1 An Agency Requirement of Responsibility

In addition to freedom and epistemic constraints, moral responsibility has agency requirements. Indeed, being an agent of a certain sort is a prerequisite for being able to satisfy the freedom and epistemic requirements of responsibility. Very young children or Irish Wolfhounds, for example, are not *morally* responsible for their behavior because (among other reasons) they fail to fulfill responsibility's agency presuppositions. To be morally responsible, then, one must be an agent of a certain sort, what I call a "morally normative agent." One agency requirement for responsibility is that the candidate be capable of intentional deliberative action. Such action, in turn, requires some psychological basis for evaluative reasoning. To be responsible, for example, one must, at least on occasion, be able to assess which line of conduct is best from one's own perspective of what is best. Revert to the scenario in which you are both tempted to smoke and tempted to refrain. We may suppose that you deliberate about or weigh these options. On the basis of such deliberation, you form a practical judgment concerning what to do that is, again, best from your own evaluative standpoint. Assume that, all things considered, you judge that it is best for you to refrain. Suppose, further, not succumbing to weakness of will, you form a decision that is in keeping with this best judgment—you decide not to smoke. You then execute this decision and refrain from smoking. With this picture in mind, we may say that an agent's deliberations that issue in a practical judgment about what to do, which in turn gives rise to a decision or intention, involve an appraisal of reasons for or against action.

The agent requires an *evaluative scheme* (or constituents of such a scheme) to entertain such reasons and to appraise them. An evaluative scheme is made up of four constituents: (a) Normative standards the agent believes (though not necessarily consciously) ought to be invoked in assessing reasons for action, or beliefs about how the agent should go about making choices. I leave it open what these standards might turn out to be, or how much weight one gives to standards that, on occasion, deliver conflicting verdicts. You might, for instance, place a lot of stock in engaging in activities, such as smoking cigars, that are sanctioned by standards that derive from your peer group—it is fashionable, in your social milieu, to puff on expensive cigars. But you might also assess courses of action on the basis of prudential considerations or long-term self-interest. If you are not prone to weakness of will or other irrational influences on a particular occasion on which you are pondering whether you should indulge in a Havana, you would have to sort out (if you haven't already done so) to which of the pertinent deliberative principles you assign greater weight: the one concerning self-interest or the one regarding peer acceptance.

What should be emphasized is that to be a fitting candidate for *moral* responsibility, the normative (or deliberative) standards of an agent's evaluative scheme must include a set of *moral* principles or norms; the agent must be minimally morally competent. She must understand the concepts of rightness, obligatoriness, or wrongness, and she must be able to appraise, morally, various choices or actions in light of the moral norms that are elements of her evaluative scheme. There is no requirement that these moral appraisals be fully considered, free of error, or even conscious. Nor is there any requirement that these norms be evidentially-based or justified in any strong sense of 'justification.' The agent may simply assimilate, without critical scrutiny, various norms of her religion or culture.

(b) Included in the agent's evaluative scheme are desires, beliefs, or plans that express the agent's long-term ends or goals he deems worthwhile or valuable. Arnold, for example, may underscore his commitment to attempt to maximize overall happiness whenever he acts.

(c) An evaluative scheme also has, as constituents, deliberative principles that the agent utilizes to arrive at practical judgments about what to do or how to act. So, for instance, the agent may endorse a principle of this sort: when self-interest conflicts with what is demanded by peer pressure, always side with self-interest. Or Arnold may believe that the best way to maximize overall happiness is to rely on rules of thumb like "keep your promises," "don't cheat," "don't steal," etc.

(d) Lastly, an evaluative scheme incorporates motivation both to act on the normative standards specified in (a) and to pursue one's goals of the sort described in (b) at least partly on the basis of engaging the deliberative principles outlined in (c).

One may opt to refine (a), (b), (c), and (d). One might, for instance, wonder whether satisfaction of any of these conditions entails that the agent is self-conscious. Here, I remain (uneasily) content with what I have written here about (a), (b), (c), and (d), fully recognizing that much more needs to be said to appreciate the complex notion of *being a normative agent*.[2]

It *suffices* for an individual's being a morally normative agent at a certain time that the individual have at that time (i) an evaluative scheme with the requisite moral elements—the agent is minimally morally competent; (ii) deliberative skills and capacities. For example, the agent has the capacity to apply the normative standards that are elements of his evaluative scheme to assessing reasons; and (iii) executive capacities—the agent is able to act on at least *some* of his intentions, decisions, or choices, or, if you want, the agent has the capacity to translate some of his intentions, decisions, or choices into action. An individual, like a toddler, who fails to have deliberative or executive capacities, will be able to exert much less control, if any, over its actions than an individual who does have such capacities. Read condition (ii) to require the agent to be able to engage in *genuine* deliberation; his deliberative activities must meet the threshold of rationality below which such activities fail to count as bona fide *deliberation*. Persons suffering from certain severe psychological ailments may not be capable of genuine deliberation.

Normal, mentally healthy, adult human beings are morally normative agents. Dogs and human babies are not such agents—they don't for instance, endorse anything like moral norms.

We can respond to the magical agent's argument, in part, by developing an account of authenticity. To facilitate construction of such an account, we exploit the distinction between the stage, roughly, of childhood, prior to which one is a morally normative agent, and the stage when or after one satisfies the agency requirements of responsibility.

2 For a thoroughly instructive discussion of free agency, see G. Strawson 2004.

7.4.2 Children and the Authenticity of their Developing Evaluative Schemes

Evaluative schemes contain both doxastic (i.e., belief) and motivational components. For brevity, the account of authenticity to be developed limits attention primarily to the latter component which includes desires. As a child matures, the child acquires an evaluative scheme; the child becomes a normative agent. The child's *initial evaluative scheme* is the evaluative scheme that the child initially acquires. One guiding idea is that if the motivational constituents of such a scheme are properly acquired, in a sense of 'proper acquisition' to be explained, then these constituents are authentic; they are "truly the child's own." Over time, the initial scheme evolves; its constituents change. If we can give an outline of when the desires that are part of an individual's initial scheme are authentic, we can then theorize that the desires of an evolved scheme are authentic provided that they causally result from modifications to the individual's initial scheme that are acceptable, again in a sense of 'acceptable' to be explained. Consider a rough analogy. Suppose we're interested in principles of just acquisition of property such as land. We might divide the task of uncovering such principles in this way: First, we defend a set of principles of how one can justly acquire previously unowned land. Then we defend another set of principles concerning how one can go about justly acquiring land from a person who has already justly acquired previously unowned land.

In what follows, I provide only an outline of authenticity. Regarding the motivational or what we may call the "pro-attitudinal" components of an *initial scheme*, such as desires, I propose that these motivational elements, if authentic, are not authentic in their own right. There exists nothing like authenticity of such motivational elements *per se* or *plain authenticity*. Rather, these motivational elements, if authentic, are *relationally authentic*: they are authentic only relative to, or in relation to, whether later behavior that causally arises from these elements is behavior for which the normative agent into whom the child matures is morally responsible. More specifically, with respect to pro-attitudinal components or would-be components of the initial evaluative scheme that the child acquires, I suggest the following:

> A pro-attitude or its mode of acquisition (the manner in which it is acquired) is *inauthentic* if that pro-attitude or the way in which it is acquired subverts moral responsibility for behavior which causally stems from this pro-attitude (typically in conjunction with other springs of action), of the normative agent into whom the child develops.

Subversion of moral responsibility would occur as a result of either epistemic, control, or other necessary requirements (*independent*, of course, of agency presuppositions) of moral responsibility being thwarted. It is in this sense that, at the pre-normative scheme stage, there is nothing like "authenticity *per se*" of pro-attitudes but only relational authenticity: "authenticity-with-an-eye-toward-moral responsibility" or "responsibility-relative authenticity."

The following examples will elucidate this idea. I said that to be morally responsible for an action, an agent must have elementary moral concepts, such as those of wrong or obligation, and she must be able to appraise morally (even if imperfectly), decisions, actions, consequences of action, etc. in light of the moral norms that are partly constitutive of her evaluative scheme. Imagine that a child, Simon, is trained in such a way that he lacks knowledge of the relevant moral concepts with the result that he is not even *minimally* morally competent. He cannot distinguish moral right from moral wrong, or he doesn't have beliefs concerning right or wrong. Then lack of instilment of the appropriate moral concepts is responsibility-subversive. Lacking such moral concepts, this child will not be *morally* responsible for any of his behavior. Or consider instilment in Simon of a pro-attitude or disposition, the influence of which on his behavior he cannot thwart. For example, imagine that, at a time when Simon does not have a fully developed evaluative scheme, irresistible desires are instilled in Simon—maybe desires that ensure that he always acts in conformity with the wishes of his zealous mother. Instilling such irresistible desires would presumably undermine responsibility for later conduct arising from these desires by undermining the control that moral responsibility requires. Or suppose callous experimenters in developmental psychology instill in Simon a powerful disposition always to act impulsively. Here, again, we would not want to hold Simon morally responsible for much of his later impulsive behavior. Or, finally, consider an interference that prevents Simon from engaging in critical self-reflection. This may subvert Simon from being morally responsible for some of his later behavior, on occasions of choice, by significantly narrowing the range of Simon's options, options he may have considered had he acquired "normal" habits of critical self-reflection.

In each of these cases Simon acquires a certain pro-attitude. The pro-attitude (or the way in which it is acquired) is such that behavior that it later causes (when Simon becomes a morally normative agent) is not behavior for which Simon will be morally responsible. His lack of responsibility for this behavior will be due to the fact that the pro-attitude, or the manner of its acquisition, ensured that some necessary condition of responsibility (such as the control condition) is not satisfied. The pro-attitude in question, for example, might be a desire that is irresistible. The action (if any) that results from such a desire at a time when Simon has become a morally normative agent will not be one for which Simon is praiseworthy or blameworthy. This is simply because Simon won't exercise the control that responsibility requires in performing an action that issues from this desire. The irresistible desire is not inauthentic in its own right. It is inauthentic (at the child's or pre-normative agent's stage) *only because* it will thwart later moral responsibility. In this way, it is relationally inauthentic.

In sum, let "interference" be a general term for things like suppression of innate propensities, or implantation of certain dispositions, or deliberate lack of instilment of various pro-attitudes. Some interferences are incompatible with the agent's being morally responsible for his subsequent behavior which issues from these interferences. Such interferences subvert later moral responsibility (as I will say) while others do not. I propose that the subversive ones are *responsibility-wise inauthentic*. Specifically, imagine an agent like a young child who does not yet have an initial scheme. Such an agent's having a pro-attitude is responsibility-wise inauthentic if his having this pro-attitude, as a result of its instilment, subverts his being morally responsible for behavior that stems from this pro-attitude; the having of this pro-attitude precludes the agent from being morally responsible for behavior stemming from this pro-attitude. 'Stems from' requires analysis which shall not be undertaken here save for the following. As we have recorded, a causal theory of action (which I endorse) assumes that actions causally arise (nondeviantly) from desires, or desire/belief pairs, or a cluster of psychological elements. On this theory, when an action issues from a certain desire (as opposed to another), this desire (as opposed to the other, typically together with other actional elements) is causally implicated in the production of the action. I presuppose whatever account of "issues from" (or "stems from") causal theories of action presuppose. Setting aside agency requirements of responsibility, if interferences of the sort at issue subvert later moral responsibility, they will do so by subverting *other* requirements of responsibility, such as epistemic or freedom requirements.

We have, so far, limited discussion to responsibility-relevant authenticity of the "objects" of instilment such as dispositions, or pro-attitudes in general. What about *modes* of instilling such things; are some responsibility-wise authentic and others not? Assume, in the interests of making progress, that to ensure prevention of subverting moral responsibility for later behavior, it is necessary to instill in the child the disposition to be moral. Different modes of instilling this disposition could affect responsibility-relevant authenticity of this very disposition itself. For example, suppose that given the mode of instilling the moral disposition in Simon, Simon finds that he cannot refrain from doing what he perceives to be morally right. Perhaps the disposition was "beaten into" Simon, or instilled via shock "therapy." On occasions of choice, he is stricken with inward terror at the faintest thought of not doing what he deems moral. Intuitively, Simon would not be morally responsible for much of his later behavior because the mode of instilling the moral disposition subverts responsibility-grounding control. Modes of instilling pro-attitudes (habits, dispositions etc.) are responsibility-wise not truly one's own if the modes subvert responsibility for later behavior. Again, putting aside agency demands of responsibility, if these modes of acquiring pro-attitudes undermine later moral responsibility, they will do so by subverting one or more of responsibility's requirements.[3]

We may now formulate a general principle about the authenticity of initial evaluative schemes. I have suggested that the having of some pro-attitudes (dispositions, etc.) may be required to ensure moral responsibility for later behavior—having them ensures that necessary conditions of moral responsibility other than those related to agency can (later) be satisfied by the agent or by her behavior that stems from them. I have also suggested that the having of some pro-attitudes (dispositions, etc.) is incompatible with moral responsibility for later behavior which issues from them; having these pro-attitudes precludes satisfaction of necessary conditions for moral responsibility other than those related to agency, such as epistemic or control conditions. Such pro-attitudes are inauthentic. Lastly, I have suggested that some modes of instilling pro-attitudes (dispositions, etc.) are incompatible with moral responsibility for later behavior; such modes of instilment subvert later responsibility by thwarting satisfaction of necessary conditions of responsibility other than those related to agency. Such pro-attitudes are also inauthentic. Limiting attention to the motivational or pro-attitudinal elements of an initial scheme, I propose this principle as one that governs responsibility-relative authenticity of *initial* schemes of "developing agents":

> **Authenticity-1**: An agent's initial evaluative scheme is responsibility-wise authentic if its pro-attitudinal elements (i) include all those, if any, that are required to ensure that the agent will be morally responsible for her future behavior; (ii) do not include any that will subvert the agent's being responsible for future behavior that issues from these elements; and (iii) have been acquired by means that, again, will not subvert the agent's being responsible for her future behavior.

I turn to further amplification of this account of initial scheme authenticity by responding to the objection that **Authenticity-1** is either *empty* or *circular*. Regarding the former, some may think that **Authenticity-1** is empty because I have left open what *all* the other requirements or dimensions of responsibility are. Also, of the dimensions that I have acknowledged—the epistemic and control dimensions—I have not said in what these consist. So the implication of **Authenticity-1** that if (during the pre-initial scheme stage), a pro-attitude, such as a desire, or its mode of acquisition, under-

3 A preliminary account of initial scheme authenticity is to be found in Haji 1998, ch. 7.

mines future responsibility for behavior that issues from it, that pro-attitude is inauthentic, is empty.

In response, setting aside responsibility's agency presuppositions, there is widespread agreement that responsibility has additional requirements. There is (general) concurrence, for example, that there are epistemic and freedom demands on responsibility. That responsibility has various requirements cannot be denied even in the face of disagreement concerning precisely *what* these requirements might be. Concerning a putative particular requirement, such as the epistemic one or the control one, theorists may well disagree on the *substantive account* of this requirement. As we have seen, some theorists propose that the control that responsibility requires is hierarchical; others claim that the control is to be understood in terms of reasons-responsiveness; still others suggest that the control is agent-causal. Yet, again, though, free will theorists do *not* deny that there is *some correct rendition* (whatever it may turn out to be) of the control requirement. Reconsider the claim that a pro-attitude acquired during the pre-initial scheme stage is inauthentic if behavior that issues from it is behavior for which the agent is not morally responsible by virtue of this pro-attitude's undercutting one or more of responsibility's requirements. On the assumption that there is a *correct* account of what the requirements of responsibility are (leaving out of consideration, again, agency requirements), and that there is a *correct* account of what each of these requirements consist in, this claim is decidedly *not* empty.

Regarding the concern of circularity, the consideration that there is a fact of the matter about what the requirements of responsibility are, and that there is a fact of the matter about what each of responsibility's requirements amounts to, also vindicates the view that **Authenticity-1** is not circular. I do not explicate the notion of initial scheme authenticity by covert appeal to the authenticity of the scheme's constituents. I reemphasize that on my view, during the pre-initial scheme stage, there is nothing like authenticity *per se* of pro-attitudes acquired during this stage. The authenticity of pro-attitudes is forward-looking, specified by way of a relation between the having of a pro-attitude at a time when the child is not yet a morally responsible agent, and behavior that issues from this pro-attitude at a time when the child has turned into a morally normative agent. Second, I account, specifically, for the authenticity in question in terms of whether an agent's behavior that owes its proximal causal genesis to this pro-attitude (typically, in association with other actional elements) is behavior for which the agent is morally responsible. I ask whether the pro-attitude subverts responsibility for such behavior by subverting one or more of the requirements (other than agency ones and so other than authenticity ones) of responsibility. Assuming that there are such requirements (whatever they may turn out to be), and that there is a correct account of what these requirements consist in, I see no circularity in **Authenticity-1**.[4]

7.4.3 Authentic Evolved Schemes

Assume that Simon has acquired an authentic initial evaluative scheme. Evaluative schemes are not static but dynamic; typically they evolve. So, for instance, Simon can renounce values formerly cherished and acquire new ones; he might come to question his belief that moral decisions should conform to the teachings of his religion and adopt a utilitarian outlook; or he might give up some of his deliberative principles such as the principle that he review his decisions frequently before implementing them. Some modifications or changes in one's evaluative scheme may be perfectly compatible with preserving responsibility-relative authenticity whereas others will subvert authenticity. To distinguish between the two sorts of change, we require a conception of *acceptable* modifications.

As one's evaluative scheme is comprised of doxastic and motivational constituents, changes in one's scheme can involve changes in one or both. The general rule for acceptable modifications in either of these types of constituents is straightforward: the modifications must be made under one's own deliberative control. With respect to changes in pro-attitudes such as desires, instilled ones or newly acquired ones are acceptable as long as the actions, if any, to which they give rise are ones over which the agent has responsibility-grounding control and the changes are initiated by the agent's exercising (or engaging) her initial scheme. The changes occur as a result of capacities, such as deliberative ones, that the agent (substantially) has in virtue of elements constitutive of her authentic scheme.[5] In brief, acceptable modifications are those that are implemented under one's own steam.

Some details: Mele plausibly proposes that most normal, healthy human agents have the following capacities in some measure: the capacity to modify the strengths of their desires in the service of their normative judgments, of aligning their emotions with relevant judgments, of mastering motivation to produce or sustain beliefs that would violate their principles for belief-acquisition and belief-retention, of rationally assessing their values and principles, of identifying with their values and principles on the basis of informed critical reflection, and of modifying their values and principles should they judge that this is called for (Mele 1995, pp. 166–72, 183–84).

4 I (and my co-author) entertain and respond to other objections in Haji and Cuypers 2008.

5 I allow for cases in which, through a series of past steps over which one has responsibility-grounding control, one deliberately instills in oneself a pro-attitude (or a cluster of such attitudes) which will give rise to actions over which one will lack such control. A person desperate to quit smoking, for example, may have implanted in her an irresistible desire to avoid cigarettes.

I do not see how it is possible to possess these capacities without having an evaluative scheme. One cannot assess values and principles, for instance, without embracing a set of normative principles. These principles are causally and, ideally, nondeviantly engaged, for instance, in one's appraisal of a thought that strikes one upon witnessing a disastrous event. If one cares deeply about another, one must be able to adjust or adapt one's emotions: appropriately favorable emotions in response to one's belief that the cared-for has fared or will fare well, and a range of unfavorable emotions in response to one's belief that the cared-for has fared or will fare poorly. One cannot do so without engaging elements of one's evaluative scheme. Here, again, there will presumably be an appropriate causal story to be told about how one brings one's relevant emotions (the having of which themselves depends upon constituents of one's evaluative scheme) in line with one's pertinent judgments. Consonant with what Mele says (see, for example, Mele 1995, pp. 166–72, 183–84; Mele 2006, pp. 166–67, 170), I propose that an agent's evaluative scheme is not engaged in acquiring a pro-attitude, if, for instance, the acquisition of this pro-attitude bypasses all of the agent's capacities of deliberative control. The modification to one's evaluative scheme resulting from its supplementation with this pro-attitude is not an acceptable one. If, in acquiring a pro-attitude, one manifests deliberative control and, thus, in this sense "engages one's evaluative scheme," the degree of deliberative control that one exercises will be a function of a number of factors. These include factors such as whether the deliberative process involves certain sorts of inefficiency and irrationality—for example, selective biasing (you ignore evidence that tells against your favored hypothesis)—and the coming to mind, while deliberating, of irrelevant considerations, or influences from the direction of weakness of will.

Assuming an appropriate account of authenticity for doxastic elements, I now formulate the following sufficient condition of scheme responsibility-relative authenticity of "developmental agents" like us.

> **Authenticity-2**: If an agent's evaluative scheme at a time, *t*, is either her initial responsibility-wise authentic scheme at that time, or is an evolved responsibility-wise authentic scheme of hers at that time, then her evaluative scheme is responsibility-wise authentic. (An evolved responsibility-wise authentic scheme of hers at *t* is a scheme resulting from *acceptable* modifications to a scheme that she possesses prior to *t* that is itself responsibility-wise authentic.)

Many more details regarding the authenticity of both initial and evolved schemes need to be supplied in a comprehensive account of authenticity. The sketch I have provided, though, should be adequate for the task at hand.

Reverting to global manipulation cases, these cases as standardly presented, such as the **Ann/Beth** cases, raise concerns not about pre- but about fully-formed morally normative agents with evolved evaluative schemes. Beth, in Mele's **Ann/Beth-1** example, is such an agent. Global manipulation has the effect of subverting normative agency in this way: pro-attitudinal and doxastic components of the individual's evaluative scheme are "replaced" by a different set. The replacement is not accomplished under the individual's own steam but occurs as a result of some process that totally bypasses the agent's capacities of deliberative or reflective control (cf. Mele 1995, pp. 166–68, 171–72, 183–84). Victimized Beth's desires are, thus, not authentic.

7.4.4 Some Objections and Responses

I now respond to three objections to the relational account of authenticity.

7.4.4.1 Evaluative Schemes and Personal Identity

The first questions the assumption that pre- and post-manipulated Beth are identical. It may be rejoined that the **Ann/Beth** case could be interpreted as follows: insofar as a person's identity is *constituted* by her values (or, more generally, her evaluative scheme), a wholesale change in values changes the person's identity. The post-transformation person, as a result, would be "Beth-2" (or, more accurately, "Ann-2," given that she would be exactly similar to Ann). But then this "newly born" person would be responsible for her actions, having just received an authentic *initial* evaluative scheme, albeit in an unconventional fashion. Indeed, if it is one's evaluative scheme that matters for both authenticity and autonomy, this seems by far the more plausible move (that is, to admit that agents are identified with their evaluative schemes, so global manipulation produces new identities—new persons).

I stress that in **Ann/Beth-1** it is not all of Beth's values that are replaced; nothing in the thought experiment requires such total change. Maybe pre-manipulated Beth is kind and generous, intellectually meticulous, and a connoisseur of food and drink. The manipulation need not affect any of the values associated with these things. Post-manipulated Beth need have no false pseudo-memories either: she may be genuinely surprised by the change in her. Moreover, she may rationalize this change. She might believe that it is time that she makes a lasting, worthwhile intellectual contribution and that she can only do so if she dedicates herself wholeheartedly to philosophical pursuit. With these stipulations, the pre- and post-manipulated agents may share many psychological connections, at least they may share a sufficient number to ensure that they are one and the same person.[6] At stake is whether post-manipulated Beth is morally responsible for actions that express the unsheddable engineered-in values, pro-attitudes, and beliefs, not those that the secretive manipulation leaves untouched.

What of the suggestion that if it is one's evaluative scheme that "matters for both authenticity and autonomy," then it ought to be that agents are to "be identified with their evaluative schemes"? One concern with this suggestion is that it implies that adult Ann is not identical to neophyte Ann; adult Ann and baby Ann have different evaluative schemes. A second primary concern is that the suggestion conflates ontological categories: whereas an agent is a *substance*, an evaluative scheme is not. A substance cannot be identical to a non-substance. Maybe there is some sense of 'identity' pertinent to responsible agency that is not the sense of 'identity' in a remark such as "Adult Ann is the same person as baby Ann." The objection, though, concerns *personal* identity: are pre- and post-manipulated Beth the same person? It makes little sense to claim that in this sense of 'identity,' pre-manipulated Beth is identical to her evaluative scheme, and then argue that pre- and post-manipulated Beth are not the same persons because their evaluative schemes differ.

7.4.4.2 Evaluative Schemes and Drastic Change

The second objection concerns actions for which an agent is allegedly morally responsible but which express changes in outlook which seemingly occur as a result of bypassing the agent's minimal capacities of reflective control. The actions in question may, for example, be expressive of certain "new values," the acquisition of which is not under the agent's control. We are invited to think of a case of this sort: Suppose that a selfish person's evaluative scheme undergoes sudden and drastic change through her witnessing some catastrophe—the devastation caused by the earthquake in Pakistan, say. And suppose that the nature of her actions is accordingly drastically changed. We would be reluctant to declare her not morally responsible for these actions, even though the change in her outlook seems not to have "engaged" her evaluative scheme and, so, seems not to have been carried out under her own steam.

In response, concerning such sudden or drastic conversion cases, Mele has argued that whether the agent *is* morally responsible for the pertinent conduct pivots vitally on the filling in of relevant details (2006, pp. 179–84). On the one hand, suppose (implausibly) that the witness to the earthquake undergoes the changes that she does because, at the time of the devastation, God implants in her a powerful disposition to be charitable, the implantation mirroring the implantation of manipulated Beth's new values. In this case, it is less than obvious whether the witness *is* morally responsible for her pertinent deed. On the other hand, imagine that the

6 The pre- and post-manipulated agents may be strongly psychologically connected, in Parfit's sense of 'connected' (Parfit 1984, p. 206).

traumatic event generates in the agent an insight into the human condition which she then evaluates, and which subsequently moves her to change her outlook. In this variation of the scenario, it is false that the agent's evaluative scheme is idle: her exercising her capacities of deliberative control is crucial in explaining the change.

7.4.4.3 Evaluative Schemes and Ambiguity of 'Autonomy'

Finally, the third objection concerns alleged equivocation on the term 'autonomy.' It may be put to us that the reason we think Beth's autonomy has been compromised is that the manipulator has indeed violated her autonomy in the *moral* sense of the word—she gave no consent to the interference. But he did not necessarily violate her autonomy in the *responsibility-providing* sense of the word. So we can certainly agree with Mele that Beth's moral autonomy has been undermined, but if we make the mistake of inferring from our agreement on that term that her responsibility was then undermined, we may very well be making a mistake: her failure to consent to the interference does not render her non-autonomous in the sense (ostensibly) required for moral responsibility.[7]

Like Mele, I take global finagling of the sort we encounter in Beth's case to be responsibility-undermining but the objector does not. Presumably, though, this objector regards *some* forms of manipulation or treatment, or *some* sorts of interference, as responsibility-subverting. Assume that Hal, in the absence of his consent, has been subject to this sort of treatment; so the objector does not take Hal to be morally responsible for various actions of his. Assume, further, that the objector's opponents do not regard this type of treatment as threatening responsibility; they think that manipulated Hal *is* responsible for his pertinent deeds. It would be ineffective (to say the least) for such opponents to argue against the objector in this way: "As Hal did not consent to the treatment, his moral autonomy has been violated. But it is a mistake to infer from this that Hal is not responsible for his pertinent behavior." Our objector would presumably not be moved by this sort of argument. She may well agree with the imagined opponents that the treatment violates Hal's moral autonomy. But further considerations would be required to persuade her, contrary to what she believes, that the treatment itself is not responsibility-undermining and hence that Hal is responsible for his pertinent behavior.

Reverting to Beth's case, it is open to the objector to supplement the "no consent argument" with additional factors that tell against Beth's not being morally responsible. For instance, the objector might appeal to "sudden conversion cases" or "sudden change of outlook" cases to convince us that in these cases, despite undergoing the sudden changes, the agents are still morally responsible for their germane behavior, and then add that Beth's case is not relevantly different from these cases. My response (really,

7 For the development of this sort of objection, see Arpaly 2003, pp. 126–28.

Mele's response) to the second objection, though, casts doubt on whether the sudden change cases can do the trick. When they are interpreted in a way in which they are analogous to Beth's case, it is contentious whether the germane agents are morally responsible for their pertinent acts. When interpreted differently in the manner suggested, the germane agents may well be responsible.

7.4.5 Reply to the Magical Agents Argument

What of Suzie Instant, though? Does her pertinent action—her *A*-ing—issue from an authentic evaluative scheme? Suzie Instant is, in certain respects, just like a young child whose evaluative scheme has not been acquired: others (or at least something, in variations of the original Suzie Instant scenario) contribute to the child's or to Suzie's acquisition of an initial evaluative scheme. Depending on how the tale is spun, Suzie Instant's initial evaluative scheme, just like that of a young child, qualifies as relationally authentic: we may assume that its pro-attitudinal and doxastic elements do not subvert responsibility for intentional behavior that has a subset of these elements as actional antecedents.

The first premise of McKenna's argument—that Suzie Instant is morally responsible for *A*-ing—hinges on the rationale that insofar as the features that ground moral responsibility are concerned, Suzie Instant is no different from Suzie Normal. We may grant this premise because we assume that when each of these agents *A*-s, her *A*-ing issues from an evaluative scheme that is authentic; Suzie Instant's initial scheme is authentic as is Suzie Normal's evolved scheme.

The second premise—if Suzie Instant is morally responsible for *A*-ing, then globally manipulated Beth, too, is morally responsible for *A*-ing—pivots on the proposal that Beth is not relevantly different regarding the features responsibility requires from Suzie Instant (or Suzie Normal). The proposal is false. Beth's *A*-ing issues from components of an evaluative scheme which are inauthentic, whereas Suzie Instant's issues from components of an authentic scheme. In Suzie Instant's case, the concern is whether an initial evaluative scheme is relationally authentic; in manipulated Beth's case, the concern is whether substantial elements that replace various elements of a prior scheme are authentic. An implication of my analysis is that not all global manipulation cases subvert responsibility, assuming that a case such as Suzie Instant's passes as a variant of a global manipulation case, and that there is a principled way, one sensitive to whether what is engineered-in is an initial scheme or "replacement elements" of a cluster of elements of a scheme already in place, to distinguish among such cases.

7.5. INTERNALISM'S DOMAIN

Turning, now, to yet another objection, one might well wonder whether this sort of differentiation of global manipulation cases merely begs the question against internalists. Internalists, roughly, insist that facts in the external world concerning how one's springs of action are acquired make no difference to moral responsibility. Siding with Mele's verdict on **Ann/Beth-1**, though, I have assumed that whether Beth's acquisition of (substantial) parts of her evaluative scheme is accomplished under her own steam *does* bear on responsibility. Hence, the complaint of question-begging is motivated. There are considerations, however, against the legitimacy of this complaint.

An important fact about authenticity of initial evaluative schemes is that there is nothing like authenticity *per se* of the doxastic and pro-attitudinal components of children who are not fully developed morally normative agents; there is only relational authenticity. I proposed that instantaneous agents are like children in the respect that their evaluative schemes are initial and not evolved schemes. It would not affect the authenticity of a set of values that were "implanted" in a child at the pre-initial scheme stage if the implantation were accomplished by harshly paternalist means, as long as the implanted values, or their means of implantation, did not compromise later responsibility for behavior issuing from these values. Similarly, it would not matter whether Suzie Instant's initial scheme were the product of deliberate engineering by a god or something created *ex nihilo*, again, provided that elements of this scheme would leave unaffected responsibility for behavior that arises from these elements. (Of course, in cases of this sort, one need not deny that moral wrong has befallen the child, or that Suzie has been unfairly treated.)

Focus on a case of instantaneous agency in which we have creation *ex nihilo* of a Suzie Instant type of agent—Suzie*. Suzie* has no history or past. Therefore, it should come as no surprise that facts about her history in the external world cannot have a bearing on the acquisition of her (fully-formed) evaluative scheme with which she is "born" and so cannot, in one way or another, affect responsibility for behavior that issues from elements of this initial scheme. Internalism—the position that the agent's history in the external world has no bearing on autonomous or responsible agency—is thus applicable to cases of magical agents. But it would be a mistake to conclude from this that past facts should not have a bearing on responsibility with agents (like us) who do have a past.

To elaborate, suppose that moments after her "birth," Suzie* falls victim to **Ann/Beth** style manipulation. I see little reason why internalists should deny that the manner in which Suzie* acquires the "new" components of her evaluative scheme has distinct implications for responsibility even though pre- and post-manipulated Suzie* are equipped with the psychology that both internalists and externalists would deem sufficient for responsibility but for its odd origins. We have noted that internalists acknowledge that freedom-affecting factors such as coercion may well be responsibility-subversive; and that factors such as deception, may compromise epistemic requirements of responsibility. But then there is no reason for internalists to resist the view that factors that compromise agency requirements of responsibility—factors, for instance, that threaten moral normative agency—may also be responsibility-subversive. In the initial scenario involving her "birth," there is no question about subversion of agency; Suzie*'s initial evaluative scheme is, we are supposing, authentic. In the latter scenario involving global manipulation, there is an obvious concern with the subversion of agency; Suzie*'s modified evaluative scheme is not authentic or it has elements that are inauthentic.

If internalists grant that factors concerning moral normative agency can affect responsibility and they grant that there is no reason to deny that, with agents who have pasts, historical factors can affect responsibility, there is every incentive for internalists to embrace the verdict that manipulated Beth is not responsible for her pertinent actions. They can do all of this consistently with holding on to internalism, or at least a crucial element of internalism. They can allow the conceptual possibility of magical agents—agents without a past—and hold that if such agents are morally responsible, *it is not a requirement of responsibility that one have a past.* This is the kernel of truth in internalism.

In summary, assume—though this is stretching things somewhat—that Suzie*'s initial scenario (in which she springs into existence) qualifies as a case of global manipulation one (though one in which a deity created her would be more apt) as does the latter scenario. In the latter scenario (in which Suzie* falls victim to **Ann/Beth** style manipulation) unlike in the former, I have proposed that internalists need not disagree that facts about Suzie*'s history in the external world do have a bearing on responsibility. These are facts regarding how Suzie* acquires components of her evaluative scheme. I can give a principled account of why internalism "holds" in the former but not in the latter scenario. Hence, one can side with the verdict that Beth is not morally responsible by calling upon a principle such as **Authenticity-1** without any question-begging against internalism.

Still, perhaps an internalist will object that what *makes* manipulated Beth not responsible is not her past but her present. What happened in the past might have produced the conditions that undermine her agency, and thus her responsibility now, but what renders her not responsible now is solely a matter of the current structure of her will. Indeed, the internalist and externalist may actually agree on the responsibility-verdict for all cases, but their dispute is over the criterion of responsibility. They disagree over what it is that makes someone responsible or not, and that dispute will remain intact through all such agreement on specific cases. Simply to assert otherwise, though, is still question-begging.

First, I respond directly to the objection. I then advance further grounds to support the contention that my strategy is not question-begging. The objection presupposes that what renders manipulated Beth not responsible is solely a matter of the current structure of her will. But this is a *non-sequitur* if Beth, just like Suzie Instant, "satisfies the juiciest nonhistorical demands" an internalist might advance. McKenna discerns no relevant difference among Suzie Instant, Suzie Normal, and victimized Beth, asserting that each *is* morally responsible. Maybe the thought is that if manipulated Beth (or her psychology) satisfies the *correct* internalist criterion of responsibility—whatever it may be—then manipulated Beth *is* responsible for her post-transformation acts. This, though, flies in the face of the objector's claims that Beth is *not* responsible and that the internalist and externalist "may actually agree on the responsibility-verdict for all cases."

In the context of this dispute between externalists and internalists, charges of question-begging are delicate. To safeguard against begging the question one way or the other, it is helpful to assume, to the extent that this is possible, the stance of theorists who have no pre-commitments to either internalism or externalism but who take seriously the following riddle: It is intuitively plausible that manipulated Beth is *not* morally responsible. It is intuitively plausible that Suzie Instant *is* morally responsible. What accounts for this asymmetry in intuitions that, in turn, may shed light on which of the seemingly competing positions is more plausible?

Adopting this sort of neutral stance, I have *not* argued in this fashion: "The initial intuition that Suzie Instant is morally responsible is questionable because, right at the outset, this intuition stacks the deck against the externalist." I do not think that this sort of move is of any help in resolving (or dissolving) the riddle anymore than would be the parry that Suzie Instant *is* morally responsible because she satisfies the juiciest internalist non-historical demands. Nor have I argued in this manner: "There is no plausible way for an externalist to explain why Suzie Instant is morally responsible consistently with the externalist's explanation of why victimized Beth is not morally responsible. So it must follow that Suzie Instant is not morally responsible." This thread of reasoning is, surely, given the dialectical context, unacceptable; it would be question-begging.

Rather, I have first conceded that Suzie Instant is morally responsible. This is an important plank in my defense against the charge of question-begging. I have then tackled head-on the challenge implicit in McKenna's paper: Suzie Instant has no past. So facts in the external world in her past can have no bearing on why, if she is morally responsible, she is so. Hence, externalists who believe that, necessarily, facts in the external world in an agent's past can have a pronounced bearing on responsible agency cannot maintain the verdict that Suzie Instant is morally responsible consistently with their explanation of why manipulated Beth is not morally responsible. I have picked up the gauntlet. I have proposed a compromise of sorts between internalism and externalism: *moral responsibility does not require that one have a past but it does require that one not have certain kinds of past.* The relational view of the authenticity of an agent's initial evaluative scheme plays a fundamental role in securing the first half of this *hybrid view*.

Here, it may be profitable to compare my view with some of Mele's pertinent views on which we are in fundamental agreement. Assume that victimized Beth is a mentally healthy, ideally self-controlled agent in every sphere of her life. Still she is not autonomous. She is not a psychologically autonomous—a "*P*-autonomous"—agent, partly because there is a sense in which she is compelled to possess her pro-attitudes. Beth comes to possess these pro-attitudes in a way that bypasses her capacities for control over her mental life; she is practically unable to shed them; the bypassing itself was not arranged or performed by her; and (assume) Beth neither presently possesses nor earlier possessed pro-attitudes that are themselves practically unsheddable products of unsolicited bypassing. With this set of conditions satisfied, Beth is (to use Mele's stipulated term) *compelled** to possess her pro-attitudes (Mele 1995, p. 172). Mele writes:

> My claim is not that *P*-autonomy regarding a pro-attitude, *P*, requires that the agent have a history of a certain kind, but rather that he lack a certain kind of history—a history yielding what I have called "compulsion*" of *P*. Imagine, if you can, an agent who magically comes into existence with a wealth of beliefs, desires, and values in place ... The point to be made is that, even assuming that such a being is possible, my proposed constraint does not entail that it lacks P-autonomy (or authenticity); for it does not entail that the being has any compelled pro-attitudes. (1995, p. 172)

Finally, any comprehensive theory of responsible agency should not shun the enormously complex issue of explaining how the child, who begins life as an individual and who is not morally responsible for any of her conduct (or who is non-autonomous), eventually turns into an agent who can be praised or blamed for various actions of hers (or who is autonomous). I have provided a sketch of certain ingredients of the story, and I have done so without presupposing internalism or externalism. Both internalists and externalist are free to co-opt what they see, if anything, of value in my contribution.

To tie some ends together: One of the primary aims of this chapter is to work toward a soft-line reply to the **Manipulation Argument.** This reply requires explaining why Plum, in Pereboom's first two cases, may not be morally responsible owing to being manipulated, while Plum, in the fourth case, may well be responsible even though all his choices and actions are deterministically caused. I proposed that an account of when our springs of action are authentic holds the key to providing such an explanation.

The guiding thought is that in Pereboom's **Case 1** and **Case 2**, Plum's actions causally derive from inauthentic springs of action (just as post-surgery Beth's actions, in either of the **Ann/Beth** cases, do), whereas Plum's actions in Pereboom's **Case 4** causally issue from authentic springs. Coupled with the principle that actions that are generated by inauthentic springs are not ones for which an agent is morally responsible, the soft-line reply is motivated. An objection, though, stood in the way of developing a soft-line response along these lines. This objection from internalism has it that victimized Plum and Beth may well be responsible despite the manipulation; how they acquire their springs of action fails to bear on whether they are free or morally responsible agents. I have responded to this objection, in part, by constructing an account of authenticity, and by exposing what I take to be the proper domain of internalism. It remains to appreciate just how the relational account of authenticity enables us to differentiate, when such differentiation is called for, among Pereboom's four cases.

7.6 A SOFT-LINE REPLY TO THE FOUR-CASE ARGUMENT

Construe **Case 1** in any reasonable way in which it is clear that Plum is not morally responsible for killing White. So, for instance, imagine that the neuroscientists at the pre-initial scheme stage implant, at the appropriate time, suitable salient action-producing events that guarantee that Plum's programmed actions meet the goals of the scientists but that undermine epistemic or control requirements of responsibility. **Authenticity-1**, with the pertinent facts, implies that Plum's initial evaluative scheme is not authentic. So he is not responsible for the murder. But now consider **Case 2** that is amenable to development in different ways. In one variation, the neuroscientists program Plum by implanting in him doxastic and pro-attitudinal elements that are constituents of his initial evaluative scheme, and none of these elements undermine responsibility for later behavior by undermining epistemic or control requirements of responsibility. Here, the process of initial scheme acquisition is speeded up considerably, assuming this is possible. Suppose that when Plum kills White, his deadly deed causally stems from an authentic evolved scheme. I, thus, see no reason to deny that he is responsible for the murder under these circumstances.

In a second variation of **Case 2**, the implanted elements constitutive of Plum's initial evaluative scheme do subvert responsibility for later behavior, including the deadly deed, that issues from these elements. In this variant, the verdict that derives from **Authenticity-1** is that Plum is not morally responsible for killing White.

In a third variation, just as in the first, the implanted initial scheme is authentic. Suppose, though, that pursuant to initial scheme acquisition, the sly neuroscientists program Plum to behave in various ways, including the following. They implant in Plum a set of relevant desires that become activated to exert influence on Plum's behavior under circumstances conducive to Plum's killing White, and they implant a set of suitable beliefs that come to Plum's mind in these circumstances. Imagine that Plum's reasoning to kill White issues from these beliefs and desires without engaging elements of Plum's authentic evolved scheme; the reasoning bypasses these elements. Then, **Authenticity-2** generates the result that Plum is not morally responsible for killing White. However nifty the manipulators, it is not possible for them to bypass an agent's capacities for control in making choices or performing actions without bypassing those capacities. And if these capacities, as in this variation, are bypassed, the agent won't be responsible for his pertinent choice, or decision, or action.

Pereboom claims that a compatibilist who takes Plum to be morally responsible in **Case 3** must show how this case differs from **Case 2**. Suppose one believes that Plum is not morally responsible in **Case 2** because one has either the second or third variation of this case in mind. **Case 3** may differ from **Case 2** in that it is akin to the first variant of **Case 2**. So, relative to the niceties of the pertinent cases, **Authenticity-1** and **Authenticity-2** allow us to draw a principled distinction between a scenario in which Plum is morally responsible and a scenario in which he is not morally responsible for the killing.[8]

Perhaps it may be objected that the neuroscientists might manipulate a person who has an authentic initial evaluative scheme in such a way that the person ends up with an *authentic* evolved scheme or with constituents of that scheme, such as desires, that are *authentic*. But then, the account of evolved scheme authenticity (see **Authenticity-2**) would imply, implausibly, that the person *is* responsible for choices or actions that causally issue from these engineered-in, intuitively inauthentic elements. This objection, though, is not cogent. Suppose Plum, who has an authentic initial scheme, acquires a "new desire." Presumably, what is being envisioned by the objector is that this desire can be implanted into Plum by the neuroscientists in such a way that it qualifies as authentic, on my account of

8 My analysis of when an initial scheme is authentic implies that Fischer and Ravizza's third condition on *taking responsibility* seems not to be correct. As I outlined, Fischer and Ravizza (1998, pp. 210–14) explain that taking responsibility for a mechanism that issues in action has three components: (i) the agent must see himself as the source of his behavior; (ii) he must accept that he is a fair target of the reactive attitudes as a result of how he exercises his agency; and, (iii), the views of himself in (i) and (ii) must be based in an appropriate way on the evidence. Suppose, at the pre-initial scheme stage, neurologists implant in Simon various pro-attitudes and beliefs, including the belief that Simon sees himself as the initiator of his behavior and the belief that he regards himself as a suitable target of the reactive attitudes based on how he exercises his agency. Suppose that none of the implanted elements, including these engineered-in beliefs, subvert moral responsibility for actions issuing from the mechanism of practical reasoning and others that include these elements. Then this sort of manipulation is not responsibility-subversive. Fischer and Ravizza's third condition implies otherwise: it is not true that Simon acquired relevant mechanisms in an appropriate way, namely, through response to moral training and acquiring knowledge of the world in normal ways.

authenticity, when it really is not authentic. So my account is faulty. On my view, though, if the new desire is acquired as a result of bypassing Plum's capacities of deliberative control, it won't be authentic. But as I cautioned when I discussed the "third variation" (two paragraphs back), however sophisticated the neuroscientists, they cannot both implant such a desire by bypassing Plum's capacities of deliberative control *and* implant it in a manner in which it engages these capacities of Plum. If the new desire is acquired as a result of totally bypassing Plum's capacities of deliberative control, my view implies that the desire is not authentic. If the desire is acquired as a result of engaging Plum's relevant capacities, then I see little reason to deny that the desire may well be authentic. In brief, it cannot be that **Authenticity-2** implies that the new desire is authentic (as the objector claims), *even though* its implantation into Plum bypasses Plum's capacities of deliberative control (as the objector needs to suppose *if* this desire is to fail to qualify as authentic by the lights of **Authenticity-2**).

In Chapter 6, we laid out the **Manipulation Argument** for incompatibilism, one essential constituent of which draws on the view that responsibility requires that we be the ultimate originators of our choices and actions. I have argued that there are various concerns with this argument. In the next chapter, we examine another pathway to incompatibilism which also pivots on a similar sort of view about ultimate origination.

8 The Impossibility Argument

8.1. INTRODUCTION

Many compatibilists and incompatibilists take seriously the "origination condition" on moral responsibility, its root idea being that if we are to be morally responsible for our actions, these actions must originate "in us"; we must be their "final source." However, they have different conceptions about what it is for our actions to originate "in us." We have noted that the **Manipulation Argument** attempts to persuade us that a causal history involving responsibility-undermining manipulation is not relevantly different from a deterministic causal history that excludes any manipulation. In cases with the former sort of history, our actions originate in the manipulator; in cases with the latter sort of history, our actions have their ultimate sources in the distant past and the laws. Strawson (G. Strawson 1986), like Pereboom, Kane, Smilansky (2000), and others, also gives the origination condition pride of place. Responsibility, he claims, does require that we be the ultimate originators of our actions. But he argues that when we understand just what is implicated in being originators of this sort, it is impossible for us to be such originators. Thus, we may regard Strawson's **Impossibility Argument** as falling into the same broad family of arguments for incompatibilism that essentially appeals to origination.

There is though, one striking difference between the **Impossibility Argument** and, for example, the **Manipulation Argument** that exploits the origination condition. Vital to the **Manipulation Argument** is some premise that invokes determinism. Specifically, it is the premise that actions resulting from a deterministic causal history are relevantly similar to those that derive from a causal history involving manipulation (in either case, the agent is not the ultimate source of her actions). The **Impossibility Argument**, in contrast, is essentially divorced from determinism. Strawson proposes that regardless of whether determinism is true or not, we cannot act freely. If we cannot act freely, then, of course, we are not morally responsible for anything that we do. So on Strawson's view, it isn't that determinism *per se* (or, for that matter, indeterminism) threatens responsibility. Rather, our acting freely logically depends upon something that is impossible—free action is contingent upon our having made an *infinite* number of choices. In loose strokes, the argument proceeds from the premise that an agent's action, if free, is free partly in virtue of being appropriately produced by various mental elements, such as the having of reasons, of the agent. Alternatively, we may say that if an agent's act is free, its being free is a function of, or determined by, how that agent is, mentally speaking (G. Strawson 1986, p. 28). But if some agent, Augustine, is not morally responsible for the way he is mentally at the time when he performs some action—say, he steals some pears—he is not morally responsible for this action owing to its deriving from how he is mentally at that time. So to be responsible for stealing the pears, Augustine must be responsible for how he is mentally at the time or just prior to the time at which he steals the pears. To be responsible, though, for how he is mentally at this time, he must have done something that gave rise to his mental constitution at this time such as performing earlier "character-forming" actions. But if Augustine were not responsible for these earlier actions, he would not be responsible for his mental constitution at the time he stole the pears. So he must have been responsible for these earlier actions to be responsible for stealing the pears. To be responsible, however, for these earlier actions, he must have been responsible for the way he was mentally at the time or just prior to the time at which he performed these earlier actions. But to be responsible for how he was mentally at these earlier times, he must have been responsible for still earlier actions that determined how he was mentally at these earlier times. And so on. It seems, then, that responsibility for an action requires performing an infinite number of actions, something that is impossible. Hence, regardless of the truth of determinism, responsibility goes by the way. Let's now formulate the argument with a bit more precision and then assess it.

8.2. THE IMPOSSIBILITY ARGUMENT

Here is Strawson's summary of the argument:

> 1. Interested in free action, we are particularly interested in rational actions (i.e. actions performed for reasons ...), and wish to show that such actions can be free.
> 2. How one acts when one acts rationally (i.e. for a reason) is, necessarily, a function of, or determined by, how one

is, mentally speaking. (One ... could add 'at the time of action' after 'mentally speaking.')

3. If, therefore, one is to be truly responsible for how one acts, one must be truly responsible for how one is, mentally speaking—in certain respects.
4. But to be truly responsible for how one is, mentally speaking, in certain respects, one must have chosen to be the way one is, mentally speaking, in certain respects. (It is not merely that one must have caused oneself to be the way one is, mentally speaking; that is not sufficient for true responsibility. One must have consciously and explicitly chosen to be the way one is, mentally speaking, in certain respects, at least, and one must have succeeded in bringing it about that one is that way.)
5. But one cannot really be said to choose, in a conscious, reasoned fashion, to be the way one is, mentally speaking, in any respect at all, unless one already exists, mentally speaking, already equipped with some principles of choice, 'P_1'—with preferences, values, pro-attitudes, ideals, whatever—in the light of which one chooses how to be.
6. But then to be truly responsible on account of having chosen to be the way one is, mentally speaking, in certain respects, one must be truly responsible for one's having *these* principles of choice P_1.
7. But for this to be so one must have chosen them, in a reasoned, conscious fashion.
8. But for this, i.e. (7), to be so one must already have had some principles of choice, P_2, in light of which one chose P_1.
9. And so on. True self-determination is logically impossible because it requires the actual completion of an infinite regress of choices of principles of choice. (G. Strawson 1986, pp. 28–29. See, also, G. Strawson 2004, pp. 371–72.)

A reformulation of the argument, (perhaps) more amenable to evaluation:

THE IMPOSSIBILITY ARGUMENT

Responsibility for a decision, choice, or overt action turns, in part, on certain psychological elements that we possess. So we may concur that what we decide to do or how we act depends on certain facts about our mental life. This gives us the first premise:

(1) The decisions or choices we make or the actions we perform depend on certain facts about what we are like in relevant mental respects, or *how we are*.

The argument continues:

(2) If (1), then to be responsible for any of our acts (mental or otherwise), we must be responsible for being in the relevant ways how we are.
(3) Therefore, to be responsible for any of our acts (mental or otherwise), we must be responsible for being in the relevant ways how we are.
(4) We cannot be responsible for being how we are unless we acted earlier in ways that made us how we are.
(5) To have been responsible for these earlier acts, we must have been responsible for how we then were, by having acted even earlier in ways that made us how we then were.
(6) If (4), and (5), then to be responsible for any of our acts, we would have to have been responsible for an infinite series of "character-forming" or "self-forming" actions.
(7) Therefore, to be responsible for any of our acts, we would have to have been responsible for an infinite series of "character-forming" or "self-forming" actions.
(8) It is not the case that we can or could be responsible for an infinite series of "character-forming" or "self-forming" actions. (That is, the proposition expressed by the consequent of (6) is false.)
(9) Therefore, it is not the case that we can be responsible for any of our actions.

8.3 ASSESSING THE IMPOSSIBILITY ARGUMENT

An implication of premises (4) and (5) is that:

> **(R)** Responsibility for any choice or action requires having made an infinitely regressive series of choices.

(R), in turn (when taken in conjunction with the proposition that we must make ourselves be the way we are in relevant respects to be morally responsible for our behavior) implies:

> **(History)** If an agent is morally responsible for something, then the agent has a history: in the pertinent way, the agent must have made herself to be that way.

8.3.1 A Problem Concerning Magical Agents and God

We have already, though, seen reason to believe that **(History)** is suspect. For instance, it is widely believed that if God exists, then God is responsible for his actions. (Or at least, it is widely believed that if God exists, and God is not responsible for his actions, it is false that he is not responsible by virtue of his actions not originating in him.) On many but not all views concerning God's existence, God is in time. Further, God is a necessary existent—if God exists, he exists in every possible world. It is not possible for a necessary existent to come into or to go out of existence. At any time, nothing makes God how he is at that time; God is not a *causa sui* (as we have explained, appealing to Strawsonian considerations, in section 6.3.1). So it's false that for God to have been morally responsible for an act, he must have been responsible for how he was at the relevant time. Of course, this first consideration against Strawson's argument may be contested: even though it may be widely believed that if God exists, he is responsible for his actions (or that if God is *not* responsible for his actions, it is *not* owing to his not being an ultimate originator of his actions), mere belief does not amount to truth.

Assuming that the concept of instantaneous autonomous agency is coherent, the possibility of magical agents such as Rosa or Suzie Instant also poses a challenge to **(History)**. Rosa's first action *may* well be free and *may* well be one for which Rosa is responsible. But this action does not derive from psychological elements for which Rosa is responsible because she enters life with her psychological repertoire fully in place. One may attempt to turn the tables on this consideration by proposing that the **Impossibility Argument** can be seen as an argument against the possibility of instantaneous autonomous agency. This is a fair, initial response. It isn't, though, evident whether the proposal that instantaneous autonomous agency is possible is less credible than the proposal that moral responsibility requires making an infinitely regressive series of choices.

8.3.2 A Problem Concerning Agency

Compatibilists (and, indeed, many libertarians) will regard premise (4) with suspicion: we cannot be responsible for being how we are unless we acted earlier in ways that made us how we are (and in ways for which we are responsible). Compatibilists (and libertarians) require a story about how (at least some) non-responsible or heteronomous children manage to become responsible or autonomous agents. Suppose part of the story that I developed in the last chapter is in the right ball park. To turn into an agent who is a suitable candidate for responsibility ascriptions, it appears that various psychological elements will have to be "implanted" into the child; at the pre-normative agent stage (when the child does not even have an initial evaluative scheme or all the constituents of such a scheme), the child will not be responsible for these implanted elements. Still, many responsibility theorists will not shy away from the view that the normative agent into whom the child develops may well be responsible for at least some of her choices or actions that causally derive from such implanted elements.

A Strawsonian may insist that to be *really* or *truly* responsible for an action, an agent must be responsible for all its pertinent antecedents; real or true moral responsibility for an action or choice, *by definition*, requires that the agent have chosen in a "reasoned, conscious fashion" an attitude or other mental antecedents that ground the choice. But then, as Mele remarks, the very definition of responsibility entails that to be responsible for any choice requires having made an infinitely regressive series of choices. But it is unclear why compatibilists or libertarians should settle for anything like this notion of responsibility, nor for any corresponding notion of free action (Mele 1995, p. 224).

8.3.3 A Problem Concerning Control

Maybe some will say that to be truly responsible for an action, one must be the *ultimate originator* of the action or one must have *ultimate control* over the action. We have noted that according to Pereboom (and others, such as Kane), ultimate origination entails the following.

> **Principle O:** If an agent is morally responsible for her deciding to perform an action, then the production of this decision must be something over which the agent has control, and an agent is not morally responsible for the decision if it is produced by a source over which she has no control.

Perhaps one might propose that premise (4) is supported by something like **Principle O**. But as we have already explained, this principle is multiply ambiguous. Once it is disambiguated, the resulting principles are highly controversial (see section 6.3.3).

Revisiting the various conceptions of ultimate control—indeterministic event-causal control (negative ultimate control), agent-causal control (positive ultimate control), and compatibilist ultimate control—helps to bring into focus what I take to be the basic concern with the **Impossibility Argument:** its conception of ultimate origination, which requires completion of an infinite number of choices, is insufficiently motivated. It is so in that no compelling reasons have been advanced to prefer this conception to rivals that are less demanding. Nondeterministic event-causal control (or negative ultimate control) is exercised by an agent in forming a decision or in performing an action when her decision or action is nondeviantly and indeterministically caused by apt agent-involving events such as the agent's having certain desires and beliefs. An agent exercises agent-causal control in forming a decision or in performing an action if she agent-causes that decision or action. Finally, compatibilist ultimate control consists in a decision or action being appropriately caused by springs of action that are truly one's own or authentic, where the notion of authenticity or ownership of one's springs is a compatibilist one.

8.3.3.1 The Impossibility Argument and Negative Ultimate Control

We reconsider, first, the negative conception of ultimate origination. Suppose that you witness a mugging in an alley. You have strong reasons to help the victim; you also have strong reasons to make it to an important meeting. Suppose there is a high probability that you will help the victim, and that if you help, your helping will be indeterministically (and nondeviantly) caused by the reasons—which include moral considerations—that you have for helping. There is a lower probability that you will attend the meeting on time, and that if you do, your doing so will be indeterministically (and nondeviantly) caused by the competing reasons of self-interest that you have for being present at the meeting. Suppose you do stop and help. Many libertarians, such as Kane (1996; 2007, p. 26) would concede that you help voluntarily (or willingly), intentionally, and rationally. Given the same past and the laws, you could have done otherwise—you could have made the meeting; and if you had made the meeting, you would have done so voluntarily (or willingly), intentionally, and rationally (Kane 2007, p. 20). On the negative conception of ultimate origination in question, you are the ultimate originator of your altruistic action, at least partly but significantly, in virtue of the fact that, prior to your helping, there are no "agent-external" causally sufficient conditions for either of your alternatives, and that when you do help, your helping is indeterministically caused by your reasons or reason states.

The Strawsonian might object that this conception of ultimate origination is too slim a basis on which to ground responsibility; for you can be "truly" responsible only if you are responsible for your nature, which is impossible. I agree that no agent—not even God in my opinion—can be a *causa sui*. But I am not sure why, *without further argument*, a proponent of the negative conception of ultimate control, should accept stronger Strawsonian demands on ultimate origination. Perhaps it might be further claimed that if, given exactly the same past and the laws, you could have done either of your options, the action that you did perform would simply be a matter of luck, and such luck is incompatible with responsibility. Maybe this is so—we shall examine this kind of **Luck Objection** much more thoroughly in the next chapter. But it is important to distinguish the problem of luck from the different problem of formulating and defending an acceptable account of ultimate origination or control. The proponent of negative ultimate control is proposing that if you have freedom of control from the past, and if your actions are suitably indeterministically caused by your reasons, then you are an ultimate originator of your actions. The **Luck Objection** does not hit against this account of ultimate control.

Well, then, the Strawsonian might take issue with this very account itself. Imagine that your actions have been indeterministically caused by your reasons, but these reasons themselves have been engineered into you by new-wave psychosurgeons (and you have no knowledge of your being finagled with). We would not want to say that you are morally responsible for your actions that express engineered-in desires, values, beliefs, etc. So the negative conception is inadequate. It is open, though, to the proponent of the negative conception to co-opt the account of authenticity that I proposed to evade this objection. The proposal would then be that if your action is suitably indeterministically caused by your *authentic* springs of action, then you are the ultimate originator of your action. Again, the Strawsonian might insist that this account of ultimate origination is not rich enough—it doesn't go far enough—to secure "true" responsibility because on this account you are not the ultimate founder of your nature. But, yet again, one might wonder why "true" responsibility requires that we go all the way to being the causes of our natures. What independent reasons are there for this stronger demand other than, perhaps mere deep faith in the truth of the stronger demand?

8.3.3.2 The Impossibility Argument and Agent-Causal Ultimate Control

We turn now to agent-causal control. On agent-causal accounts an agent's directly free actions are caused by the agent; neither a directly free action, nor the event that is the agent's bringing about a directly free action is deterministically caused by other events; and the causation by the agent of a directly free action does not consist in causation by events. On such a view of control, since the free actions that are agent-caused have no deterministic event-causes, the view allows for genuine alternative possibilities: given the same past and the laws, the agent could have done otherwise. Further, as an uncaused cause of her free actions, the agent is the ultimate initiator of these actions. Finally, agent causalists add that having the power to agent-cause her actions provides the agent-cause with a power to influence causally which open alternative will be made actual. These salient features of typical agent-causal views, taken together, paint a rich portrait of ultimate control or ultimate origination. It is a picture that, again, is estranged from the view that ultimate origination requires a regress of free choices; it does not require that one be a *causa sui*.

It may be objected that the agent-causal picture of ultimate origination is, in the end, unacceptable because it appeals to a view of causation—agent-causation—that is not conceptually adequate. Or even if such a view of causation were coherent, there is little reason to believe that we would have free will because there is little reason to believe that we are agent-causes. Regarding the former concern, theorists such as Clarke (2003a), O'Connor (2000), and Pereboom (2001), have done much in the way of giving an explication of agent-causation that is every bit as coherent as explications of rival non-agent-causal accounts of control.

Regarding the latter concern, even if free will requires that we be agent-causes, and we are not agent-causes, this is insufficient reason to renounce the view of ultimate origination that the agent-causalist proposes. (Indeed, if the Strawsonian view of ultimate origination were correct, we would lack free will as well since it is not possible for any person to complete an infinitely regressive series of choices.)

Strawson does consider a libertarian view—he calls it the "Leibnizian View"—that resembles agent-causal views but that requires no regress. He claims, though, that the Leibnizian view fails to secure the *rationality* of free decisions—such decisions won't be made for reasons. On this view, the will is likened to

> a queen seated on her throne, whose minister of state is the understanding, while the passions are her courtiers or favorite ladies, who by their influence often prevail over the counsel of her ministers. One will have it that the understanding speaks only at this queen's order; that she can vacillate between the arguments of the minister and the suggestions of the favorites, even rejecting both, making them keep silence or speak, and giving them audience or not as seems good to her. (Leibniz [1710] 1985, p. 421)

The Leibnizian View, Strawson comments, prompts the question, "upon what, exactly, are the agent's decisions about actions now supposed to be based, other than upon its reasons?" (G. Strawson 1986, p. 53). The decisions cannot be based on further "principles of choice" because then the agent could not be self-determining with respect to these principles without generating the infinite regress of the sort that is implicated by the **Impossibility Argument.**

> But if [the agent] does not have any such further desires or principles of choice, then the claim that it exercises some special power of decision or choice becomes useless in the attempt to establish its freedom. For if it has no such desires or principles of choice governing what decisions it makes in the light of its initial reasons for action, then the decisions it makes are rationally speaking random: they are made by an agent-self that is, in its role as decision-maker, entirely non-rational in the present vital sense of 'rational': it is reasonless, lacking any principles of choice or decision. The agent-self with its putative, freedom-creating power of partially reason-independent decision becomes some entirely non-rational (reasons-independent) flip-flop of the soul. (G. Strawson 1986, pp. 53–54)

Strawson's concerns about the Leibnizian view amount to the following. We are to suppose that on this view, the agent's reasons (her desires and beliefs, for instance), are one causal (mental) constituent of a supposedly free decision (or choice) that this agent makes. These reasons incline to but do not necessitate the making of this decision; they do not, on their own, cause the agent to decide as she does. So, Strawson asks, what makes the difference that accounts for the agent's deciding as she does? Not *further* "principles of choice," he proposes, for in this case, we would spiral down the sort of regress that the **Impossibility Argument** brings to light, and the Leibnizian View is supposed to avoid such a regress. Rather, what makes the relevant difference is the *agent's* causal contribution to the decision: she agent-causes this decision, and this is the second mental constituent of a free decision. On the Leibnizian View, then, free decisions are to be co-caused by a mental reasons constituent and a mental agent-causal constituent.[1] But Strawson proposes that rational decisions (or actions in general) must have a full causal explanation solely in terms of the agent's reasons. More exactly, rational decisions must have an explanation in terms of reasons the agent has that reflect *all* of what there was about the agent, mentally speaking, that causally brought it about that she performed the action that she did. For if not, only the reasons constituent of the decision's cause would be rational; the remaining agent-causal constituent, dissociated from reasons, would not be. But then the Leibnizian View countenances a dilemma. On the one hand, if it is only the reasons constituent that causally brings about the putatively free decision, the agent-causal constituent seems superfluous to free action. We would, it appears, not have a rational explanation of why one set of reasons for one decision rather than a competing set for another decision "prevailed." Further, on the Leibnizian View, the decision would not, it seems, be free because it would not be co-caused by a reasons constituent *and* an agent-causal constituent. On the other hand, if the agent-causal constituent does play a causal role in bringing about the decision, this constituent, independent as it would be of any influence from reasons, would not be rational. In this event, the allegedly free action that is co-caused would not be rational.

It is open, though, to a proponent of a traditional agent-causal view or a Leibnizian-like view to claim that the role of reasons in causing a free decision, and the role of the agent in agent-causing the decision, are not independent of each other (Clarke 2003a, pp. 173–76; Pereboom 2001, 67-68), thereby blocking the dilemma. A traditional agent-causalist who proposes that free decisions have agent-causes but no event causes can hold that an element of one's agent-causal powers is the capacity to consider and weigh reasons, and thereby to guide one's causing of decisions or choices. On this view, having judged that the reasons in favor of one's

1 The Leibnizian view resembles Clarke's integrated agent-causal account (which we examine, in more detail, in the next chapter).

decision outweigh those in favor of another, one would agent-cause the one rather than the other. One could, though, consistent with the past and the laws remaining fixed, still have agent-caused the alternative that is less favored by one's reasons (Pereboom 2001, p. 67). An advocate of a hybrid or integrated agent-causal view according to which free decisions have both agent-causes and event causes, may theorize that one would agent-cause a (free) decision only if this decision were indeterministically caused by one's reasons (Clarke 2003a, p. 176).

Assuming that Strawson has no other concerns with either traditional agent-causal views or Leibnizian-like integrated views—concerns having to do specifically with ultimate origination—these agent-causal perspectives present an engaging alternative to Strawson's conception of ultimate origination, a conception that falls prey to the regress that we previously described.

8.3.3.3 The Impossibility Argument and Compatibilist Ultimate Control

Finally, we reintroduce compatibilist accounts of ultimate origination. The account that I adumbrated in the previous chapter is compatibilist. On this view, if an agent's decisions or choices causally derive from an authentic evaluative scheme, then these decisions or choices are "truly the agent's own." During childhood when the individual is not yet a morally normative agent, components of the individual's evaluative scheme may be relationally authentic; they will be so if they do not undermine responsibility for decisions that express these components at a time when the individual can be morally responsible for her behavior. At the post-normative agent stage, newly acquired actional springs will not be the agent's own (or authentic) if they are acquired by processes that fail to engage the agent's capacities of deliberative control.

Perhaps one will object that the common problem with all compatibilist accounts of authenticity (or origination, or sourcehood) is that if determinism is true, then the sources of one's actions reside in the distant past and the laws. If so, one has no say—no control—over the "ultimate origins" of one's decisions and choices; they are already "in the cards." Hence, determinism rules out one's being the final source or ultimate originator of one's actions.

I believe that this sort of concern is misguided. Recall the negative conception of ultimate control. According to this conception, you are the ultimate originator of a decision largely by virtue of the fact that, prior to making your decision, you have genuine alternatives (you could have decided otherwise), there are no "agent-external" causally sufficient conditions for any of your alternatives, and when you do make whatever decision you make, that decision is indeterministically (and nondeviantly) caused by your reasons or reason states. I proposed that this account is inadequate; the conditions that it lays down for being an ultimate originator can all be satisfied by an agent who is a Beth-like victim of crafty enough manipulation. To circumvent this difficulty, I suggested that a proponent of the negative view could add to this view the additional requirement that one's springs of action be authentic in the compatibilist sense of authenticity that I proposed. But then it is puzzling why the other two requirements are needed for a robust enough account of origination: the requirement of access to alternatives, and the requirement of indeterministic causation of the decision. Regarding the former, an agent in a Frankfurt-type case has no (pertinent) alternatives; still, if her action causally issues from authentic springs, she may well be the ultimate originator of her actions. What, though, of the worry that if this agent's actions are deterministically caused by prior antecedents, her actions, in the end don't really originate in her? The plausibility of this concern can be tested against a hybrid compatibilist/non-traditional agent-causal view of control. We noted previously that if an event can, in principle, be both agent-caused and indeterministically caused, then it should also be the case that that event can, in principle, be both agent- and deterministically caused (Clarke 2003a, pp. 148, 182). It is open to compatibilists to enrich their account of free action by insisting that an agent performs an action freely only if it is both deterministically caused by apt agent-involving events, such as prior reasons of the agent, and it is agent-caused by that agent. Since the complex event, *the agent's agent-causing an event*, it seems cannot itself have a cause, the agent will be the ultimate cause or initiator of her free actions even though these actions will be co-determined by event causes.[2] In this fashion, a compatibilist theory can incorporate both a control component (appropriate deterministic causation of a free action) and a sourcehood component (agent-causation of a free action) of the freedom dimension of responsibility.

One need not, of course, accept the hybrid compatibilist account. It is outlined simply to draw attention to the following points. First, alternative possibilities are *not* necessary for the variety of robust ultimacy at issue.[3] Second, suppose apt prior reasons of some agent, call him Mork, deterministically cause his decision to lie. Such event causation of his decision is consistent with Mork's co-determining his decision by agent-causing it. It seems that there would be no relevant difference in Mork's being a robust ultimate initiator in this deterministic scenario, and his being such an initiator in an indeterministic scenario, as close as possible in all details to the first, save for the difference that in this second scenario, Mork's decision to lie is indeterministically caused by prior reasons of his and agent-caused by him. In the second scenario, there is no prior causally sufficient condition of the decision that Mork makes. In the first, however, not only is there

2 An argument for the view that the complex event that is an agent's agent-causing something cannot itself have a cause, appears, for example, in O'Connor 2000, pp. 52–53. See, also, Clarke 2003a, pp. 154–58.

3 This appears to be consonant with Pereboom's view on the matter (2001, pp. 18–22).

such a condition but Mork lacks control over this condition. Despite there being such a condition, and despite his lacking control over it, it seems that he is just as robust an initiator of his decision in the deterministic scenario as he is in the indeterministic one.

We may model the first scenario in the fashion in which we modeled Pemba's case (in section 3.5). We can assume that Mork's agent-causing his decision to lie is causally sufficient for his making this decision. We may further assume that there is an independent deterministic causal pathway to this very same decision, and that its constituent elements do not in any manner interfere in the way in which Mork himself brings about his decision. Now, again, we may compare this scenario with the second scenario in which Mork's decision to lie is agent-caused by Mork and indeterministically event caused by prior reasons of Mork. Mork appears to be just as robust an ultimate initiator in either of these scenarios despite his not having freedom from the past in the first deterministic one.

One might rejoin that in the deterministic scenario, Mork's agent-causing his decision is explanatorily irrelevant to the decision's occurrence, while it is relevant in the indeterministic scenario. Presumably, if the following counterfactual is true, then *Mork* is explanatorily irrelevant to his making his decision: If Mork had not agent-caused the decision, the decision still would have occurred. This counterfactual appears to be true in the deterministic case. But its truth-value is, at best, indeterminate in the indeterministic scenario, compatible with the explanatory relevance of Mork's agent-causing his decision.

In response, a proponent of the hybrid view, whether the view is of Clarke's or of the compatibilist's variety, should insist that there is a distinction between Mork's decision's occurring and Mork's decision's *freely* occurring. Free action, on the hybrid views in consideration, requires initiation, at least in part, by the agent, something that the requirement of agent-causation, it is proposed, captures.[4] Mork's agent-causing his decision, then, *is* explanatorily relevant to the decision's being *free*.

I conclude that there are good reasons to be skeptical of the view that ultimate origination requires completion of an infinitely regressive series of choices. This skepticism, in turn, casts suspicion on the **Impossibility Argument**.

4 See, for example, Clarke 1996, p. 32.

9 Libertarianism and the Luck Objection

9.1 LIBERTARIANISM AND LUCK

Van Inwagen has affirmed that the following argument is "the strongest argument for the existence of free will"; indeed, he says, it is "the *only* strong argument for the existence of free will": "moral responsibility requires free will and we *are* responsible for at least some of the things we have brought about" (1983, p. 188). The first conjunct of this argument is widely accepted. With respect to the second, van Inwagen writes:

> if we examine our convictions honestly and seriously and carefully, we shall discover that we cannot believe that this assent [to the thesis that "responsibility exists"] is merely something forced upon us by our nature and the nature of human social life.... [W]e shall discover that we cannot but view our belief in moral responsibility as a justified belief, a belief that is simply not open to reasonable doubt. I myself would go further: in my view, the proposition that often we are morally responsible for what we have done is something that we all know to be true. (1983, p. 209)

One might well have reservations about this justification for the thesis that responsibility exists (consult, for example, Mele 1995, pp. 244–46). Nevertheless, that this thesis is true has struck many as highly credible (see, for instance, P. Strawson 1962). Assume, then, that you are convinced about the reality of moral responsibility. But assume, also, that, overall, in your estimation, the case in disfavor of compatibilism is powerful. You may, for instance, believe that responsibility requires that we be the ultimate originators of our choices and actions, but that no compatibilist view can sustain a robust enough account of ultimate origination. Since you endorse the thesis that responsibility exists, you will then be drawn to libertarianism (on the supposition that nature cooperates and allows for the germane indeterminacies in persons' brains or elsewhere). But if some account of libertarianism is true, then, of course, incompatibilism carries the day, as libertarians are just incompatibilists who believe that at least some of us, on occasion, perform free actions for which we are morally responsible. Assume (and this is a weighty assumption, as hard incompatibilists will be quick to remind us) that the thesis that responsibility exists is not in contention. Some theorists may want to think twice about this final route to incompatibilism that we examine in this work, if it can be argued that leading libertarian contenders succumb to serious concerns. In this chapter, I address a worry about luck that I believe is the bane of prominent varieties of libertarianism. I shall by and large confine discussion to two species of libertarianism: a so-called "action-centered modest event causal" view and Clarke's hybrid agent-causal incarnation.[1]

9.2 EVENT CAUSAL MODEST LIBERTARIANISM

In section 2.4.2.3, we outlined two compatibilist accounts of moral responsibility, a hierarchical account and a reasons-responsive one. Reconsider the former. You identify with a first-order desire insofar as you have an unopposed second-order desire that this first-order desire move you all the way to action. The hierarchical account has it that if your action is nondeviantly caused by a first-order desire with which you identify, then (assuming other conditions of responsibility are satisfied), you are morally responsible for this action. I have left unspecified whether the causation at issue is deterministic or indeterministic. Suppose that the causation is indeterministic: given exactly the same past and the laws, although you "acted on" this first-order desire, there is a chance that you would not have done this. This sort of hierarchical account would then qualify as a *modest* libertarian account. Or reconsider Fischer and Ravizza's brand of compatibilism. According to this sort of compatibilism, assuming all other requirements of responsibility have been met, you are responsible for an action that causally arises nondeviantly from a moderately reasons-responsive mechanism for which you have taken responsibility. Suppose, again, that the causation is indeterministic. Then this account would be a modest libertarian one as well. With these examples in mind, we may now generalize and outline the principal characteristics of modest libertarian accounts of free action and responsibility.

1 Non-causal variants will not be scrutinized.

Such accounts, as our two examples illustrate, share important features with the most promising compatibilist views on free action.[2] They require that to choose or to act freely, an agent must have the capacity to engage in practical reasoning and to guide her behavior in light of the reasons that she has. In addition, structured after their compatibilist rivals, such accounts are *modest* in that they make no appeal to Kantian noumenal selves, Cartesian minds, or other metaphysically exotic agents, and avoid forms of causation with metaphysically demanding commitments such as agent-causation. Further, like their compatibilist competitors, they dictate that the choices—the decisions or intentions—or overt actions for which an agent is morally responsible be the outcomes of causal processes. Specifically, they require that, for instance, a free decision be made for reasons, and its being made for reasons consists, partially, in its being caused in an appropriate and nondeviant way by the agent's having those reasons. An indirectly free action is an action whose freedom derives from the freedom of other actions to which this action is suitably related. A directly free action is a free action but not indirectly so. Standard libertarian views allow that an indirectly free action may be determined by its immediate causal precursors. Modest libertarian theories differ from compatibilist ones in that they imply that even the immediate causal antecedents of a directly free action do not determine that action: given these antecedents, and the natural laws, there is some chance that that action will not occur.[3] In other words, on a modest libertarian view, a directly free action must be indeterministically caused by antecedents such as desires and beliefs. This requirement of indeterministic causation is partly designed to meet the libertarian's demand that (directly) free actions have no deterministic causes; given the same past and the laws, the agent could have decided or done otherwise.

9.2.1 Nonaction-Centered Modest Libertarianism

Clarke usefully distinguishes between nonaction-centered and action-centered versions of modest libertarianism (Clarke 2000, p. 23). To understand these versions, the following partial picture of deliberative intentional action, one we have called upon before, is helpful. Claudia is deliberating about whether to buy a Coke or some fizzy water. Trying to cut down on caffeine, there is a reason for her to favor the water. But she enjoys caffeinated Coke more than she enjoys fizzy water; so she has a reason to favor the Coke. Beliefs involving these and other considerations come to Claudia's mind as she weighs her options. These considerations causally give rise to an all things considered best judgment—best from Claudia's

2 Such accounts have been defended or discussed by Clarke 1996; 2000; 2003; Dennett 1978, pp. 286–99; Fischer 1995; Kane 1996; and Mele 1995.

3 A recent defense of this sort of view is to be found in Kane 1996.

point of view—about what drink to buy. She judges that it is best for her to buy the water. This best judgment then nondeviantly causally issues in Claudia's forming an intention (her arriving at a decision) to buy the water. Finally, she executes this intention and buys the fizzy water.

Nonaction-centered libertarian accounts locate indeterminism relatively early in the causal pathway of an action at some point *before* making a decision, and they require that the events that are indeterministically caused not be *actions* of any sort. For instance, when Claudia engages in full-blown intentional action, a number of considerations, including various beliefs, present themselves to her mind during her deliberations, prior to her forming a best judgment about what beverage to purchase. If it is causally undetermined whether certain nonoccurrent beliefs will enter into one's reflections and causally affect what best judgment is reached, then forming one's best judgment—an event not deemed to be an action—will be indeterministically caused. In Claudia's case, we imagined that various beliefs concerning the merits of buying the water and shortcomings of buying the Coke (in conjunction with other actional elements, such as desires) indeterministically cause Claudia's best judgment. On a nonaction-centered account, the causal pathway from the formation of a best judgment to the performance of the action is deterministic. So, for instance, on such an account, Claudia's decision to buy the fizzy water is deterministically caused (in part) by her best judgment, although this judgment itself is indeterministically caused (in part) by prior beliefs. I distinguish this sort of modest libertarianism only to set it aside. It is action-centered accounts that are of concern to us.

9.2.2 Action-Centered Modest Libertarianism

According to *action-centered modest libertarianism*, the event that is indeterministically caused is the making of a decision, a mental *action*; hence, the label "action-centered" (Clarke 2000, p. 23). The recipe for generating a working version of this sort of libertarianism is to start with our best compatibilist view of freedom—whatever it turns out to be—and then to add to this "host" the requirement that free decisions themselves are to be indeterministically caused. The resulting event causal action-centered libertarianism specifies that an agent's control—"active" (or "proximal") control—in making a decision consists in apt agent-involving events, such as the agent's having a desire, an agent's entertaining certain beliefs, or an agent's making of a best judgment, nondeviantly causing that decision. We said that such control is a species of causal control. This sort of control concerns the direct causal production of agent-involving events, such as the agent's having certain values, desires, and beliefs, his making a certain evaluative judgment, his forming a certain intention or arriving at a certain decision, his executing an intention, and his performing a non-mental action. The degree of active control the agent exercises depends on which agent-involving events actually cause the decision and on their causal histories. If, for example, Claudia makes her decision on the basis of her best judgment, she will exercise greater active control in making this decision than she would have if, from weakness of will, she decided to buy the water instead. On such a libertarian view, the factors that constitute an agent's active control in making a free decision are the very ones shared by this view and its compatibilist host: roughly, deliberative processes with appropriate causal histories nondeviantly causing the decision. In short, the modest libertarian account will differ from its compatibilist "host" principally in requiring that a free decision is to be *indeterministically* caused by whatever causal precursors its compatibilist host recognizes as required elements for free action. So both the compatibilist "host" and the modest libertarian account "derived" from this host will, it appears, not differ in their requirements of active control for free action; they differ simply in that in one (the "host") the relevant causation is deterministic; in the other (the derived modest libertarianism) the relevant causation is indeterministic.

9.3 INTRODUCING THE LUCK OBJECTION

Some philosophers have thought that modest libertarianism undermines free action, responsibility, or freedom-relevant control. This is a surprising objection, on the assumptions that modest libertarianism does not vary from its best compatibilist rival with respect to active control, and that its best compatibilist competitor (whatever it may be, perhaps its "host") does not share these faults. Dwell a bit further on Claudia's case. In the example, Claudia decides to buy the water, and this decision is indeterministically caused by prior beliefs, desires, values, and the like. Since the causation is indeterministic, given *exactly the same* past and the laws, Claudia could have decided to buy the Coke instead.[4] Had she indeed decided in favor of the Coke, it is not that she would have deliberated differently from the way in which she actually did. Nor would it have been the case that she would have entertained other beliefs than the ones she entertained. Nor, again, is it true that she would have given more weight to Coke-favoring considerations than she did. We are to imagine that *everything* is to remain *exactly* as it is in the scenario in which Claudia decides to buy the water save for her final decision; she ends up deciding to buy the Coke. Hence, the decision to buy the water that Claudia (indeterministically) makes seems to be a matter of luck provided it is true that given an identical past

4 Kane claims that exact "sameness or difference of possible worlds is not defined if the possible world contains indeterminate efforts or indeterminate events of any kinds" (1996, p. 172). I'm not sure that this concern is correct. Even if with indeterminate events of any kind, sameness of possible worlds is not defined, "near sameness" or "as close as possible" will do nicely to motivate the **Luck Objection**.

(and the laws), she could have decided to buy the water instead. The difference between the actual world in which Claudia decides at the time at which she does to buy the water, and possible worlds with the same past and the laws in which she decides at this time to buy the Coke, is a matter of luck. If, contrary to fact, we imagine that Claudia had decided to buy the Coke and (for convenience) we call Coke-deciding Claudia "Claudia*, then it appears that Claudia's decision to buy the water is luck-infused; this is richly suggested by the following query: why did Claudia* decide to buy the Coke when *under (type- or near type-) identical conditions of the past*, Claudia decided to buy the water? There seems to be no good explanation of this fact.

Another example from a previous work of mine should help bring into sharp relief this concern about luck (and control):

> Suppose Peg is mulling over whether to keep a promise to visit Al. She judges that, all things considered, she ought to keep the promise, though reasons of self-interest tempt her to refrain. She decides to keep the promise, and her having certain reasons to do so, including her making the all things considered judgment that she ought, on this occasion, to keep the promise, indeterministically causes her to make this decision. On an action-centered libertarian view, since Peg's decision to keep the promise is indeterministically caused, there was a chance that her deliberative process would terminate in a decision not to keep the promise. Had Peg made this other decision, it would have been indeterministically caused by her having reasons of self-interest. *Everything* prior to the decision that Peg actually makes, including every feature of Peg, might have been just the same, and yet she could have made the alternative decision instead. To underscore this point, consider the nearest possible world with the same past as the past in Peg's world. This world will have a past in which Peg's prior deliberations have resulted in the best judgment that the promise ought to be honored but Peg (or if we want, one of Peg's counterparts, Peg*) decides not to keep the promise. In so deciding, Peg* acquires an intention not to keep the promise. The acquisition of this intention—the making of the decision to refrain from keeping the promise—is seemingly not explained by anything. At least, Peg*'s prior deliberations do not explain why she makes this decision. This is because these deliberations exactly mirror those of Peg's but Peg's deliberations indeterministically give rise to the opposed decision to keep the promise. As Alfred Mele has commented, if one agent does one thing and another refrains from doing that thing, "and there is nothing about the agents'

> powers, capacities, states of mind, moral character, and the like that explains this difference in outcome, then the difference really just is a matter of luck."[5] Luck of this sort seems incompatible with free action or moral responsibility. (2005, pp. 323–24)

If we add what I think is not essential to the **Luck Objection** but has a measure of plausibility nonetheless—that the sort of luck at issue is a matter of something's not being in one's control—then it is not farfetched to suppose that Peg's decision is not free or that she is not morally responsible for it because she lacks freedom-level control in making it. (Again, it's worth emphasizing that the **Luck Objection** can be energized independently of this claim about control. I return to this below.) But now we should tread carefully. With respect to the decision that she makes, precisely what sort of control, if any, does Peg lack? Not active control (it seems); not, that is, the sort of causal control that one exercises in forming a decision when that decision nondeviantly issues from one's reasons. Why not? Well, we are entertaining the supposition that if Peg decides to keep the promise, this decision is nondeviantly and indeterministically caused by prior antecedents of action; and just as surely, if Peg decides to break the promise, this decision is also nondeviantly and indeterministically caused by a different set of prior antecedents of action. So in either case, Peg exercises active (causal) control in making the decision that she does. If Peg doesn't lack active control in making whatever decision that she makes, what sort of control (if any) does she lack?

Elsewhere, I have referred to this sort of control as "*antecedent proximal control*" (2002, p. 110–11). To explain, with fixed pasts, the difference in outcome in Peg's and Peg*'s cases appears to be merely a function of the indeterminacy in actional pathways leading to choice. It seems that no agent, however self-controlled, could exert active (causal) or any other sort of control over such indeterminacy to ensure a particular outcome. Amplifying somewhat, if *t1* is the time at which Peg makes whatever decision she makes, then if she is still alive then (it is not indeterministic, for instance, whether Peg will suffer a fatal stroke then), unlike an otherwise similar deterministic counterpart Annie-D, Peg does not have the ability or power to ensure that at *t1* she decides in accordance with her decisive best judgment about what to do: she lacks antecedent proximal control in deciding as she does. She may judge that it is best for her to keep the promise, may muster all the powers of self-control that would ordinarily suffice for her deciding in accordance with this best judgment, but still fail to so decide. She could so fail because, given a fixed past and the laws, the other decision was in the offing. So in Peg's case, her prior actional antecedents seem not to contribute sufficiently to control. With Annie-D, though, things

5 Mele 1999, p. 280.

are different. Suppose, like Peg, deterministic Annie-D judges that it is best to keep the promise. Being self-controlled, she can ensure that she decides on the basis of this best judgment; there will be no surprises at the end of the day concerning what decision she will make.

Consider this sort of objection to my view that antecedent proximal control may well be required for free action and responsibility: "Assume that Annie-D is just like Peg save that she is a deterministic agent—she occupies a world at which determinism is true. Imagine that she faces a conflict similar to the one that Peg faces—she can either keep or break a promise. These alternatives are compatibilist in that it is true that in some compatibilist sense of 'can,' Annie-D has the ability to make a decision other than the one she actually makes. Suppose Annie-D, just like Peg, judges that it is best for her to keep the promise. You claim that Annie-D has the power to ensure that she can decide on the basis of this best judgment; but Peg, because her decision is indeterministically caused by prior antecedents, including the making of her best judgment, cannot ensure that she decides in accordance with her best judgment. In your terminology, whereas Annie-D exercises antecedent proximal control in deciding as she does, Peg does not. You claim, further, that lack of such control (as in Peg's case) may well undermine responsibility. But this can't be so. Why? First, simply introduce 'agent *external* indeterminism' into the picture in this way: owing to certain properties of Peg's brain it is indeterministic whether or not she will suffer a massive stroke at *t1*. So there is now a genuine chance that, rather than make the decision in question at *t1*, she will die of a stroke at *t1*. Yet it is obvious that if, as things actually unfold, they unfold smoothly and Peg makes the decision in question—nobody coerces her into making the decision, she is not duped about relevant facts, she is not insane, etc.—then she is as morally responsible as she would have been if there had been no possibility of anything else happening, like her being dead at *t1*. Second, if the indeterminism is *internal* to Peg's decision-making processes rather than external, this does not make any difference in terms of the reliability with which she can ensure a particular decision is made. In other words, if it is indeterministic whether Peg will make decision *X* or be dead at *t1* (as in a case of external indeterminism), or indeterministic whether Peg will make decision *X* at *t1* or decision *Y* at *t1* (as in a case of internal indeterminism), Peg's ability reliably to ensure that she makes decision *X* is equally damaged in both cases. Peg can no more antecedently ensure that she makes decision *X* at *t1* when the source of the control-diminishing indeterminism is *external* to her will, than she can when it is coming from *within* her own will. But we have already seen that in the case involving external indeterminism, the fact that the agent cannot antecedently ensure a particular outcome does not, in any way, compromise control and so responsibility. Why, then, should responsibility be threatened in the case of internal indeterminism? Hence, antecedent proximal control is not required for free action and moral responsibility."[6]

I agree with the objector that in the scenario with indeterminism external to the decision-making process, the indeterminism does not preclude the agent from making a particular decision at the relevant time, *t1*, and that if the actual sequence unfolds in the absence of ordinary freedom- or responsibility-subversive factors, the agent *would* be responsible for the decision. It is, after all, not controversial that if it is indeterministic whether Peg will make decision *X* at *t1* or be dead at *t1*, Peg cannot *ensure* that she makes decision *X* at this time; and that if she does decide to *X* at *t1*, and there are no responsibility-undermining factors in the causal sequence of events that culminate in Peg's decision to *X* at *t1*, then Peg may well be responsible for making this decision at *t1*. I do not, however, see how any of this undermines the view that antecedent proximal control may well be required for free action and responsibility. To flesh this out, consider, first, a deterministic world in which it is *not* true that the agent, Annie-D, will suffer a fatal stroke at *t1*. Rather, given her compatibilist alternatives, Annie-D will either decide to keep the promise or to break it. Imagine that the actual sequence culminating in Annie-D's decision contains no responsibility-undermining factors. Supply the best compatibilist story about how Annie-D resolves her conflict concerning what decision she should make (assuming she is torn between keeping her promise and breaking it). If she is self-controlled, Annie-D has the ability to ensure that she decides in accordance with her best judgment.

Peg, in her indeterministic world, is pertinently like Annie-D: whatever compatibilist story we tell about how Annie-D resolves her conflict, we advance this very same sort of story about how Peg attempts to resolve her conflict; the relevant segment of the actual sequence of events in the trajectory leading to Peg's decision in Peg's scenario, right until just prior to the moment at which Peg decides, is type- or near-type identical to the "corresponding" segment in Annie-D's case. Still, assuming that it is not indeterministic that Peg will suffer a fatal stroke at *t1*, and that she will not die at *t1*, Peg cannot ensure that the decision that she will make at *t1* will accord with her previously formed best judgment, even though the relevant segment of the causal trajectory is free from otherwise responsibility-subverting factors, such as, the influence of clandestine manipulation. I, thus, reject the objector's claim that if the indeterminism is internal to the agent's decision-making processes rather than external, that does not make any difference in terms of the reliability with which the agent can ensure that a particular decision is made. In the scenario in which the indeterminism is external, provided Peg does not die at *t1*, or, more generally, provided that other external things, such as Peg's suffering a massive but non-fatal stroke that leaves her permanently unconscious, do not transpire, nothing else

---

6 This sort of objection has been advanced by Harrison 2007.

can, so to speak, go "wrong" at *t1*; if Peg is self-controlled, there will be no surprises in what decision she makes; she will decide on the basis of her best judgment. But in the scenario in which the indeterminism is internal, things can go very "wrong": even if Peg* differs not a whit from Peg, Peg may end up deciding akratically.

In a number of places, I have granted that an agent such as Peg may exercise (active) control *in* making the decision that she does; still, she does not have control *over* which decision "prevails." I have, at times, expressed this sort of concern about control in the following way. The **Luck Objection** is intriguing precisely because it points to factors that undermine responsibility even on the assumption that these factors do not affect *active* control. An agent such as Peg does not have what we may call "dual directional control over her actions": she seems not to have antecedent control over doing one action rather than another. Libertarians like Kane have conceded this, but have suggested that lack of *such* control leaves untarnished the active control that an agent exercises in performing actions. Further, they have proposed that if active control is not undermined, there is little reason to suppose that when, for instance, Peg decides to keep her promise, her deciding is a matter of luck. Disputing this claim, I have underscored the point that the actions of a libertarian agent such as Peg are luck-infused in a manner that compromises responsibility. That there is a problem of luck is brought out by the fact that there seems to be no adequate action explanation of the akratic action of Peg's counterpart, Peg*. (I revert to this point concerning explanation shortly.) Thus, I am strongly drawn to the view that luck can undermine responsibility without influencing active control. An enticing implication of the **Luck Objection** is that, in addition to standard requirements of responsibility including the one for active control, there is yet an additional insulated-from-luck requirement (see, for instance, Haji 2003, pp. 270–71).

I agree with Clarke that theorists inclined toward libertarianism should be wary about modest versions. Among other reasons, they should be wary about these versions because on these versions it is false that the agent has some *further* power to influence causally which of her alternatives she realizes. These versions have no provisions to ensure that when an agent chooses among two or more alternatives, the agent has a power over and above the mere chance of acting differently from the way in which she did; they do not secure for the agent a power over and above the power to exercise active control in making whatever decision that she does (1996; 2003a). Clarke, as we summarized, proposes that a free decision is one that is indeterministically caused by apt agent-involving events, such as the agent's prior reasons, *and* co-produced by the agent's agent-causing it (2003, ch. 8). Augmentation of the indeterministic causation of the decision (which ensures, under normal circumstances at least, that the agent had genuine alternatives) with the agent-causation of it, on Clarke's view, secures for the agent the exercise of further positive powers extending beyond the powers the agent would have had in the absence of agent-causing that action. These powers influence causally which of the agent's open alternatives, just prior to her doing what she did in his indeterministic world, will become actual (Clarke 2003a, pp. 96, 105, 133). It is not improbable to conceptualize these powers as consisting, at least partly, in the powers that the indeterministic agent has to ensure that she decides in accordance with her best judgment provided that she is sufficiently self-controlled. A compatibilist who wants little to do with agent-causation (because, for instance, she finds agent-causation mysterious) may suggest that, at least with respect to ensuring that the free agent can decide in accordance with her best judgment when self-controlled, the agent should be able to exert antecedent proximal control in deciding as she does. But then barring any appeal to agent-causation, it would seem that a modest libertarian should either accept the constraint of antecedent proximal control or provide an alternative that, again, secures for the agent the power to ensure that (in the absence of responsibility-undermining factors and unexpected death) the agent can decide in accordance with her decisive best judgment if the agent is adequately self-controlled.

9.4 LUCK, EXPLANATION, AND CONTROL

I have suggested that the problem that modest libertarians encounter about control is intimately tied to lack of an explanation, in terms of prior reasons, of why an agent such as Peg* makes the decision that she does when her relevant counterpart, Peg, makes a different decision under type- or near type-identical conditions. Lest I be misunderstood, I stress that the pertinent explanation is not a *contrastive* one—it is not an explanation of why one thing rather than another occurred. Rather, I'm concerned with straightforward or "plain" action explanation.

9.4.1 Akratic Action

I elucidate: Assume, as the event causal libertarian insists, that Peg*'s decision (under appropriate conditions) is free. Assume, further, that it is a decision that is contrary to her decisive best judgment, the content of which is that it is better for her to keep the promise. Peg*s decision is, thus, or at least appears to be, a strict akratic action; it is a free, intentional (mental) action that is contrary to what we stipulate is her consciously held best judgment. On customary accounts of akratic action, when an agent performs a strict akratic action, there is a misalignment between the motivational strength of the desire on which she acts (the motivationally strongest desire) and her best judgment. Elaborating, Mele proposes that (i) best judgments normally are formed at least partly on the basis of our evaluation of the "objects" of our desires—what is desired, and (ii) that the motivational force of our desires does not always match our evaluation of their objects (Mele 1987; 2004, p. 243; see, also, Watson 1975). If both these things are true, then it should not be surprising that sometimes, although we decisively judge it better to *A* than to *B*, we are more strongly motivated to *B* than to *A*. Mele remarks:

> Thesis ... [(i)] is a major plank in a standard conception of practical reasoning. In general, when we reason about what to do, we inquire about what it would be best, or better, or "good enough" to do, not about what we are most strongly motivated to do. When we ask such questions while having conflicting desires, our answers typically rest significantly on our assessments of the objects of our desires—which may be out of line with the motivational force of those desires, if thesis ... [(ii)] is true.... Thesis ... [(ii)] is confirmed by common experience and thought experiments and has a foundation in empirical studies. Desire-strength is influenced not only by our evaluation of the objects of desires, but also by such factors as the perceived proximity of prospects for desire-satisfaction, the salience of desired objects in perception or in imagination, and the way we attend to desired objects.... Factors such as these need not have a matching effect on assessment of desired objects. (2004, p. 243)

Summarizing some of the salient points of interest to us concerning strict akratic action: Imagine, again, that Claudia both has a desire to drink Coke and a competing desire to drink fizzy water. Suppose, after some reflection, she judges that it is best for her to drink fizzy water. She forms this judgment largely on the basis of evaluating how good the objects of each of the desires are for her—is the Coke or the water better for her? We can presume that though she judges that the water is better for her, despite this evaluative judgment, her desire for the Coke is stronger than is her desire for the water. In this fashion, the motivational strength of her desire for Coke is misaligned with her evaluation of the object—how good the Coke is for her—of this desire. At the time she decides to buy the Coke, she still consciously holds the judgment that it is best for her to buy the water. Her akratic decision is to be explained, in part, by drawing on resources such as Claudia's selectively focusing on certain elements concerning Coke and fizzy water. For example, she downplays detrimental long-term effects of caffeine, exaggerates the anticipated pleasures of drinking Coke, tones down the benefits of drinking water, and so on (see, for e.g., Mele 1987).

9.4.2 Modest Libertarianism, Luck, and Akratic Action

Reverting, now, to the case of Peg and Peg*: Peg does not act from weakness of will. So we may safely assume that Peg's desire to keep the promise has *greater* motivational clout than her competing desire and, further, that there is no misalignment between this stronger desire and Peg's judgment that it is better for her to keep the promise; this stronger desire and her best judgment are in harmony. Unlike Peg, though, Peg* *does* act akratically. If we accept typical accounts of akratic action, Peg*'s best judgment—the judgment that she ought to keep the promise—should stand opposed to her stronger desire—her desire to break the promise. With Peg*'s libertarian free decision, though, we see no such misalignment because Peg* shares the relevant past with Peg. Given her past, Peg*'s desire to keep the promise does not differ in motivational strength from this desire of Peg's. But in the example it is false that Peg's desire to break her promise is stronger than her desire to keep the promise. So we have a pretty obvious problem: how are we to explain Peg*'s akratic decision?

Perhaps a libertarian might claim that the misalignment in question does not occur *prior* to choice but at the moment of choice. The desire to break the promise, it may be suggested, does not become Peg*'s strongest desire until she makes it so at the moment of choice. On this view, it is false that akratic misalignment preexists the pertinent choice. Rather, such misalignment is created by the akratic agents themselves when they choose (Kane 1999, p. 114, n. 7). What, precisely, though, does the akrates do to shift the balance of motivational strength in favor of the desire that is allegedly out of kilter with her best judgment? How, exactly, at the very moment of choice, does Peg* "make" her desire to break the promise the stronger of the two competing desires? As we suggested, various explanations of the balance have been proposed, ones that make use of such things as selective focusing, failing to remind oneself how one will feel later knowing that one has acted contrary to one's better judgment, and, conversely, thinking of how good one will feel afterward in light of being aware that one has successfully resisted temptation, and failing to make an effective attempt at self-control.[7] On the view that akratic misalignment occurs at the moment of choice, Peg*'s situation may be depicted in this way: Let t be the time at which Peg* makes the decision (to break the promise) that she does. Unlike Peg, at t, Peg* selectively focuses, fails to make a concerted attempt at self-control, and so forth. At t, these activities (as we may say) of Peg*, in turn, bolster the motivational strength of her desire to break the promise, which, at t, causally gives rise to her decision to break the promise, despite her consciously held better judgment at t that she ought to keep

7 For the first and third of these explanations, see Mele 1987, chs. 5–6; for the second of these explanations, see, for example, Milo 1984, esp. ch. 5.

the promise. "So there," one might claim, "we have a perfectly reasonable action explanation of Peg*'s akratic decision."

I am not convinced. I limit comment to two concerns with this picture.[8] First, the actual world, where, at *t*, Peg decides to keep the promise, and possible world, *W*, in which she decides at *t* to break the promise, do not differ in *any* respects until *t*. It is, consequently, a mystery why, at *t*, Peg* engages in the activities that we have outlined when Peg, at this time, fails to engage in these activities, given identical pasts. (I guess, I just plain don't get it.) Engaging in these activities, or failing to do so, seems itself to be a matter of luck. Second, either these activities are free or they are not. If they are not free, there is strong reason to doubt that the decision that Peg* makes is free as this very decision stems from activities (that allegedly occur at the time when the decision is itself made) that are themselves not free.[9] If some of these activities, such as selective focusing, are not actions, if free, they will be indirectly free. If they are actions—an intentional omission would qualify as an action—then, again, if free, they would presumably be indirectly free. If the latter—if, that is, these activities *are* free—and if it is false that free events are uncaused, as the event causal libertarian assumes—these activities (if they are events) must themselves be indeterministically caused. Again, given that the actual world and world *W* are indiscernible right up until *t*, it is a mystery what the causal antecedents of these activities could be. More cautiously, if these activities have causal precursors, and Peg* engages in these activities, then again it seems to be entirely a matter of luck that Peg fails to engage in these activities.

In sum, the event causal libertarian says that, consistent with the past and the laws being what they are, at *t* Peg can either freely decide to keep the promise, or at *t* she can decide to break the promise, and that whatever decision she makes at *t*, there is an action explanation of that decision. Roughly, apt reasons, it is claimed, indeterministically cause the decision that the agent makes. It seems that this view is not quite on target, as Peg*'s scenario illustrates. As we have remarked, active control is a function of one's actions being *appropriately* caused by agent-involving springs of action. It appears that an agent who decides akratically exercises less active control in deciding as she does than an otherwise similar agent who decides continently. So it would be too quick to claim, without further explanation, that indeterministic Peg*, who decides akratically, exercises the same degree of active control in making the decision that she does as deterministic Annie-D would in making a type- or near type-identical decision when Annie-D is perfectly self-controlled.

Still, one might wonder about what precisely is the connection between lack of an action explanation of Peg*'s akratic action and responsibility-

8 Other concerns are discussed in my 2005, sec. 2.

9 I am not ruling out the possibility that if one event causes another, these two events may occur simultaneously.

level control. Kane, an event causal libertarian, explains that an agent's decision is free only if that agent exercised plural voluntary control in making that decision. Plural voluntary control presupposes that the agent had genuine alternatives; consistent with the past and the laws remaining fixed, the agent (like Peg*) could have made an alternative decision. Assuming that the agent had these genuine options, she had plural voluntary control over these options only if she was able to bring about whichever of the options she willed (or desired) when she willed to do so, for the reasons she willed to do so, on purpose, rather than accidentally or by mistake, without being coerced or compelled in doing so or in willing to do so, or otherwise controlled in doing or in willing to do so by other agents or mechanisms (Kane 2005, p. 138).[10] If Peg*, then, has plural voluntary control over her akratic decision, that decision must be suitably (indeterministically) caused by her reasons or reason states. But if there is no apt explanation of her akratic decision in terms of prior reasons, then we have reason to doubt that she exercises such control in making this decision.

9.4.3 Luck's Persistence

So far, I have pursued the thought that modest libertarianism erodes control. But there is also another strand (to which I have alluded above) concerning the sort of luck that is associated with modest libertarianism. It is simply that, independently of eroding control, the type of luck at issue undermines free action or moral responsibility (see, for example, Haji 2000b, p. 223). Assume that Peg exercises active control in deciding as she does in the actual world and that she would have exercised this sort of control had she decided otherwise. Still, her very exercises of active control seem to be a matter of responsibility-subverting luck. Under type- or near type-identical conditions she (Peg*) would have acted akratically.[11] The difference at the time Peg decides between the actual world, in which she decides to keep the promise then, and worlds with the same past and laws in which she decides to break the promise then, is just a matter of luck.

9.5 CLARKE'S HYBRID ACCOUNT AND THE LUCK OBJECTION

Does Clarke's hybrid (or, as he says, "integrated agent-causal view") escape the **Luck Objection**? We begin with a more detailed explication of the integrated view than the brief summaries we have been content with in previous sections.

Clarke (1996, p. 31; 2003a, p. 25) endorses an event causal account of action according to which an event is an action only if certain conative and

10 These conditions pertain to self-forming decisions.

11 Compare this with Mele 2005, pp. 398–99.

cognitive states of the agent appropriately causally produce this event (see section 2.4.1.1). A *free* action (mental or otherwise) is both indeterministically caused by apt-agent involving events, such as the agent's prior desires, intentions, and beliefs *and* co-produced by the agent's agent-causing it.

Invoking agent-causation in explicating free action immediately invites concerns about the very coherence of this concept of causation. Clarke believes that the concept *is* intelligible and argues that it is not as mysterious as it has frequently been made out to be, though he doubts whether such causation is possible (2003a, ch. 10). Affirming that agent-causation is, in a straightforward sense, *causation* achieves a degree of demystification. Clarke contends that the sole fundamental difference between agent-causation and event causation is that, with the former, the first relatum of the causal relation is a substance, while with the latter, the first relatum is an event; with either relatum, the causal relation is *exactly* the same.

9.5.1 Accounts of Causation

As Clarke himself notes, explaining agent-causation along these lines is tenable only if certain accounts of causation in general prove correct. A reductive analysis of causation that explains causation in terms of non-causal phenomena, such as a *regularity account* or a *counterfactual account*, would not be friendly to Clarke's approach. To illustrate this concern, consider, first, a regularity (or Humean) account. According to this account, causation reduces to regularity among events. On some such accounts, to say that event *A* causes event *B* is just to say that there is a constant conjunction between the occurrence of *A*-type events and *B*-type events; whenever events of type *A* occur, events of type *B* occur as well. With agent-causation, the first relatum of the causal relation is a substance and not an event. It would be nonsense to claim that whenever substance *S* "occurs," some other event occurs as well. It is true that substances persist; at best, it is misleading to say that they "occur." Further, suppose what is directly agent-caused by an agent is a decision. Suppose one claims that the analog of events of type *A* (the first relatum in an instance of event-event causation on the Humean account) should be construed as the agent's agent-causal activity. It is false, though, that whenever the agent agent-causes something, that thing is a decision of the same type. There is no constant conjunction, for example, between the decision to eat noodles and instances of agent-causal activity.

Consider, second, the counterfactual account. According to this account, causation reduces to counterfactual dependence of events. On this view, the causal claim, *my flicking the pen caused the pen to move*, is to be analyzed as follows. If I had flicked the pen, then the pen would have moved; and if I had not flicked the pen, then it would not have moved. Again, this account of causation reduces causation to a relation among events. Suppose you agent-caused the decision to eat noodles. The following is false. If you had agent-caused the decision, then that decision would have occurred; and if you had not agent-caused that decision, that decision would not have occurred. Surely, a decision can occur even if it is not agent-caused.

However, it is not clear that these two accounts of causation are correct. Further, there are rival accounts that, it seems, can accommodate agent-causation. According to these rival views, the causal relation is an irreducible relation, one that, for example, cannot be reduced to constant conjunction among events or counterfactual dependence among events. These views are sometimes called "realist" views of causation. To summarize these views, it might be best to quote Clarke: "Realists take the causal relation to be among the basic constituents of the universe, something not reducible to noncausal properties and relations. Causation, a realist holds, is producing, bringing about, making happen" (2003a, p. 187). On the realist's approach, agent-causation is, in a straightforward sense, causation. The only fundamental difference between agent-causation and event causation is that, with the former, the first relatum of the causal relation is a substance, while with the latter, the first relatum is an event. When an agent agent-causes an event, the relation in which the agent stands to that event is the very same one in which one event stands to another when the first event causes the second. There is nothing more to an instance of direct agent-causation (1996, pp. 21–23; 2003a, p. 186).

9.5.2 Clarke's Hybrid Agent-Causal Account

As we have mentioned, Clarke says that a "determinant" is any entity that is a cause of an event (1996, p. 28). On traditional agent-causal views, the agent is the sole determinant of the free event she directly agent-causes. On Clarke's hybrid view, she is one determinant among others, the others being event causes. The agent-cause co-determines the free action as does the action's event causes (the agent's pertinent reasons).

Clarke hypothesizes that, as a matter of nomological necessity, that is, as a matter, roughly, of the natural laws or as a matter of law-like necessity, with free decisions, whichever of the "open" decisions the agent makes, prior reasons of the agent will indeterministically cause the decision made only if the agent agent-causes that decision. Such joint causation of a decision by its agent and by the reasons possessed by its agent is meant, among other things, to account for the timing and the rational explanation of human actions, things with which, it is claimed, traditional agent-causal views have difficulty. Since, on the hybrid view, a free decision or action is event-caused, Clarke can conveniently adopt the causal theory of what it is for an event to be an action. In addition, he can espouse the causal account of action explanation according to which we explain why an agent performs some action at a time in terms of the reasons of the agent that actually cause that action. We can explain why you opened the window, for instance, by citing the reasons that you had that caused your action.

In addition, on the integrated view one can explain why an agent agent-caused an action at a particular time simply by citing the time at which the event that is the action's co-determining event cause occurs (Clarke 1996, pp. 39–40).

Supplementing the indeterministic event-causation of the agent's decision, with the substance-causation of it by its agent, Clarke affirms, secures for the agent further positive powers to influence causally which of the open alternative courses of action an event causal libertarian view permits will become actual (1996, pp. 25–26; 2003a, chs. 7–9). An agent who is, in this way, a co-determinant of her action will, thus, exercise "determining control" in its production: she will *determine* which of two or more alternatives become actual. Further, when an agent agent-causes a free action, she herself is an uncaused cause of that action; the agent as substance is not the kind of thing that can be an effect (2003a, p. 134). In this way, Clarke contends, she is an ultimate originator of her action, and she exercises greater active control in its causal production than do either her deterministic or indeterministic counterparts whose actions are not co-generated (1996, pp. 27–30).

9.5.3 The Hybrid Account and Luck

Reverting to the **Luck Objection**, as I have argued in prior works, even granting that a co-determinant of Clarke's variety exercises augmented control in the performance of what is allegedly a free action, I doubt whether the integrated account escapes this objection (Haji 2004; 2005).[12] The crux of the problem is not difficult to discern. Clarke argues that causal theories of action have a distinct advantage over noncausal ones in giving an account of acting for reasons and in explaining rational actions. The event-causal component of the integrated view carries the primary burden of action explanation: as we have noted, on this view, we can explain what an agent did or why she did something at a certain time by citing relevant events, such as the agent's prior reasons, in the event causal chain leading to her action. Noting that an agent is also the cause of her free action, Clarke affirms, indicates a further cause of that action, and it indicates that a necessary condition of the agent's acting with a variety of enhanced control is met. But Clarke admits that it is "unclear whether noting this contributes to an explanation of the action" (1996, p. 39). One's agent-causing one's action does not help answer why one performed that action; "the reasons explanation that cites event-causes of the action does that" (1996, p. 39).[13]

12 On thoughts about whether such a co-determinant does indeed exercise augmented control, see my 2004.

13 But see Clarke 2003a, p. 200.

Our previous discussion of Peg's predicament revealed that there was no difference in the worlds of Peg and Peg* to account for the discrepancy in their behavior. The disparity in behavior, thus, seemed to be just a matter of responsibility-subverting luck. If the event causal component of the integrated view bears the burden of action explanation, it seems that this view cannot account for the difference in behavior either. It cannot do so because in the Peg/Peg* scenarios, the event causal components of conduct—for instance, the agents' reasons for doing what they did—are held constant.

Against this skeptical verdict, one might rejoin that the integrated view does have the wherewithal to account for the difference in action: if Peg freely decides to keep her promise, she does so only if she *agent-causes* her decision to keep the promise; similarly, if Peg* freely decides to break the promise, she so decides only if she *agent-causes* this decision. So the integrated agent-causal view introduces a layer of complexity or control that is absent in event causal modest libertarian views: on the integrated view, there is a supplemental degree of control involved in the production of a free decision or action that the agent herself provides. This dissimilarity, however, does nothing to dispel the fundamental riddle. For, surely, the pertinent question requiring response, unanswered by conceding this dissimilarity, is this: if the past is fixed, there is nothing that Peg did differently in her world prior to her, Peg's, agent-causing her decision to keep the promise than Peg* did in her world prior to her, Peg*'s, agent-causing her decision to break the promise. Why, then, did Peg* agent-cause what she did, and in so doing acted akratically, when Peg agent-caused something quite different, and in so doing acted continently? If plain event causal action-centered modest libertarianism generates a puzzle regarding Peg*'s forming an intention to do one thing when her pertinent counterpart forms an intention to do something distinctly different (given a fixed past), why does a similar concern not simply reemerge in association with the assumed agent-causal activity of these counterparts? I suggest that however complex the control supplied by the co-determinant of the allegedly free decision that is the agent, or by other co-determinants, such as the decision's event causes, the **Luck Objection** will rear its ugly head if, holding fixed the past (and laws), the agent can bring about one decision rather than another.

9.6 MELE'S DARING SOFT-LIBERTARIAN REPLY

In his wonderful 2006 book, Mele advances a daring reply, on behalf of those he calls "soft libertarians," to the problem of luck. Soft libertarians "leave it open that free action and moral responsibility are compatible with determinism but they maintain that the falsity of determinism is required for a more desirable species of free action and a more desirable brand of moral responsibility" (Mele 2006, p. 95). Think of soft libertarians as non-traditional libertarians. Traditional libertarians affirm that determinism is incompatible with free action and responsibility. Soft libertarians deny this incompatibility but claim, nonetheless, that the falsity of determinism makes room for what they take to be a more valuable variety of free action and responsibility. The falsity of determinism, from the perspective of such non-traditional libertarians, allows for agents to be the ultimate initiators or originators of their actions: "a soft libertarian may value being the kind of agent of whom it is false that his every thought and action is part of a deterministic causal chain stretching back to the vicinity of the big bang. He may value the ability to make contributions to the world that are not part of such a chain" (2006, p. 99). One should, then, bear in mind that the soft libertarian, where 'soft libertarian' is a technical label, is not a libertarian of the conventional variety who denies that determinism is incompatible with free action or moral responsibility. This aspect of soft libertarianism is of no substantial concern in what follows in the remainder of this section.

With respect to the problem of luck, how might a daring soft libertarian defend the claim that Peg freely decides at *t* to keep the promise, given that the actual world and a world in which Peg (or counterpart Peg*) instead decides at *t* to break the promise do not differ in any way prior to *t*? A soft libertarian is daring insofar as this libertarian affirms that the relevant cross-world difference is consistent with Peg's freely deciding then and being morally responsible for her decision. The relevant cross-world difference, recall, is the difference at *t* between the actual world, in which Peg decides to keep her promise then, and worlds with the same past and laws in which she decides to break her promise then.

9.6.1 Akratic Action vs. Actions that Manifest Agency Breakdown

Assume that there are cases in which an agent's decision is directly free in the libertarian sense of 'free' (consistent with the past and the laws remaining as they were, the agent could have made an alternative decision instead), and that the alternative decision, had the agent made this alternative decision, would have been directly free as well. Regarding this assumption, Mele draws a distinction between indeterministically caused akratic actions and indeterministically caused actions that manifest a radical breakdown of agency. A case illustrative of the latter sort of action is that of Cathy, a woman in her mid-fifties who has always been a sweet, harmless person. She decides one day, though, to kill her loud, obnoxious neighbor, George, despite her all-things-considered best judgment that while killing him would be good, it would be best not to do it at the end of a long busy day. After watching the 10:00 p.m. news, Cathy executes her plan for George's murder. She slips her hands into some new latex gloves, breaks into George's house, sneaks into his bedroom, and stabs him through the heart. She then returns home, destroys the gloves, crawls into bed, and falls into a deep sleep (n.d., p. 268). Mele remarks that this "is all very strange, and the fact that the murder was wildly out of line with Cathy's history and character contributes to the strangeness" (n.d., pp. 268-69). Assuming that Cathy was not moved to kill George owing to a fanciful kind of hypnosis, brainwashing, or psychosurgery, Mele adds:

> [Imagine that] there was ... an extremely improbable indeterministically caused pair of glitches in Cathy's head that day.... Normally, when Cathy has thoughts about doing something or other that for her would be very strange ... she simply sets it aside as a fleeting fantasy. As a consequence of her first glitch that day, the thought of killing George was not set aside. As a consequence of the second, Cathy became so bizarrely fixated on and emotionally detached from the thought of killing George that killing him seemed to her to be an absolutely normal, unpleasant activity—rather like filling out her income tax forms. If we had to attach an everyday label to Cathy's psychological condition at the time of the killing it would be "insanity." One final detail: it was possible the whole day, even as Cathy was in the process of executing her deadly plan, that she would snap out of her bizarre psychological condition, but there was nothing she could do to snap herself out of it. (n.d., p. 269)

Mele proposes that there are two principal differences between akratic actions preceded by indeterminism at the moment of decision and indeterministically caused actions, such as Cathy's. One difference between actions of the former kind and Cathy's killing George is that the "former are not relatively direct products of extremely improbable but enormously powerful flukes" (p. 269). A second is that "Cathy's insanity gets her off the hook for the killing. Cathy seems not to be morally responsible for the killing and not to have performed it freely, in a sense of *freely* closely associated with moral responsibility" (n.d., pp. 269–70).

Cathy's case, I take it, is supposed to differ from Peg's (or any relevantly similar Peg-like case in which the agent's akratic decision is indeterministically caused) in these respects: In the non-actual possible world (as in the actual world), unlike Cathy, Peg is not crazy. In the non-actual possible world, Peg freely decides, and is morally responsible for her decision (from the perspective of the soft libertarian); her decision in the non-actual world is not fluky. There is, however, a leftover worry with Peg's case: Peg in the non-actual possible world supposedly acts akratically, or so we are assuming; in the actual world, her action is not the relatively direct product of extremely improbable but enormously powerful flukes. But with the past fixed (as I explained previously), there seems to be no account of why she acted akratically. Further, there appears to be no explanation of a related cross-world difference. At a single time—the time when Peg decides to keep her promise in the actual world, and when she decides (akratically) to break her promise in the non-actual world—both worlds have identical pasts and laws. The difference is just a matter of luck.

9.6.2 The Daring Reply

Now to turn to the core of the daring soft libertarian's reply to the **Luck Objection**. Mele draws our attention to the fact that the probabilities of either of the decisions that Peg makes at *t* will partly depend on Peg's relevant psychological attitudes and traits, and that Peg's having these attitudes and traits will, in normal cases, have resulted, partly, from many of Peg's previous actions (2006, pp. 122–23). Through their past behavior, "agents shape present practical probabilities [probabilities, for instance, of actions], and in their present behavior they shape future practical probabilities" (2006, p. 122). Peg's desire, for example, not to be branded as untrustworthy, her desire to avoid other possible detrimental consequences of her not keeping her promise (such as being shunned by her friends), and her desire to cultivate a good character, may all contribute to raising the probability that she will decide to keep the promise. Daring soft libertarians maintain that in the vast majority of cases of directly free actions, agents have some responsibility for the relevant probabilities.[14] For example, they have some responsibility for the chance that they will act akratically and for the chance that they will act continently. "These chances are not dictated by external forces, and they are influenced by basically free and morally responsible actions the agents performed in the past" (n.d., p. 264). Mele ventures that daring soft libertarians "take these claims to soften worries about present luck, but they realize that they have more work to do" (n.d., p. 264).

Assume that the probability of Peg's actions have been shaped by her past actions—that she has learned pertinent lessons from her past successes and failures, and used them to influence future probabilities of whether she will act akratically or continently. And assume that, as a result, she decides at *t* to keep her promise. If her mental action of deciding then is directly free, then in at least some non-actual worlds with the same past and laws up to or just prior to *t*, she decides (akratically) at *t* to break her promise then. Her ability to shape probabilities of her future actions adds little to Peg's story to illuminate why she decides akratically in the non-actual possible worlds in which she does, worlds with the same past as the actual world up to or just prior to the time in which she decides continently. What explains her akratic action in the non-actual worlds in

14 In this sentence, I have replaced Mele's "basically free actions" with "directly free actions." Suppose an agent performs some action *A* at some time. Mele calls any free *A*-ings that occur at times at which the past (up to those times) and the laws of nature are consistent with the agent's not *A*-ing then "basically free actions" (n.d., p. 255).

which she acts akratically? (See section 9.4.2.) If anything, if through her past actions, Peg has raised considerably the probability of her keeping future promises and reduced substantially the probability of breaking such promises, then this phenomenon of probability shaping brings into stark perspective the problem of cross-world luck: *despite* her shaping the probabilities in the way in which she did, in the pertinent non-actual possible worlds, Peg decides akratically; further, there appears to be no adequate action explanation of why she decides akratically. It seems, consequently, that the ability of an agent to shape the probabilities of future actions that she will perform does not, itself, assuage the problem of luck.

As part of their response to the problem of luck, in addition to calling attention to an agent's ability to influence the probabilities of what future actions she will perform, Mele claims that daring soft libertarians still have their work cut out for them. The further work they have to do concerns the following. If responsibility for a decision (or overt action) of the brand the soft libertarian finds attractive can only derive from an *undetermined* directly free action, any responsibility that Peg has for the probabilities of her making certain decisions at *t*, will have to stem from some prior undetermined actions of hers. Won't, then, the problem of luck merely re-emerge in connection with these prior actions? On the daring soft libertarian's view of free and responsible action, if there is a problem of luck concerning Peg's act of promise-keeping, why isn't there also such a problem concerning Peg's "earlier" probability-influencing actions, whatever these actions turn out to be? Has the problem of luck not just been pushed further back?

Fully cognizant of this concern, Mele invites us to reflect on a case in which a four-year-old child—Tony—performs his earliest, his first, directly free action. Tony is tempted to snatch a toy from his sister. Seeing his father stand nearby, and recalling some of the unpleasant experiences associated with his snatching something from his sibling on previous occasions when his father caught him in the act, Tony decides not to take the toy and refrains from taking it. Suppose that Tony's decision at *t* is indeterministically caused; although he made this decision, until *t* there remained a significant chance that he would not make this decision and that he would have made some alternative decision instead. Mele writes:

> The difference at *t*...between the actual world and a world with the same past and laws in which Tony decides at *t* to snatch the toy is just a matter of luck [or so some might argue]. That should be taken into account when asking about Tony's moral responsibility for deciding not to take the toy. Only a relatively modest degree of moral responsibility is at issue, and the question is whether the cross-world luck—or the luck together with other facts about the case—entails that the degree is zero. I doubt that the knowledge that all actual

> decision-making children are indeterministic decision makers like Tony would lead us to believe that no children are morally responsible at all for any of their decisions.... Views according to which agents' past decisions can contribute to their moral responsibility for their present decisions naturally lead us to wonder about the earliest decisions for which agents are morally responsible. When we do wonder about that, we need to keep firmly in mind how young these agents may be and how trivial their good and bad deeds may be by comparison with the full range of good and bad adult deeds. Tony's making the right or the wrong decision about the toy is not that big a deal, and that is something for theorists to bear in mind when trying to come to a judgment about whether Tony is morally responsible for his decision. If, when pondering whether an indeterministic decision maker can make a first decision for which he is morally responsible, a theorist is focusing on scenarios in which adults make decisions about important moral matters, cross-world luck at the time of decision should strike the theorist as at least seriously problematic on grounds associated with the worries presented ... [previously]. But this focus is very wide off the mark [when the decision maker is a child like Tony]. (2006, pp. 130–31)

We should readily grant that there are degrees of moral responsibility. A person who is morally blameworthy for an act that is not a big deal—perhaps an act that is a minor faux pas—may be blameworthy for it to only a nominal degree. Suppose Peg decides to perform such an act and then performs this act. The difference at *t* (the time of Peg's decision) between the actual world and a world with the same past and laws in which Peg decides at *t* to refrain from performing this act is a matter of luck. Its being the case that this cross-world difference is a matter of luck should undermine Peg's responsibility for the not-a-big-deal act, even though past actions of hers may have influenced the probability that she would make the decision that she did on this occasion, and even though, had she been responsible for this decision, she would have borne only a small degree of responsibility for it; she would have been blameworthy, say, to a nominal degree. Why, then, should things be any different with little Tony? Suppose Tony is *genuinely* morally responsible for his decision to refrain from snatching the toy; he is normatively and not merely causally responsible in that he is *deserving* of even a nominal degree of moral praise for his decision. Then it seems that his decision cannot be relevantly like Peg's—it *can't* be a matter of luck. Luck does not discriminate among degrees of responsibility. If luck presents a problem for responsibility, it presents a problem no matter what the degree of responsibility in question. The **Luck Objection**, then, it seems, is equally effective in cases that involve (or would involve) only relatively modest degrees of moral responsibility. This is so even if the pertinent agents would have been responsible in the absence of luck, and even if the past behavior of these agents had significantly influenced the probabilities of the decisions at issue.

Commenting further on Tony's case, Mele writes:

> *If* young children and adults are morally responsible for some of what they do, it is plausible, on grounds of the sort I mentioned, that young children are not nearly as morally responsible for any of their deeds as some adults are for some of their adult deeds. When we combine our recognition of that point with the observation that the good and bad deeds of young children are relatively trivial in themselves, we should be struck by the implausibility of stringent standards for deserved moral praise and blame of young children—including standards the satisfaction of which requires the absence of present luck. And once even a very modest degree of moral responsibility is in the picture, ... [daring soft libertarians] can begin putting their ideas about the shaping of practical probabilities to work. (n.d., p. 274)

It is one thing, though, to grant that if young children are morally responsible for what they do, they are responsible to a relatively nominal degree, but quite another thing to suggest that "we should be struck by the implausibility of stringent standards for deserved moral praise and blame of young children—*including standards the satisfaction of which requires the absence of present luck* (emphasis added)." The concern can be summarized in this way: The advocate of the **Luck Objection** pushes for the view that the cross-world luck at issue undermines free action and moral responsibility. It is partly for this reason that I suggested above that, perhaps, in addition to epistemic and control requirements on responsibility, there is some insulated-from-luck requirement as well. If little Tony's decision is infected with the problem of cross-world luck, his action is not free. And if his action is not free, then he cannot be morally responsible to any degree for this action. In short, there certainly are factors that affect degree of responsibility without undermining responsibility. Cross-world luck, though, does not seem to be a factor of this sort; if such luck affects responsibility, it is a responsibility-subversive factor.

9.7 BRIEF WRAP-UP

Summing up, I have considered a number of arguments for incompatibilism: the **Original Consequence Argument**, the **Reformulated Consequence Argument**, the **Basic Argument**, the **Direct Argument**, the **Deontic Argument**, the

Manipulation Argument, and the **Impossibility Argument**. I have exposed what I take to be various concerns with these arguments. I have been selective in having focused on problems that I believe reveal something significant about free action or responsibility, problems that incompatibilists should be motivated to address. I have not argued that these problems or concerns are insurmountable. As I stated earlier, in my view the **Basic Argument** seems to be the most promising of the lot. I then proposed that the attraction of incompatibilism to some people may derive somewhat indirectly from belief in the thesis that the existence of responsibility is a reality—we *are* responsible for at least some of our choices or actions. If you take this thesis seriously, and, further, if you are convinced that no compatibilist can deliver the goods, then you will be drawn to libertarianism, and via this route to incompatibilism. I argued, though, that the **Luck Objection** dampens optimism concerning the prospects of primary (action-centered) libertarian candidates.

So we find ourselves in a bit of a quandary. I mention two avenues to pursue. First, if like van Inwagen, one is strongly drawn to the reality of responsibility thesis, and like van Inwagen one finds the **Consequence Argument** (perhaps the **Basic Version**) compelling, and, further, one believes that the **Luck Objection** is telling, one might want to develop the semicompatibilist's stance. One might want to develop this stance provided that one believes, perhaps on the basis of Frankfurt examples or considerations of luck, that responsibility does not require freedom to do otherwise. The semicompatibilist affirms that though determinism undermines freedom to do otherwise, it does not undermine moral responsibility because moral responsibility does not require such freedom.

Alternatively, if one regards neither libertarian nor compatibilist accounts of free action and responsibility as particularly promising, then one will be drawn to the sort of position that hard incompatibilists find congenial: assuming we are not agent-causes, no one acts freely or is morally responsible for anything that one does.

References

Aristotle. 1966. *De Interpretatione*. In R. McKeon, ed., *The Basic Works of Aristotle*. NY: Random House.

Armstrong, David. 1983. *What is a Law of Nature?* Cambridge: Cambridge UP.

Arpaly, Nomy. 2003. *Unprincipled Virtue: An Inquiry Into Moral Agency*. NY: Oxford UP.

Audi, Robert. 1997. "Acting for Reasons." In A. Mele, ed., *The Philosophy of Action*. Oxford: Oxford UP.

Austin, J.L. 1961. "Ifs and Cans." In J.O. Urmson and G. Warnock, eds., *Philosophical Papers*. Oxford: Clarendon Press.

Ayer, A.J. 1954. "Freedom and Necessity." In *Philosophical Essays*. NY: St. Martin's Press.

Beebee, Helen. 2000. "The Non-Governing Conception of the Laws of Nature." *Philosophy and Phenomenological Research* 56: 571–94.

Beebee, Helen. 2003. "Local Miracle Compatibilism." *Nous* 37: 258–77.

Beebee, Helen, and Alfred Mele. 2002. "Humean Compatibilism." *Mind* 111: 201–23.

Brand, Miles. 1984. *Intending and Acting*. Cambridge, Mass.: MIT Press.

Brandt, Richard. 1958. "Blameworthiness and Obligation." In A.I. Melden, ed., *Essays in Moral Philosophy*. Seattle: U of Washington P.

Chisholm, Roderick. 1982. "Human Freedom and the Self." In Gary Watson, ed., *Free Will*. Oxford: Oxford UP.

Chisholm, Roderick, and E. Sosa. 1966. "Intrinsic Preferability and the Problem of Supererogation." *Synthese* 16: 321–31.

Clarke, Randolph. 1996. "Agent Causation and Event Causation in the Production of Free Action." *Philosophical Topics* 24: 19–48.

Clarke, Randolph. 2000. "Modest Libertarianism." *Philosophical Perspectives* 14: 21–45.

Clarke, Randolph. 2003a. *Libertarian Accounts of Free Will*. NY: Oxford UP.

Clarke, Randolph. 2003b. "Freedom of the Will." In Stephen P. Stich and Ted Warfield, eds., *The Blackwell Guide to the Philosophy of Mind*. Oxford: Blackwell.

Conee, Earl. 1987. "Against Moral Dilemmas." In Christopher Gowans, ed., *Moral Dilemmas*. NY: Oxford UP.

Corwin, Miles. 1982. "Icy Killer's Life Steeped in Violence." *Los Angeles Times* (May 16).

Creswell, Hugh. 1972. "The World is Everything that is the Case." *Australasian Journal of Philosophy* 50: 1–13.

Davidson, Donald. 1980. *Essays on Actions and Events*. Oxford: Clarendon.

Dennett, Daniel. 1978. "On Giving Libertarians What They Say They Want." In D. Dennett, *Brainstorms*. Montgomery, VT: Bradford Books.

Donagan, Alan. 1987. "Consistency in Rationalist Moral Systems." In Christopher Gowans, ed., *Moral Dilemmas*. NY: Oxford UP.

Driver, Julia. 1992. "The Suberogatory." *Australasian Journal of Philosophy* 70: 286–95.

Feldman, Fred. 1986. *Doing The Best We Can*. Dordrecht: D. Reidel Publishing.

Feldman, Fred. 1990. "A Simpler Solution to the Paradoxes of Deontic Logic." *Philosophical Perspectives* 4: 309–41.

Fischer, John M. 1994. *The Metaphysics of Free Will*. Oxford: Blackwell.

Fischer, John M. 1995. "Libertarianism and Avoidability: A Reply to Widerker." *Faith and Philosophy* 12: 119–25.

Fischer, John M. 1999. "Recent Work on Moral Responsibility." *Ethics* 110: 93–139.

Fischer, John M. 2004a. "The Transfer of Nonresponsibility." In Joseph Keim Campbell, Michael O'Rourke, and David Sheir, eds., *Freedom and Determinism*. Cambridge, Mass.: The MIT Press.

Fischer, John Martin. 2004b. "Responsibility and Manipulation." *The Journal of Ethics* 8: 145–77.

Fischer, John M. 2005. "Reply: The Free Will Revolution." *Philosophical Explorations* 8: 145–56.

Fischer, John M. 2006a. "The Cards That Are Dealt You." *The Journal of Ethics* 10: 107–29.

Fischer, John M. 2006b. "Free Will and Moral Responsibility." In *My Way: Essays on Moral Responsibility*. NY: Oxford UP.

Fischer, John M. 2007. "Compatibilism." In J.M. Fischer, R. Kane, D. Pereboom, and M. Vargas, *Four Views on Free Will*. Oxford: Blackwell Publishing.

Fischer, John Martin, and Mark Ravizza. 1998. *Responsibility and Control: A Theory of Moral Responsibility*. Cambridge: Cambridge UP.

Frankfurt, Harry. 1969. "Alternate Possibilities and Moral Responsibility." *Journal of Philosophy* 66: 829–39. Reprinted in H. Frankfurt, *The Importance of What We Care About*. Cambridge: Cambridge UP, 1988.

Frankfurt, Harry. 1971. "Freedom of the Will and the Concept of A Person." *Journal of Philosophy* 68: 5–20. Reprinted in H. Frankfurt, *The Importance of What We Care About*. Cambridge: Cambridge UP, 1988.

Frankfurt, Harry. 1975. "Three Concepts of Free Action." *Proceedings of the Aristotelian Society*, supp. vol. IL: 113–25. Reprinted in H. Frankfurt, *The Importance of What We Care About*. Cambridge: Cambridge UP, 1988.

Frankfurt, Harry. 2002. "Reply to John Martin Fischer." In S. Buss and L. Overton, eds., *Contours of Agency. Essays on Themes from Harry Frankfurt*. Cambridge, Mass.: The MIT Press.

Ginet, Carl. 1966. "Might We Have No Choice?" In Keith Lehrer, ed., *Freedom and Determinism*. NY: Random House.

Ginet, Carl. 1990. *On Action*. NY: Cambridge UP.

Ginet, Carl. 1996. "In Defense of the Principle of Alternative Possibilities: Why I Don't Find Frankfurt's Arguments Convincing." *Philosophical Perspectives* 10: 403–17.

Ginet, Carl. 2003. "Libertarianism." In M.J. Loux and D.W. Zimmerman, eds., *The Oxford Handbook of Metaphysics*. NY: Oxford UP.

Glannon, Walter. 1998. "Moral Responsibility and Personal Identity." *American Philosophical Quarterly* 35: 231–49.

Goetz, Stewart. 1998. "A Noncausal Theory of Agency." *Philosophy and Phenomenological Research* 49: 303–16.

Gowans, Christopher. 1987. "Introduction: The Debate On Moral Dilemmas." In Christopher Gowans, ed., *Moral Dilemmas*. NY: Oxford UP.

Haji, Ishtiyaque. 1998. *Moral Appraisability: Puzzles, Proposals, and Perplexities*. NY: Oxford UP.

Haji, Ishtiyaque. 2000a. "Death and Asymmetries in Moral Appraisals." *Midwest Studies in Philosophy* 24: 135–50.

Haji, Ishtiyaque. 2000b. "Indeterminism, Explanation, and Luck." *The Journal of Ethics* 4: 211–35.

Haji, Ishtiyaque. 2000c. "Alternate Possibilities and Responsibility." *Journal of Social Philosophy* 31: 259–67.

Haji, Ishtiyaque. 2002. *Deontic Morality and Control*. Cambridge: Cambridge UP.

Haji, Ishtiyaque. 2003. "Alternative Possibilities, Luck, and Moral Responsibility." *The Journal of Ethics* 7: 253–75.

Haji, Ishtiyaque. 2004. "Active Control, Agent-Causation, and Free Action." *Philosophical Explorations* 7: 131–48.

Haji, Ishtiyaque. 2005. "Libertarianism, Luck, and Action Explanation," *The Journal of Philosophical Research* 30: 321–40.

Haji, Ishtiyaque. 2006. "The Principle of Alternate Possibilities and a Defeated Dilemma." *Philosophical Explorations* 9: 179–202.

Haji, Ishtiyaque, and Michael McKenna. 2004. "Dialectical Delicacies in the Debate about Freedom and Alternative Possibilities. *Journal of Philosophy* 101: 299–314.

Haji, Ishtiyaque, and Michael McKenna. 2006. "Defending Frankfurt's Argument in Deterministic Contexts: A Reply to Palmer." *Journal of Philosophy* 103: 363–72.

Haji, Ishtiyaque and Stefaan E. Cuypers. 2004. "Responsibility and the Problem of Manipulation Reconsidered." *International Journal of Philosophical Studies* 12: 439–64.

Haji, Ishtiyaque, and Stefaan E. Cuypers. 2006. "Education for Critical Thinking: Can it be Non-Indoctrinative?" *Educational Philosophy and Theory* 38: 723–43.

Haji, Ishtiyaque, and Stefaan E. Cuypers. 2008. *Moral Responsibility, Authenticity, and Education*. NY: Routledge, forthcoming.

Harman, Gilbert. 1997. "Practical Reasoning." In A. Mele, ed., *The Philosophy of Action*. Oxford: Oxford UP.

Harrison, Gerald. 2007. "Libertarian Free Will and the Erosion Argument." *Polish Journal of Philosophy* 1: 61–75.

Henderson, G.P. 1966. "'Ought' Implies 'Can.'" *Philosophy* 41: 101–12.

Heyd, David. 1982. *Supererogation*. Cambridge: Cambridge UP.

Hudson, Stephen D. 1986. *Human Character and Morality*. London: Routledge and Kegan Paul.

Huemer, Michael. 2000. "Van Inwagen's Consequence Argument." *The Philosophical Review* 109: 525–44.

Hume, David. [1748] 1978. *Enquiry Concerning Human Understanding*. Edited by P.H. Niditch, Oxford: Clarendon Press.

Hunt, David. 1999. "On Augustine's Way Out." *Faith and Philosophy* 16: 3–26.

Hunt, David. 2005. "Moral Responsibility and Buffered Alternatives." *Midwest Studies in Philosophy* 29: 126–45.

Kane, Robert. 1985. *Free Will and Values*. Albany, N.Y.: State U of NY P.

Kane, Robert. 1996. *The Significance of Free Will*. NY: Oxford UP.

Kane, Robert. 1999. "On Free Will, Responsibility, and Indeterminism: Responses to Clarke, Haji and Mele." *Philosophical Explorations* 2: 105–21.

Kane, Robert. 2000. "The Dual Regress of Free Will and the Role of Alternative Possibilities." *Philosophical Perspectives* 14: 57–79.

Kane, Robert. 2005. *A Contemporary Introduction to Free Will*. NY: Oxford UP.

Kane, Robert. 2007. "Libertarianism." In J.M. Fischer, R. Kane, D. Pereboom, and M. Vargas, *Four Views on Free Will*. Oxford: Blackwell Publishing.

Lehrer, Keith. 1964. "'Could' and Determinism." *Analysis* 29: 29–32.

Leibniz, G.W. [1710] 1985. *Theodicy: Essays on the Goodness of God, the Freedom of Man and the Origin of Evil*. Trans. E.M. Huggard. La Salle, Ill.: Open Court.

Lemmon, E.J. 1987. "Moral Dilemmas." In Christopher Gowans, ed., *Moral Dilemmas*. NY: Oxford UP.

Lewis, David. 1968. "Counter-part Theory and Quantified Modal Logic." *Journal of Philosophy* 65: 113–26.

Lewis, David. 1979. "Counterfactual Dependence and Time's Arrow." *Nous* 13: 455–76.

Lewis, David. 1981. "Are We Free to Break the Laws?" *Theoria* 47: 113–121.

Loewer, B. 1996. "Humean Supervenience." *Philosophical Topics* 24: 101–27.

Marcus, Ruth Barkan. 1987. "Moral Dilemmas and Consistency." In Christopher Gowans, ed., *Moral Dilemmas*. NY: Oxford UP.

McConnell, Terrance. 1987. "Moral Dilemmas and Consistency in Ethics." In Christopher Gowans, ed., *Moral Dilemmas*. NY: Oxford UP.

McKay, Thomas J., and David Johnson. 1996. "A Reconsideration of an Argument against Compatibilism." *Philosophical Topics* 24: 113–22.

McKenna, Michael. 2001. "Source Incompatibilism, Ultimacy, and the Transfer of Non-Responsibility." *American Philosophical Quarterly* 38: 37–51.

McKenna, Michael. 2003. "Robustness, Control, and the Demand for Morally Significant Alternatives: Frankfurt Examples with Oodles and Oodles of Alternatives." In Michael McKenna and David Widerker, eds., *Freedom, Responsibility, and Agency: Essays on the Importance of Alternative Possibilities*. Aldershot, UK: Ashgate Press.

McKenna, Michael. 2004. "Responsibility and Globally Manipulated Agents: Why Mele's Beth Might be Blameworthy." *Philosophical Topics* 32: 169–92.

McKenna, Michael. 2008a. "A Hard-line Reply to Pereboom's Four-Case Manipulation Argument." *Philosophy and Phenomenological Research*. 76: 142–59.

McKenna, Michael. 2008b. "Saying Goodbye to the Direct Argument the Right Way." *Philosophical Review*.

Mele, Alfred. 1987. *Irrationality: An Essay on Akrasia, Self-Deception, and Self-Control*. NY: Oxford UP.

Mele, Alfred. 1995. *Autonomous Agents: From Self-Control to Autonomy*. NY: Oxford UP.

Mele, Alfred. 1999. "Ultimate Responsibility and Dumb Luck." *Social Philosophy and Policy* 16: 274–93.

Mele, Alfred. 2000. "Goal-Directed Action: Teleological Explanations, Causal Theories, and Deviance." *Philosophical Perspectives* 14: 279–300.

Mele, Alfred. 2003. *Motivation and Agency*. NY: Oxford UP.

Mele, Alfred. 2004. "Motivated Irrationality." In Alfred Mele, ed., *The Oxford Handbook of Rationality*. NY: Oxford UP.

Mele, Alfred. 2005. "A critique of Pereboom's 'Four-Case Argument' for Incompatibilism." *Analysis* 65: 75–80.

Mele, Alfred. 2006. *Free Will and Luck*. NY: Oxford UP.

Mele, Alfred. n.d. "A Libertarian View of Akratic Action." *Studies in Philosophy and the History of Philosophy*.

Mele, Alfred, and P. Moser. 1997. "Intentional Action." In A. Mele, ed., *The Philosophy of Action*. Oxford: Oxford UP.

Mele, Alfred, and David Robb. 1998. "Rescuing Frankfurt-Style Cases." *Philosophical Review* 107: 97–112.

Mele, Alfred, and David Robb. 2003. "Bbs, Magnets and Seesaws: The Metaphysics of Frankfurt-Style Cases." In Michael McKenna and David Widerker, eds., *Freedom, Responsibility, and Agency: Essays on the Importance of Alternative Possibilities*. Aldershot, UK: Ashgate Press, pp. 127–38.

Milo, R. 1984. *Immorality*. Princeton, NJ: Princeton UP.

Moore, G.E. 1911. *Ethics*. Oxford: Oxford UP.

O'Connor, Timothy. 2000. *Persons and Causes*. NY: Oxford UP.

O'Connor, Timothy. 2002. "The Agent As Cause." In Robert Kane, ed., *Free Will*. Oxford: Blackwell Publishers.

Parfit, Derek. 1984. *Reasons and Persons*. Oxford: Oxford UP.

Parfit, Derek. n.d. *Rediscovering Reasons*.

Pereboom, Derk. 1995. "Determinism *al Dente*." *Nous* 29: 21–45.

Pereboom, Derk. 2000. "Alternative Possibilities and Causal Histories." *Philosophical Perspectives* 24: 119–37.

Pereboom, Derk. 2001. *Living Without Free Will*. Cambridge: Cambridge UP.

Pereboom, Derk. 2002. "Living Without Free Will: The Case For Hard Incompatibilism." In Robert Kane, ed., *The Oxford Handbook of Free Will*. NY: Oxford UP.

Pereboom, Derk. 2003. "Source Incompatibilism and Alternative Possibilities." In Michael McKenna and David Widerker, eds., *Freedom, Responsibility, and Agency: Essays on the Importance of Alternative Possibilities*. Aldershot, UK: Ashgate Press.

Pereboom, Derk. 2005. "Defending Hard Incompatibilism," *Midwest Studies in Philosophy* 29: 228–47.

Pereboom, Derk. 2007. "Hard Incompatibilism." In J.M. Fischer, R. Kane, D. Pereboom, and M. Vargas, *Four Views on Free Will*. Oxford: Blackwell Publishing.

Plantinga, Alvin. 1974. *The Nature of Necessity*. Oxford: Clarendon Press.

Ravizza, Mark. 1994. "Semicompatibilism and the Transfer of Non-Responsibility." *Philosophical Studies* 75: 61–94.

Reid, Thomas. 1969. *Essay on the Active Powers of the Human Mind*. Cambridge, Mass.: The MIT Press.

Rescher, Nicholas. 1975. *A Theory of Possibility*. Pittsburgh, Penn.: U of Pittsburgh P.

Richman, Robert. 1983. *God, Free Will, and Morality*. Dordrecht: D. Reidel Publishing.

Robinson, Richard. 1971. "Ought and Ought Not." *Philosophy* 46: 193–202.

Rowe, William. 1991. *Thomas Reid on Freedom and Morality*. Ithaca, NY: Cornell UP.

Sartre, Jean-Paul. 1975. "Existentialism Is a Humanism." Trans. Philip Mairet. In W. Kaufmann, ed., *Existentialism from Dostoevsky to Sartre*. NY: Meridian-New American.

Saunders, John Turk. 1968. "The Temptations of 'Powerlessness'." *American Philosophical Quarterly* 5: 100–08.

Sinnott-Armstrong, Walter. 1988. *Moral Dilemmas*. Oxford: Basil Blackwell.

Slote, Michael. 1982. "Selective Necessity and the Free Will Problem." *Journal of Philosophy* 79: 5–24.

Smilansky, Saul. 2000. *Free Will and Illusion*. Oxford: Oxford UP.

Smith, Michael. 2003. "Rational Capacities, or: How to Distinguish Recklessness, Weakness, and Compulsion." In S. Stroud and C. Tappolet, eds., *Weakness of Will and Practical Irrationality*. Oxford: Clarendon Press.

Stocker, Michael. 1990. *Plural and Conflicting Values*. Oxford: Clarendon Press.

Strawson, Galen. 1986. *Freedom and Belief*. Oxford: Clarendon Press.

Strawson, Galen. 2004. "Free Agents." *Philosophical Topics* 32: 371–402.

Strawson, Peter F. 1962. "Freedom and Resentment." *Proceedings of the British Academy* 48: 1–25.

Stump, Eleonore. 1996. "Libertarian Freedom and the Principle of Alternative Possibilities." In Daniel Howard-Snyder and Jeff Jordan, eds., *Faith, Freedom, and Rationality*. Lanhan, MD.: Rowman & Littlefield.

Stump, Eleonore. 1999. "Alternative Possibilities and the Flicker of Freedom." *The Journal of Ethics* 3: 299–324.

Stump, Eleonore. 2000. "The Direct Argument for Incompatibilism." *Philosophy and Phenomenological Research* 61: 459–66.

Stump, Eleonore. 2002. "Control and Causal Determinism." In Sarah Buss and L. Overton, eds., *The Contours of Agency: Essays in Honor of Harry Frankfurt*. Cambridge: The MIT Press.

Taylor, Richard. 1966. *Action and Purpose*. Englewood Cliffs, NJ.: Prentice Hall.

Taylor, Richard. 1974. Metaphysics. Englewood Cliffs, NJ.: Prentice Hall.

Thalberg, I. 1984. "Do Our Intentions Cause Our Intentional Actions?" *American Philosophical Quarterly* 21: 249–60.

Thomson, Judith Jarvis. 1991. "Self-Defense." *Philosophy and Public Affairs* 20: 283–310.

Van Fraassen, Bas. 1987. "Values and the Heart's Command." In Christopher Gowans, ed., *Moral Dilemmas*. NY: Oxford UP.

van Inwagen, Peter. 1983. *An Essay on Free Will*. Oxford: Oxford UP.

Vihvelin, Kadri. 1991. "Freedom, Causation, and Counterfactuals." *Philosophical Studies* 64: 161-84.

Vihvelin, Kadri. 2000. "Freedom, Foreknowledge, and the Principle of Alternate Possibilities." *Canadian Journal of Philosophy* 30: 1–23.

Vihvelin, Kadri. 2004. "Free Will Demystified: A Dispositional Account." *Philosophical Topics* 32: 427–50.

Warfield, Ted. 1996. "Determinism and Moral Responsibility are Incompatible." *Philosophical Topics* 24: 215–26.

Warfield, Ted. 2003. "Compatibilism and Incompatibilism: Some Arguments." In M.J. Loux and D.W. Zimmerman, eds., *The Oxford Handbook of Metaphysics*. NY: Oxford UP.

Watson, Gary. 1975. "Free Agency." *Journal of Philosophy* 72: 205–20.

Watson, Gary. 1993. "Responsibility, and the Limits of Evil: Variations on a Strawsonian Theme." In John Martin Fischer and Mark Ravizza, eds., *Perspectives on Moral Responsibility*. Ithaca, NY: Cornell UP.

Widerker, David. 1995. "Libertarianism and Frankfurt's Attack on the Principle of Alternative Possibilities." *The Philosophical Review* 104: 247–61.

Widerker, David. 2002. "Farewell to the Direct Argument." *Journal of Philosophy* 99: 316–24.

Widerker, David. 2006. "Libertarianism and the Philosophical Significance of Frankfurt Scenarios." *Journal of Philosophy* 103: 163–87.

Widerker, David, and Michael McKenna. 2003. *Freedom, Responsibility, and Agency: Essays on the Importance of Alternative Possibilities*. Aldershot, UK: Ashgate Press.

Wiggens, David. 1973. "Towards a Reasonable Libertarianism." In Ted Honderich, ed., *Essays on Freedom and Action*. London: Routledge & Kegan Paul.

Williams, Bernard. 1987. "Ethical Consistency." In Christopher Gowans, ed., *Moral Dilemmas*. NY: Oxford UP.

Yaffee, Gideon. 2005. "More on 'Ought' Implies 'Can' and the Principle of Alternate Possibilities." *Midwest Studies in Philosophy* 29: 307–12.

Zagzebski, Linda. 2000. "Does Libertarian Freedom Require Alternate Possibilities?" *Philosophical Perspectives* 14: 231–48.

Zimmerman, David. 1999. "Born Yesterday: Personal Autonomy for Agents Without a Past." *Midwest Sudies in Philosophy*: 236–66.

Zimmerman, David. 2003. "That Was Then, This Is Now: Personal History vs. Psychological Structure in Compatibilist Theories of Autonomous Agency." *Nous* 37: 638–71.

Zimmerman, Michael. 1987. "Remote Obligation." *American Philosophical Quarterly* 24: 199-205.

Zimmerman, Michael J. 1988. *An Essay on Moral Responsibility*. Totowa, NJ: Rowman & Littlefield.

Zimmerman, Michael J. 1996. *The Concept of Moral Obligation*. Cambridge: Cambridge UP.

Zimmerman, Michael J. 1997. "A Plea for Accuses." *American Philosophical Quarterly* 34: 229–43.

Zimmerman, Michael J. 2002. "Taking Luck Seriously." *Journal of Philosophy* 99: 553–76.

Zimmerman, Michael J. 2006. "Moral Luck: A Partial Map." *Canadian Journal of Philosophy* 36: 585–608.

Index